# Comprehensive Literacy Basics

## AN ANTHOLOGY BY CAPSTONE PROFESSIONAL

Nancy Boyles

Kathy Brown

Nicki Clausen-Grace

Charlene Cobb

Connie Dierking

Michael P. Ford

Shari Frost

Michelle J. Kelley

Kristin Lems

Adele T. Macula

Sarah Martino

Mary C. McMackin

Becky McTague

Barbara Nelson

Margaret Mary Policastro

Timothy V. Rasinski

Sharon Vaughn

Elaine M. Weber

Nancy L. Witherell

Hillary Wolfe

Chase Young

*Edited by Karen Soll*

MAUPIN HOUSE BY
CAPSTONE PROFESSIONAL
a capstone imprint

*Comprehensive Literacy Basics: An Anthology by Capstone Professional*

© Copyright 2017. Capstone. All rights reserved.

Cover Design: Charmaine Whitman
Book Design: Charmaine Whitman and Daren Hastings

Library of Congress Cataloging-in-Publication Data

Cataloging-in-publication information is on file with the Library of Congress.

978-1-4966-0832-1 (pbk.)
978-1-4966-0833-8 (eBook PDF)
978-1-4966-0834-5 (eBook)

**Image Credits:**
Capstone: *I Am a Scientist* cover, 25, *Lacey Walker, Nonstop Talker* cover, 31; Courtesy of or adapted from authors Michelle Kelley and Nicki Clausen-Grace, 144, 150, 175; Courtesy of or adapted from authors Kathy Brown and Sarah Martino, www.canyoureadityesyoucan.com, 23, 24, 27, 29, 30, 32, 34, 35; Courtesy of Margaret Policastro, 185; Shutterstock: Betelgejze, 61 (river), Christos Georghiou, 23 (senses icons), Double Brain, 61 (ocean), Kotkoa, background design, MiguelAngelDelCarpio, 61 (valley), Mjosedesign, 23 (mouth icon), NEILRAS, 61 (mountains), Olga Kuevda, 61 (lake), s_oleg, 65, StockSmartStart, 23 (kids icon), Xelfit, 125, zzveillust, 61 (plains)

Maupin House publishes professional resources for K-12 educators. Contact us for tailored, in-school training or to schedule an author for a workshop or conference. Visit www.capstonepd.com for free lesson plan downloads.

This book includes websites that were operational at the time this book went to press.

Maupin House Publishing, Inc. by Capstone Professional
1710 Roe Crest Drive
North Mankato, MN 56003
www.capstonepd.com
888-262-6135
info@capstonepd.com

# Table of Contents

# Introduction

## Karen Soll

. . . . . . . . . . . . . . . . . . . . . . . . . . . . . . . . . . . . . . . . . . . . . . . . . . . . . . . . . . . . . . . . . . . . . . . . . . . . . . . . . . . . . . .

Over the years I have seen elementary educators experiencing similar challenges. Educators are tasked to teach literacy skills and content while also tailoring instruction to each student's individual needs. They are challenged to monitor students who are working independently while conducting small group instruction. And they must focus on providing differentiated support with a rather complicated text. No easy feat.

With increased attention to rigor, requirements, and personalized instruction, it can be a challenge to make sure all students are receiving instruction that is just right to improve growth. *Comprehensive Literacy Basics: An Anthology by Capstone Professional* grew out of the need to create a resource for today's elementary English language arts teacher. We contacted Capstone Professional authors, and a few additional contributors, to help us write a book on best practices. Chapters focus on each part of the literacy and language arts block. The quick tips, suggestions, and research base within will reinforce current practices while providing an invaluable go-to reference.

Although a chapter on whole group also focuses on supporting learners in small group settings, the book is naturally sequenced from whole group support to small group support to individualized instruction. A brief description of each chapter follows.

Margaret Mary Policastro sets the stage by discussing the read-aloud. She explains its evolution from past to present and provides suggestions for maximizing instruction with the end goal of improving comprehension. Included are examples from her observations and tips for a collaborative, schoolwide approach to read-alouds.

Shared reading is an enjoyable experience in the elementary classroom. As the teacher sits in front of children with a big book in hand, the children eagerly await the next part of the story. Kathy Brown and Sarah Martino discuss ways to make this whole group experience interactive by providing tips and ideas for connecting shared reading to skills and strategies.

The building blocks in learning to read include phonics and word recognition. Sharon Vaughn provides instructional routines that aid in teaching and learning these foundational skills. She also answers frequently asked questions about instruction, including whether there's a correct sequence for teaching phonics and whether students can apply their knowledge of phonics to multisyllabic words.

Part of the whole group experience is sharing background knowledge, but as author Shari Frost explains, "The playing field is not level . . . ." Frost explains why background knowledge is important, gives ideas on ways to assess students' background knowledge on a given topic, and provides suggestions for activating and building that knowledge during whole group instruction.

Tied to background knowledge is vocabulary. Without an understanding of the vocabulary, the content of a text is lost on students. Charlene Cobb gives tips and strategies for incorporating vocabulary instruction during literacy instruction as well as identifies what this looks like in both the primary and intermediate classrooms. Ideas for promoting vocabulary instruction across the content areas are also shared.

Elaine M. Weber and Barbara Nelson explain how to teach comprehension strategy instruction in order to create active, engaged, reflective, and critical readers with the end goal of independent use of strategies. The authors describe how to incorporate these strategies for analytic reading, close reading, guided highlighted reading, profundity scales, and levels of meaning.

When students are struggling in reading, sometimes the issue is with fluency. Chase Young and Timothy V. Rasinski define reading fluency and provide several models that can be used in the classroom. Whether students require significant attention or instruction can be conducted during whole group, the tips and strategies provided will help students become more engaged readers.

Students today are writing in response to reading; writing as an exit out the door; or writing an argument, informative/expository, or narrative text. Clearly writing has become an integral component of the language arts program. In this chapter Hillary Wolfe offers best practices based on five key components: building a culture that supports writing, including writing every day, tying writing to reading, modeling and providing strategy instruction, and using assessment practices to support growth.

Students at all levels can manage the rigor of close reading. Nancy Boyles provides step-by-step directions for implementing small group close reading lessons in the classroom with the end goal of students being able to read deeply on their own. The chapter includes ideas for what to teach, how to teach the text, and examples of metacognitive questions.

Michael P. Ford explains what guided reading was like in years past and how it has shifted to become more intentional. He outlines basic elements to include in a guided reading program, such as the integration of guided reading with other components of the literacy program, selection and use of appropriate texts, planning, decisions for work away from the teacher, and guided reading as an intervention.

Independent reading is helpful and necessary for students' continued growth with reading. This chapter explores the rationale and best practices for implementing independent reading. Authors Michelle J. Kelley and Nicki Clausen-Grace also describe a model that supports a differentiated approach.

How can teachers make sure that the practice away from the teacher is well spent and differentiated? In this chapter on literacy centers, Connie Dierking explains how to set up centers with integrity to the curriculum and differentiation in mind. She also provides suggestions for centers and activities at grades K–2 and 3–5, with a sample model of a mini-lesson with differentiated centers.

Sharing and assessment go hand-in-hand, and the benefits are student engagement and accountability as well as a deepened sense of community within the classroom. But what might this look like in the literacy and language arts classroom? Adele T. Macula explains how to approach sharing and assessment in the classroom along with research-based practices.

The final two chapters focus on the learners in the classroom. Authors Becky McTague and Kristin Lems suggest ways teachers can support English language learners. The chapter begins with an explanation of how learners acquire a second language and identifies some of the characteristics of which to be mindful. The authors also explain five effective classroom practices for English language learners.

Students enter the classroom at various levels and with various needs. In this final chapter, authors Nancy L. Witherell and Mary C. McMackin explain how teachers can meet the needs of all students during the English language arts block. Whether the child requires a challenge or needs intervention, the authors propose modifying content, process, or product to meet intended outcomes. The chapter is rounded out with two model lessons, showing how to provide for differentiation.

All of the components of a comprehensive literacy program are necessary because they have different purposes, scaffolds, and goals. And all build on each other by deepening knowledge, increasing achievement, and building classroom community. It has been an honor and a pleasure to work with the authors on this anthology. I hope you enjoy this resource and return to it throughout your career.

# Celebrating the Magnificent Read-aloud: Unending Classroom Possibilities

Margaret Mary Policastro

## Introduction

The practice of reading aloud has steadily and swiftly evolved, and it is now one of the most important, vital, and common classroom practices used by primary teachers. Meller, Richardson, and Hatsch (2009) refer to read-alouds as planned oral readings of children's books that are a vibrant part of literacy instruction in the primary grades.

In balanced literacy classrooms, the read-aloud has a prominent position and is built in as part of the literacy block or routine. In some classrooms the daily read-aloud, which was once reserved for a single reading, often takes place several times throughout the day. Over time children in the early grades grow accustomed to this routine and come to school eager and expecting read-alouds. Little did we realize how much this important pedagogy would evolve into such a dynamic and critical practice and experience for teachers and children alike.

In the past a read-aloud was done in a rather swift and terse manner, often without a lot of planning and reflection. Today, the intentional and deliberate decision-making that goes into the selection of the text, the interactive strategies, questioning techniques, and more provide unlimited possibilities for whole group classroom instruction. Therefore, the purpose of this chapter will be to explore the following:

- Background on reading aloud, including the evolution and changes in classroom practices from past to present.

- Ideas for the selection of texts that align with instructional goals and maximize every moment of instruction.

- Purposes for reading aloud, along with strategies to implement before, during, and after the read-aloud, including formative assessment.

## Evolution of Read-alouds

During my career I have experienced and participated in thousands of read-alouds either by reading a text to children or observing teachers and children in action. As a result of these experiences, I know reading aloud is a joyful experience children look forward to. The beauty of reading aloud is it allows children to sit back, listen, and not be concerned with decoding the text. Rather, children are actively participating and involved in their learning as they listen to their teacher and peers create and construct new meaning. To help students construct meaning, the teacher stops and asks questions to elicit meaningful discourse and discussion.

| Read-aloud Practices | Then | Now |
|---|---|---|
| Text Selection | more narrative than nonfiction, private teacher choices | informational text, more complex, teacher collaboration, and sharing of choices |
| Purposes and Strategies | less interactive | more interactive, promoting classroom discourse and risk-taking |
| Frequency | not always part of a daily literacy routine, done sporadically | done daily to several times a day, integral to the literacy block |
| Questioning Techniques | questions that require students to remember and have some level of understanding | questions that require students to analyze and evaluate as well as find evidence, argue, give opinions, and debate |
| Language Focus | lots of listening | shared talking and social discourse |
| Length of Instruction | approximately 10 minutes, terse | up to approximately 20 minutes, pace is deliberately slower |
| Who's Reading | mostly prekindergarten and primary English language arts teachers | prekindergarten, primary, intermediate, upper grade level, and content-area teachers |

There has been a thoughtful evolution in the read-aloud practice over the last several decades. For example, there have been changes in the selection of texts from narrative to nonfiction (Duke 2004, 2007; Bradley and Donovan 2010); children only listening to text to now participating in interactive read-alouds (Barrentine 1996); and the use of strategies before, during, and after the read-aloud (Kindle 2010). Further, the read-aloud takes more time than in the past as the teacher pauses while reading to give children time to reflect and interact with the text and others. The table above represents some of the changes in practice of the read-aloud from the past several decades to today.

The onset and development of the Common Core State Standards (CCSS) helped create an even clearer shift in thinking about all classroom instruction. This shift has involved the use of more informational and complex text and an emphasis on close reading, finding evidence from text, building argument, developing opinion, and more (Shanahan 2013). With these shifts came a new direction for the read-aloud (Policastro and McTague 2015). These gradual but distinctive changes have been a revealing voyage with interesting detours and skillful maintenance.

With CCSS, text selection practices for read-alouds took a remarkable turn as narratives were traded for informational and complex texts. The shift demanded at least 50 percent of the texts used for classroom instruction be informational and complex texts (Policastro and McTague 2015). With this change in practice, teachers had to rethink their choices, and schools needed to look into access to these types of books. Informational texts in many classrooms were sparse at best. During this transition, many schools made a lot of great changes. For example, I saw and continue to see informational texts covering new territory and knowledge for students and teachers alike. When working with a school that decided to read the text *Brave Girl: Clara and the Shirtwaist Makers' Strike of 1909* by Michelle Markel (2013), teachers learned side by side with their students about the 1909 shirtwaist makers' strike. The music teacher researched the period and music of the time. The math teachers had students calculate wages earned during 1909, and the art teacher had them create strike signs after researching unions. This was just one example where the shift in text selection brought forth noticeable and marked changes schoolwide. The teacher collaboration piece added an important dimension as teachers worked together to discuss the read-aloud selection.

The purpose of the read-aloud has also changed over the years. The teacher now embeds instruction strategically within the lesson, making the read-aloud more interactive in nature. Barrentine (1996) discusses interactive read-alouds as the teacher posing questions during the reading that enhance meaning and modeling how one can glean meaning from the text. With the noticeable change in text selection to more informational and complex text, the nature of the interaction has indeed become more rigorous. This interaction also includes a focus on language during the read-aloud. The classroom landscape has been well prepped with texts that yield and promote high levels of discussion and discourse. Thus, attention has moved from children listening to a concentrated effort of classroom dialog. Inherent in these discussions is the dialogic nature of talk. Lennox (2013, 382) states, "Before, during, and after reading, adults may use opportunities to incorporate dialogic strategies. These are strategies that actively engage children in reciprocal, conversational exchanges with participants sharing ideas with each other and listening to alternative perspectives." Children are engaged in sharing ideas with the entire group, a small group, or a partner. They are also listening and constructing new meaning as the shared talk takes on a special interaction in and of itself. Hearing everyone's ideas and having an opportunity to share is very important (Policastro 2016–2017). As the children listen to the read-aloud, they make connections to the text from their own life and background knowledge, other texts, and the world around them. As they listen to their peers, their comprehension and meaning making is further expanded and deepened.

As text selection for the read-aloud shifted, questioning techniques have expanded to reflect higher-order thinking. In the primary grades, teachers typically focused on levels of questioning techniques that had to do with "remembering" and "understanding." Remembering questions focus on recalling basic concepts and ideas while understanding questions seek to explain concepts and ideas. Today, teachers pose questions that focus on applying, analyzing, evaluating, and creating. Although there is room for remembering and

understanding questions, the emphasis is on higher-order thinking skills that include a taxonomy for learning (Anderson and Krathwohl 2001). These skills are based on Bloom's Taxonomy and include questions related to applying and solving problems, analyzing text by making inferences, finding evidence to support generalizations, developing and defending opinions through argument, and proposing alternative solutions.

Finally, important to note has been the length of the read-aloud, the frequency, and who is doing the reading. In the past, it was a quicker practice that started and stopped in approximately 10 minutes. With the new text selections and more sophisticated interactive strategies and questions asked, the read-aloud can last as long as 20 minutes or more. The length of time does not determine the extent to which a read-aloud is necessarily effective. Rather it is the thoughtful and reflective practices implemented that are important. Slowing the pace of the read-aloud and taking more time for questions and responses allow for a deeper application of the process to unfold. In addition, the read-aloud once was not part of the "daily routine or literacy block," but today it is common practice to see the read-aloud as a routine within the balanced literacy classroom. And often it is done more than once a day. Finally, once reserved as a practice for the primary and English language arts teachers, today the read-aloud is noticed schoolwide.

## Selection of Texts

Selecting texts for a read-aloud has become a thoughtful process. Teachers are deliberate decision-makers to the type of text (e.g., narrative, nonfiction) and the complexity of the text. Lennox (2013, 383) states, "Teachers have an influential role in choosing books. Selecting the right book contributes towards successful read-alouds; the repertoire should include a variety of well-illustrated, quality literature, fiction, poetry and information books." Often teachers are collaborating in teams to choose texts, which enhances the expertise of the teacher (Hattie 2015). What I have observed in the schools is capacity building through collaboration. What this means is that within both literacy and grade level team meetings, school leaders and teachers are discussing and deciding upon the forthcoming texts. Often books are selected as part of a schoolwide theme. Moreover, the read-aloud is shared publicly so all can celebrate it. Read-aloud titles are posted outside each classroom, or the book jacket or covers are displayed prominently in the hallway in an effort to share the read-aloud practice. Thematic-based units are kept in mind during text selection, so the read-aloud can be integrated throughout the entire curriculum. Further, the careful selection of read-alouds is enhanced with the alignment to curriculum standards and instructional shifts. Selecting texts that allow students to develop arguments, form opinions, find evidence from the text, and develop debate skills will enable the shift in instruction to align with standards.

When considering texts, teachers must have easy access to the books they have selected together. By creating a read-aloud library, the books are available in a central location. Several areas within the school work well, including the "book room," the teacher's lounge, and the school library. In one school the assistant principal decided to house the read-aloud collection in her office, a space where ongoing professional development takes place daily. The benefits of housing these selections in a school leader's office sends a message to teachers that reading aloud is important—a priority schoolwide. Another benefit is teachers and school leaders have ongoing conversations about the books, new selections, and implementation strategies. I have also seen schools develop a read-aloud collection or library, so teachers can have access to quality resources throughout the day (Policastro and McTague 2015).

Erdos Brocious (2016) reported that the Virginia State Reading Association took on a statewide initiative to promote informational texts within schools and classrooms. From this special example, and others no doubt, all are excited about selecting the read-aloud texts. Teachers and students unite in the celebration.

Not only is the collaborative selection of texts important, it is also crucial that teacher collaboration and expertise exists in order to implement strategy instruction for the read-aloud. Most recently we worked with a group of teacher leaders across several schools from our Improving Teacher Quality (ITQ) grant. The teachers were reporting out on the book *Last Stop on Market Street* by Matt de la Peña (2015). When the discussion started, the collaborative conversation centered on sharing all the things they had seen in their schools. Time and time again, we would hear the teachers saying things like, "Oh, I never would've thought of that idea" and "I'm going to go back and share that with other teachers and make sure that we offer that idea at our school."

In the book *Last Stop on Market Street*, the character CJ rides the bus with his grandmother, with the route ending at a soup kitchen. He asks many questions about the neighborhoods, people, and more. The bus ride helps him see the beauty and fun in the world around him, otherwise taken for granted. One fifth grade teacher used the read-aloud as a mentor text for a lesson called *Last Stop on 63rd St.* He designed lessons that took the children on an inquiry ride through the neighborhood and the street surrounding the school, focusing on appreciating the different aspects around them. The teacher also included a service project for the students to complete. A teacher at a different school had the children write their own books called *Last Stop on Halsted Street.* This lesson had children research and write about the historic districts in the neighborhood. In both examples, the mentor text was used as an exemplar model and anchored the lessons and planning. Both of these examples were spearheaded by the power of collaboration among the teachers across schools.

While working in our ITQ grant schools, we have introduced social justice literature for classroom read-alouds. The titles included narrative nonfiction, informational, and complex texts. Having worked at a university with a mission dedicated to social justice, this alignment was quite natural and easy. One way to introduce topics of social justice is to "weave social justice concepts and processes into your existing curriculum" (Hernandez 2016, 21). Introducing social justice concepts through literature is a subtle way to teach and empower students to understand peace, equity, and other important global issues.

When we first introduced some of these selections to school leaders and teachers, they were concerned about presenting books with sensitive information and topics and worried about how the parents would respond. As time went on and teachers worked collaboratively schoolwide to introduce and present these texts through classroom read-alouds, the level of instruction deepened. What makes these informational books special is they help children understand important content knowledge that might not otherwise be presented.

Schickedanz and Collins (2013) discuss the importance of reading informational narratives to young children. They stress that giving children the opportunity to understand the content knowledge central to the story is key. Setting the stage and building background knowledge for the read-aloud helps children increase their comprehension of the text. Building background knowledge can be as simple as talking about the topic of the book and asking children what they already know about the subject. Children love to talk about their own experiences and share with others. Showing children pictures or objects representing the subject matter is another way of assessing how much they already know. Asking prediction questions, such as what they think the text will be about can get them thinking about the topic.

One example is with the book *Mama's Nightingale: A Story of Immigration and Separation* by Edwidge Danticat (2015). Presenting information about a family experiencing separation through immigration is a delicate subject. Teacher leaders agreed that this informational text would require special planning in order to implement it and made sure students were introduced to the topics gradually. Currently, teachers are in the planning stages of this selection. Current events and news on immigration generated much conversation within the schools on how to proceed

with implementation. Planning the lessons ahead of time and considering the background knowledge children bring to the text is critical to the success of the lesson. Also, when teachers collaborate and plan together, all content areas are included. Further, working schoolwide allows for exploring and learning together. Should this be something teachers incorporate schoolwide, proper planning with school leaders and communication with parents are elements to consider.

There are several excellent examples that teach children other social justice topics. *Who Said Women Can't Be Doctors?: The Story of Elizabeth Blackwell* by Tanya Stone (2013) and *Razia's Ray of Hope* by Elizabeth Suneby (2013) can help students understand how far women have come and how much work there is yet to do in the world. A book written in verse that captures the struggle of a young girl's dream of becoming an engineer is *Rosie Revere, Engineer* by Andrea Beaty (2013).

**Tips and Considerations for Text Selection**
- Have team and community shared planning meetings and make choices with the team.
- Encourage thoughtful planning around topics and themes that include social justice and more.
- Consider a range of picture books, poetry, nonfiction, and fiction.
- Consider the types of strategies for implementation during the selection process.

**Read-aloud Tips for Informational Text:**
- Talk about the author and illustrator of the book.
- Discuss the cover, title, photographs, and illustrations.
- Point out any awards the book has received and what they mean.
- Have students make connections to their own lives.
- While reading, stop and ask higher-order questions, such as those that prompt students to compare and contrast, argue, defend, and judge.
- For narrative informational text, always stop periodically and ask a prediction question like, *What do you think will happen next?*

## Purposes, Strategies, Tips, and Formative Assessment

Text selection and purpose go hand in hand. Duke (2004, 42) states, "Teachers can use many strategies to create authentic purposes for reading informational text." Identifying a purpose of the read-aloud lesson will help ensure children are aware of what they are learning, and they are ready for the lesson that is to take place. Whether it's to simply enjoy the text read aloud or to reinforce content or to re-examine a comprehension strategy, the read-aloud can be used in many different ways. The end result is a routine that is an integrated part of the English language arts block and content area lessons.

Teachers can vary the strategies and questioning techniques used before, during, and after the read-aloud. Formative assessment can take place during the read-aloud as the teacher collects important data, provides feedback, and assists students in their own self-monitoring (Policastro, McTague, and Mazeski 2016). Focusing on four key areas will help strengthen the classroom read-aloud:

1. **Developing the joy and pleasure for reading:** Children should have many opportunities to engage in literacy as a joyful experience; read-alouds offer this opportunity. Research supports read-alouds as a way to introduce students to the joy of reading and listening (Morrow 2003). An important goal is for students to feel successful and become lifelong readers. In order to develop

the read-aloud routine, English language arts teachers need to make sure the read-aloud is built into the literacy block. Content area teachers need to integrate it as part of their lessons. In both instances, the deliberate time set aside for the read-aloud is essential. Children easily adapt to classroom routines, and when the read-aloud routine is established schoolwide, children not only expect it but are eager and ready for it as well. It is within this routine that the habits of participating in a read-aloud develop. These habits include listening and speaking and developing the love of literacy. As the excitement grows during the reading, the children will scoot closer, get up and point to pictures, and show a definite interaction with the text. This is something that happens across grade levels.

Encouraging parents to read aloud at home is an important contribution to growing these literacy habits. Lane and Wright (2007, 673) state, "Teachers and schools can assist parents in their read-aloud efforts by ensuring plentiful access to appropriate books." Helping and supporting parents to read aloud at home will increase the home-to-school connections (Policastro 2017). One way to support parents is to set up a Read-aloud Family Lending Library. It's the perfect way to help them have access to books at home. This library can be part of the overall parent library, or it can be a separate library for the parents. Children can also take out books for their parents to read to them or take out books to read to their siblings.

2. **Engaging students in meaning-making processes during the read-aloud:** Children should have many opportunities to seek and construct new meaning and see reading as a meaning-making process (Barnhouse and Vinton, 2012) through purposeful read-alouds and classroom discourse. Reading aloud to the whole class is the perfect venue for children to experience shared talking. Hearing everyone's ideas and having an opportunity to share out is most important. Lawson (2012, 266) states, "the pleasure of

everyday discourse is in social interaction." I have seen children respond by making connections to the teacher reading. For example, I observed a teacher reading about a character in a book, and a student naturally and authentically started talking about his father and how he had similar characteristics. It made me think how children naturally want to respond to the text the teacher is reading.

Classroom discourse typically refers to the language students and teachers use to communicate with each other, including talking, discussions, conversations, and debates. Moore and Hoffman (2012) discuss discourse as language interactions among students and teachers that form the way they both create meaning and further their understanding. It is through these meaning-making episodes that children, who would not normally be exposed to higher-level, complex texts because of their reading levels, are able to make sense of the text. Discourse allows for scaffolding and support as students construct their own meaning and draw upon their own background knowledge and experiences. This talk is important before, during, and after the read-aloud.

Teachers need to make sure they are providing opportunities for extended and productive discourse with students and among students during the read-aloud. All students should be provided with opportunities to create and respond to multiple perspectives, use background knowledge, and make new connections and meaning. Most important, the teacher must ensure the classroom environment promotes risk-taking and enables participation from all students. Creating a culture of shared talk requires a classroom environment that is safe and encourages students to take risks. Students need to know what they say will be valued by all in the classroom. Talk is promoted when it is always respected, encouraged, and developed within a zone where children explore new ideas (Policastro 2016–2017).

3. **Engaging students in self-monitoring during read-alouds:** Children need to develop both their metacognitive and self-monitoring skills. Read-alouds are perfect for allowing children to take charge and be responsible for their own learning. Making the read-aloud interactive provides an opportunity for the listener to respond and participate in creative ways, building language and classroom discourse all along (Policastro, McTague, and Mazeski 2016). Moreover, through the interactive nature of the read-aloud, children are able to constantly monitor their understanding and learning. Whole group read-alouds provide opportunities for children to learn from each other and construct new ideas and meaning. During shared talk, children can actively monitor their learning. As they listen to the responses of others, they can "fix up" their own responses, enhance their own comprehension, and construct new ideas. Andrade and Valtcheva (2009) discuss self-assessment as a process of formative assessment during which students reflect on the quality of their work, judge the degree to which it reflects the lesson's purpose, and revise accordingly. Especially effective is when the teacher stops, poses questions, and allows children time to respond using whiteboards and share their responses with others. Through this interaction, students can compare their responses with others, hear and see multiple perspectives, correct or change misconceptions, and construct new meaning.

We have also had great success with read-aloud exit slips as both "whole group exit slips" and "individual exit slips." See examples of exit slips on page 19. By starting with the whole group exit slip, students have an opportunity to discuss what they learned and what they still have questions about. Doing this as a whole group allows students to hear what others learned and, more important, what they still need more information about or what they didn't understand. Reluctant students will find it comforting to see and hear other students take risks publicly. Individual exit slips allow students to focus on just their own thoughts about the text. These exit slips provide powerful tools for both students and teachers alike. This process brings forth differentiated instruction in an authentic manner. Once the exit slip information is collected, teachers can consider how to adjust instruction for the group and individual students.

4. **Using key strategies effectively in the read-aloud process:** Teachers have the opportunity to implement many different learning and questioning strategies before, during, and after the read-aloud. Complex texts aid in this process. Hoffman, Teale, and Yokota (2015, 9) state, "Read-alouds that engage children with complex texts rely on interactive discussions focused on interpretation of texts that may vary with the backgrounds, perspectives, and experiences of the children listening. In other words, discussing multiple interpretations of text helps children realize that there are many possible responses to complex literature." Although an interactive read-aloud has many dimensions and qualities, it is the student-to-student interaction that is so rich. The interaction begins when the teacher introduces the text, asks questions, and begins the experience. When the teacher introduces the text, he or she can ask background knowledge and prediction-based questions. During the read-aloud the teacher continues to pose questions and allow students time to respond. One of the most important questions that a teacher can ask is, *What do you think is going to happen next?* Prediction skills are an essential aspect of comprehending text as students can confirm their responses by finding the evidence in the text. Thinking ahead and generating thoughts of what the text might be about draws on personal background knowledge. Drawing upon finding the evidence within the text also helps in developing argument and debating skills. Most important is the students have time to share, listen, and respond to each other. Encourage students to respond using whiteboards. Responses can be

in the form of drawings, text, or both. Students are quite comfortable sharing the boards with another student or groups of students. The use of whiteboards works across the grades. Most recently, I observed upper grade level students responding to the read-aloud *The Crossover* by Kwame Alexander (2014). This book is written in verse and elicits interesting predictions and rigorous conversations when responses are put on the whiteboards and shared by all. As children make connections to the text and the shared talk, new and deeper meaning is constructed throughout the read-aloud lesson.

---

**Snapshot of a 20 Minute Read-aloud**

- Always practice reading the read-aloud.
- Introduce the book by talking about the author and or illustrator. (Show pictures of author/illustrator if available.)
- Discuss the cover, title, and illustrations. (Use sticky notes to remind yourself of the illustrations and more that you want to point out and discuss.)
- Point out award-winning medals and awards if appropriate.
- Have students make connections from the book information to their own lives.
- Use whiteboards and have children draw or write their predictions of what they think the text will be about.
- Allow time for the students to share responses with each other.
- As you read, stop and ask higher-order questions that require students to compare and contrast, argue, defend, judge, and more.
- Always stop periodically and ask a prediction question like, *What do you think will happen next?* Use sticky notes to remind yourself where to stop and ask questions.
- Do a group exit slip with the students to find out what they learned and still have questions about.

---

Formative assessment is integrated throughout the read-aloud as teachers have the opportunity to assess what students have learned. Timely feedback to students during and after the read-aloud allows for students to make adjustments to their learning (Policastro, McTague, and Mazeski 2016). Celebrating the classroom read-aloud in these ways brings joyful learning to the children, especially when meaning making through discourse and other strategies are the focus. This kind of instruction, which includes formative assessment, puts children in charge of their own learning—a responsibility that is lifelong.

## Conclusion

There is no doubt the classroom read-aloud has come a long way over the past several decades. Today, the time for read-alouds is valued and protected as a critical and essential routine in the literacy block. Moreover, it is common practice for content area teachers to spend time reading aloud as well. Selecting texts to read is now a collaborative process and casts a net to include more nonfiction, informational, and complex texts than in the past. The strategies implemented during the read-aloud encourage interactions that move beyond teacher-to-student questions and embrace student-to-student discourse. Meaning making is at the heart of the read-aloud as students connect their own knowledge to the text, listen to others, and construct their own meaning. Formative assessment is integrated into all aspects of the read-aloud as teachers can collect data, provide feedback, and assist the students in self-monitoring their learning. Indeed, there is much to celebrate with the magnificent read-aloud.

### References and Resources

Alexander, K. 2014. *The Crossover*. New York, NY: HMH Books for Young Readers.

Anderson, L. W., and D. R. Krathwohl, eds. 2001. *A Taxonomy for Learning, Teaching, and Assessing: A Revision of Bloom's Taxonomy of Educational Objectives*. Abridged Edition. Boston, MA: Allyn and Bacon.

Andler, K. 2014. "Nonfiction in the Classroom: Exciting Adventure or Perilous Journey." *Illinois Reading Council Journal* 42 (1): 13–22.

Andrade, H., and A. Valtcheva. 2009. "Promoting Learning and Achievement Through Self-Assessment." *Theory into Practice* 48: 12–19.

Barnhouse, D., and V. Vinton. 2012. *What Readers Really Do: Teaching the Process of Meaning Making*. Portsmouth, NH: Heinemann.

Barrentine, S. J. 1996. "Engaging with Reading through Interactive Read-Alouds." *The Reading Teacher* 50 (1): 36–43.

Beaty, Andrea. 2013. *Rosie Revere, Engineer*. New York, NY: Abrams.

Benham, B., and P. Yassamin. 2009. "Classroom Discourse: Analyzing Teacher/Learner Interactions in Iranian EFL Task-Based Classroom." *Porta Linguarym* 12: 117–132.

Bradley, L. G., and C. A. Donovan. 2010. "Information Book Read-Alouds as Models for Second-Grade Authors." *The Reading Teacher* 64 (4): 246–260.

Danticat, E. 2015. *Mama's Nightingale: A Story of Separation and Immigration*. New York, NY: Penguin Group.

de la Peña, M. 2015. *Last Stop on Market Street*. New York, NY: Penguin Group.

Duke, N. 2003. "Beyond Once Upon a Time." *Instructor* November/December: 23–26.

———. 2004. "The Case for Informational Text." *Educational Leadership* 61 (6): 40–44.

———. 2007. "Informational Text and Young Children: When, Why, What, Where and How." *Best Practices in Science Education*. Cengage Learning. http://ngl.cengage.com/assets/downloads/ngsci_pro0000000028/am_duke_info_txt_yng_child_scl22-0469a.pdf.

Erdos Brocious, T. 2016. "Got IT? Virginia State Reading Association's Statewide Initiative to Promote Informational Texts." *Literacy Today* 34 (3): 34–35.

Hattie, J. 2015. *What Works Best in Education: The Politics of Collaborative Expertise*. London: Pearson.

Hernandez, M. 2016. "Social Justice in a Digital Age: Promoting Empathy, Equity and Cultural Literacy Through Digital Storytelling." *Literacy Today* 34 (3): 18–21.

Hoffman, J. L., W. H. Teale, and J. Yokota. 2015. "The Book Matters! Choosing Complex Narrative Texts to Support Literacy Discussion." *Young Children* 70 (4): 8–15.

Kindle, K. 2010. "Vocabulary Development During Read-Alouds: Examining the Instructional Sequence." *Literacy Teaching and Learning* 14 (1 & 2): 65–88.

Lane, H. B., and T. L. Wright. 2007. "Maximizing the Effectiveness of Reading Aloud." *The Reading Teacher* 60 (7): 668–675.

Lawson, K. 2012. "The Real Power of Parental Reading Aloud: Exploring the Affective and Attentional Dimensions." *Australian Journal of Education* 56 (3): 257–272.

Lennox, S. 2013. "Interactive Read-Alouds—An Avenue for Enhancing Children's Language for Thinking and Understanding: A Review of Recent Research." *Early Childhood Education Journal* 41 (5): 381–389.

Markel, Michelle. 2013. *Brave Girl: Clara and the Shirtwaist Makers' Strike of 1909*. New York, New York: Blazer-Bray, a division of Harper Collins.

Meller, W. B., D. Richardson, and J. A. Hatch. 2009. "Using Read-Alouds with Critical Literacy Literature in K–3 Classrooms." *Young Children* 64 (6): 76–78.

Moore, J. E., and J. L. Hoffman. 2012. "Rebuilding Teaching Professionalism: Teacher Reflection and Instructional Redesign through Classroom Discourse Analysis." *Ohio Journal of English Language Arts* 52 (1): 27–38.

Morgan, K. 2016. "What Is the Difference Between a Nonfiction Narrative & Informational Text." *Synonym*. http://classroom.synonym.com/difference-between-nonfiction-narrative-informational-text-2922.html.

Morrow, L. 2003. "Motivating Lifelong Voluntary Readers." In *Handbook of Research on Teaching the English Language Arts*. 2nd ed. Edited by J. Flood, D. Lapp, J. Squire, and J. Jenson, 857–867. Mahwah, NJ: Erlbaum.

Pantaleo, S. 2007. "Interthinking: Young Children Using Language to Think Collectively During Interactive Read-Alouds." *Early Childhood Education Journal* 34 (6): 439–447.

Policastro, M. M. 2015. "Word Walls to Language Walls: A Natural Evolution in the Balanced Literacy Classroom." *Illinois Reading Council Journal* 43 (3): 15–22.

———. 2016–2017. "Discourse: The Importance of Talk in the Balanced Literacy Classroom." *Illinois Reading Council Journal* 45 (1): 3–11.

———. 2017. *Living Literacy at Home: A Parent's Guide*. North Mankato, MN: Capstone Professional.

Policastro, M. M., and B. McTague. 2015. *The New Balanced Literacy School: Implementing Common Core*. North Mankato, MN: Capstone Professional.

Policastro, M. M., B. McTague, and D. Mazeski. 2016. *Formative Assessment in the New Balanced Literacy Classroom*. North Mankato, MN: Capstone Professional.

Policastro, M. M., Mazeski, D. K., and McTague, B. 2010–2011. "Creating Parent Libraries: Enhancing Family Literacy Through Access to Books." *Illinois Reading Council Journal* 39 (1): 60–64.

Schickedanz, J. A., and M. F. Collins. 2013. *So Much More Than the ABCs: The Early Phases of Reading and Writing*. Washington, DC: National Association of the Education of Young Children.

Shanahan, T. 2013. "Common Visions, Common Goals: Preparing Schools, Colleges and Universities for the New Standards and Assessments." Common Visions, Common Goals. Lecture conducted from Bone Student Center, Center for the Study of Education Policy, Illinois State University, Normal, IL, October 17.

Shedd, M. K., and N. K. Duke. 2008. "The Power of Planning Developing Effective Read-Alouds." Beyond the Journal, *Young Children on the Web*. http://www.naeyc.org/files/yc/file/200811/BTJReadingAloud.pdf.

Stone, T. L. 2013. *Who Said Women Can't Be Doctors?: The Story of Elizabeth Blackwell*. New York, NY: Henry Hold and Company, LLC.

Suneby, E. 2013. *Razia's Ray of Hope: One Girl's Dream of an Education*. CitizenKid. Tonawanda, NY: Kids Can Press Ltd.

Wiseman, A. 2011. "Interactive Read-alouds: Teachers and Students Constructing Knowledge and Literacy Together." *Early Childhood Education Journal* 38 (6): 431–438.

# Formative Assessment: Group Self-Monitoring

## Group Exit • Read-aloud

Title: _____

Purpose of the lesson:

We learned about:

We weren't sure of:

# Student Self-Monitoring

## Read-aloud Exit Slip

Purpose of the lesson:

I learned about:

I wasn't sure of:

I need to ask my teacher about:

# Engage, Interact, Inspire: Creating Young Thinkers During Shared Reading

Kathy Brown and Sarah Martino

## What Is Shared Reading?

Shared reading is just what it sounds like: A teacher shares the enjoyment of reading with his or her students. Yet shared reading is truly so much more! It is an extremely powerful approach that when implemented correctly infuses enthusiasm and skill instruction. The teacher uses authentic literature as a tool to introduce students to a variety of rich texts while explicitly modeling how to use multiple reading strategies to make meaning. An effective shared reading lesson blends elements of guided reading with a read-aloud lesson. Shared reading lessons vary in length, and focus skills depend upon the needs of the students at that grade level. Fountas and Pinnell (1996) stated that in shared reading, children participate in reading, learn critical concepts of how print works, get the feel of learning, and begin to perceive themselves as readers.

Don Holdaway (1979) is often credited with creating the shared reading philosophy. Holdaway recommended that teachers teaching the early years use big books and enlarged texts to help young learners feel like they were being read to in a cozy home environment. Nowadays, teachers don't need to purchase enlarged texts to put Holdaway's theories into practice. Educators in the age of technology can easily project texts, creating instant on-screen big books. As children become older and further develop their reading skills, big books are not as critical. In fact, in the intermediate grades students typically participate in shared reading experiences with their own copy of the text.

In kindergarten through second grade, students benefit from balanced literacy instruction that includes read-alouds, shared reading, guided reading, interactive writing, and shared writing. It is important to note that shared reading is a fundamental component of this approach. Here is how shared reading could look in kindergarten. The teacher typically sits in a comfy reading chair and gathers the students around. Students begin to feel like they are part of a community of readers and thinkers as the teacher actively **engages** them in examining the pictures and words. The teacher reads, but the students don't just listen. They are encouraged to think and to **interact** with the text and one another.

FIGURE 1 SHARED READING FOCUS AND SUPPORTING SKILLS

| Foundational | Comprehension | Speaking and Listening |
|---|---|---|
| title/title page/author/illustrator/front and back cover | questioning | participates in turn-and-talk conversations |
| words vs. illustrations | connecting | actively listens |
| text types (fiction vs. nonfiction) | predicting | asks questions to gain understanding |
| conventions (spacing, punctuation, capitalization) | inferring | describes with detail people, places, things, and events |
| letters and sounds | comparing/contrasting | explains ideas/thoughts |
| sight words | retelling/summarizing | fluently reads in choral reading opportunity |
| rhyming | sequencing | participates in group reading experiences |
| sentence patterns | story elements (characters, setting, plot) | asks and answers questions about new vocabulary |
| directionality (top to bottom/left to right) | visualizing | uses new vocabulary learned from reading experiences |
| text features (table of contents, graphs, charts, headings, diagrams, etc.) | main idea and details | expresses ideas clearly |

A successful shared reading lesson bundles multiple skills and standards simultaneously. (See Figure 1.) For example, the teacher directs students to attend to foundational skills, like print concepts and text features, while inspiring higher-level thinking, like connecting, comparing, and contrasting. Before the lesson, the teacher carefully plans questions and talking points and after reading, often revisits the story to give students more opportunities to discuss and comprehend the text. Sometimes fluency can be the goal of a shared reading experience. In this case, choral reading and echo reading are great strategies to build oral reading confidence. Other times, the goal is to increase comprehension. Most important, no matter what specific skills are practiced, shared reading should **inspire** students to develop a love of literature and a passion for reading!

## Routines for Shared Reading Success

So how does one begin? Never underestimate the power of routines. Children thrive on routines to help them successfully navigate their school day and to build confidence as learners. As teachers, we must carefully craft routines that will guide our students in achieving the rigorous academic demands expected of them. Most of us love to read to our students because it is so enjoyable. We want to share our love of reading. But do we strategically set the stage for reading success by incorporating routines into our everyday shared reading time? What we do before, during, and after we read to children is essential in creating young thinkers. You can create shared reading routines to help you and your students be successful.

## Engagement and Interaction: The Turn-and-Talk Routine

Begin by cultivating a climate of collaborative conversation where all students are routinely engaged as they interact with one another and the text. Don't be afraid to let your students' voices roar. Also strategically engage your audience in active listening and thinking. Effective teachers preview their shared reading texts and post sticky notes on pages where they can stop and ask guiding questions. Remember, as the National Association for the Education of Young Children (NAEYC) and the International Reading Association (IRA) clearly stated, it is important to talk about what you are reading before, during, and after reading. "It is the talk that surrounds the storybook reading that gives it power, helping children to bridge what is in the story and their own lives" (IRA and NAEYC 1998, 32).

When peers challenge one another during shared reading conversations, students are participating in higher-level thinking like clarifying and explaining. To engage all students in shared reading conversations simultaneously, set parameters. This will help ensure students understand purposeful and productive talk that helps them learn. To do so, you need a conversation routine called a Turn-and-Talk Routine.

FIGURE 2 TURN-AND-TALK ROUTINE
www.canyoureadityeswecan.com

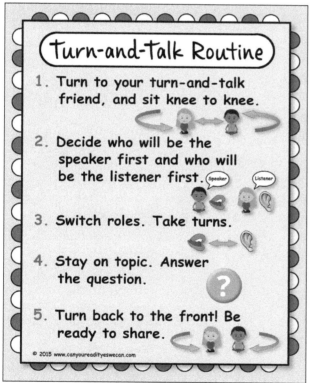

First, teach your students the role of a speaker and the role of a listener. This will require explicit modeling and a gradual release approach of practicing being good speakers and listeners. Then, students need a conversation partner. You can assign turn-and-talk friends, or you can quickly let students find

a partner. Do what works best for your classroom. Next, make sure they know how to take turns and have a conversation, so they switch roles. After they have been the speaker, then they must be a good listener and vice versa. Also, remind students to stay on topic and be sure to give them a cue for what to do when their conversations are complete. Create a class anchor chart as a visual reminder of the steps to follow during your turn and talk routine. (See Figure 2.) Be sure to review this chart every time before you engage students in a turn and talk. Walk around as students are turning and talking, providing praise and feedback, so you intentionally cement appropriate conversation behaviors. Then, encourage students to share their thoughts or the thoughts of their partner with the whole group. Celebrate the diversity in responses. If you teach the turn-and-talk routine early in the school year, you can strategically use it all year long to activate higher-level thinking. Spark speaking and listening in your shared reading block by using this turn-and-talk routine. Watch your students benefit as they learn not only how to be better readers but also learn how to appreciate diversity in others!

## Be Strategic and Enthusiastic: The Reading Routine

When you sit down in your reading rocking chair, do you have a clear plan to engage each learner in active listening and thinking? Do your students know what to do? Do you and your students know what standards you are teaching? Do you know where you might stop and facilitate discussions? Do you know what questions you are going to ask? How will you know if they are learning? How will you support their learning at home? Creating a reading routine during your shared reading block will optimize reading success.

First, determine the most important things you always do when you read aloud. Then, create a reading routine anchor chart. You can display this for yourself, or you can share it with your students. Figure 3 on the next page is a great sample reading routine for young learners.

FIGURE 3 READING ROUTINE

## Reading Routine

★ **Warm Up:** Activate Prior Knowledge, Discuss Front Cover, Title Page, Author, Author's Purpose, Text Type, and Take a Picture Walk

★ **Display & Discuss the Focus Standard**

★ **Display & Sing the Song Anchor Chart**

★ **Read & Model Metacognition**

★ _Engage_ **Students in Discussing Guiding Questions**

★ **Encourage Students to** _Interact_ **with Text and with One Another**

★ **Reread &** _Inspire_ **A Love of Literature**

★ **Display and Discuss Graphic Organizer**

★ **Respond with Writing**

★ **Provide Powerful Parent Practice**

A reading routine will pay dividends for both you and your students. Your students will know exactly what is expected during shared reading time. The consistency will provide them an opportunity to enjoy literature as they build their confidence and develop their reading skills. You won't have to start from scratch every time you write a shared reading lesson. You will have a successful routine to guide your shared reading instruction. The key is to refer to the routine as you purposefully plan, so you have a consistent approach. However, in an effort to be strategic, don't forget to model enthusiasm as you read. This will inspire your students to love reading, too!

Your shared reading block is an important anchor for reading instruction in your classroom. It needs to be built around routines that can help learners actively participate and grow as thinkers. You can use strategic routines like the turn-and-talk routine and the reading routine to help you make the most out of your shared reading lessons. In the remainder of this chapter, we are going to share an overview of how you can use these routines with both a nonfiction and fiction mentor text. These routines can be adapted for any text. In fact, you will notice that the routine for fiction and nonfiction are intentionally based on similar techniques in an effort to foster familiarity and confidence.

Once your purpose for reading is set, select a shared reading text that matches instruction, is highly engaging, and will ignite the interest of your students. Develop a list of open-ended questions that can build upon what children already know as well as activate higher-level thinking. Depending upon the grade level and the text, your reading routine can take multiple days and multiple rereadings to complete.

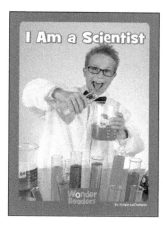

## I Am a Scientist
by Angela LaCompte

**Summary:** *I Am a Scientist* is an informational text that introduces students to the beginning concepts of science. Scientists ask and answer questions about the world around them. Learn what it means to be a scientist and what scientists do.

| Focus Skill | I can identify the main idea and give details about the text. | | |
|---|---|---|---|
| **Supporting Skills** | title/title page/author/ illustrator/front cover/ back cover | directionality (top to bottom/left to right) | makes predictions |
| | text types (fiction vs. nonfiction) | text features (table of contents, graphs, charts, headings, diagrams, etc.) | participates in turn-and-talk conversations |
| | asks questions to gain understanding | uses new vocabulary learned from reading experiences | actively listens |

Display the book. **Warm up** readers by activating prior knowledge, discussing author's purpose, examining text features, and determining text type. Read the title and ask students about their prior knowledge of the topic. *Class, today we are going to read a book called I Am a Scientist. Let's think about what we already know about scientists.* You can record responses, or you can have students share verbally through turn and talks or whole group responses. *Great job readers! We know a few things about scientists, but I am really excited to learn some new information about scientists, too.*

*Let's look more closely at the book. Good readers always carefully look at the front cover, back cover, and title page before they read to help them predict what the book might be about. It helps them get ready to read and to learn.* Engage students in reviewing the title, author, front cover, back cover, and title page. Discuss with the whole group or with turn-and-talk partners.

Examine and discuss the table of contents. *Look at this page. It is called a Table of Contents. A Table of Contents tells us where we can find important information in the book. Good readers always read this part of the book carefully to get their brains ready for the book. Reading the Table of Contents is like getting a preview of what is inside.* Display and read the Table of Contents page. Discuss. *Wow, great job readers. We can learn so much about a book by looking carefully at its parts before we read.*

*Illustrations are another important part of a book. The illustrations are the pictures. They help us understand the story. Let's take a picture walk by flipping through and looking at all the pictures before we read the words. Looking at the illustrations can give us some more ideas to help us predict what the story might be about.* Take a quick picture walk by turning each page and looking carefully at the illustrations. Stop and discuss individual pages or wait until the end to discuss them all.

Engage students in a turn and talk about their predictions. *Boys and girls, now that we have examined the parts of the book, turn to your turn-and-talk partner and predict what you think the book will be about.* Walk around and provide feedback as students are engaged in conversations. Discuss several responses with the whole group. *Great job friends! Wow! You are super-duper predictors. I love the way you used the illustrations, the title, and the table of contents to predict what we might learn about in this book.*

*Now we need to get our brains ready for the type of book we are going to read. An author can write a fiction story with characters, a setting, and a plot, or an author can write a nonfiction book that tells information about a main idea. As readers, we need to know what kind of book we are reading before we begin reading all of the words. Discuss with your turn-and-talk partner if you think this book is a fiction or a nonfiction book. Be sure to explain why.* Discuss responses and explanations. Affirm that it is a nonfiction book. *The author wrote this book to share information with us about what a scientist does. We call this type of book a nonfiction book. Nonfiction books are special because they help us learn new things.*

*We read books because they are so fun to read but also to help us learn. So let's make sure we know what important reading skill we are going to learn about as we read our scientist book today.* **Display and discuss the focus standard**. *Our reading learning goal today is: I can identify the main idea and give details about the text.* Have students echo the goal. *When we read nonfiction books we have to get our brains ready to remember the main idea and important details. Let's make sure we know what main idea and details are. The main idea is the one big idea of the book. The main idea is the glue that holds all the other parts together. The details are the parts of the book that give us examples about the main idea. Main idea and details are very important to remember whenever we read nonfiction. So I have a song that will help us think about the main idea and important details.* **Display the Main Idea Anchor Chart Song** at the easel. (See Figure 4.) Have students echo sing the main idea song multiple times to the tune of "Bingo." Post the Main Idea Anchor Chart Song in the classroom as a visual prompt to refer to when reading nonfiction.

FIGURE 4 MAIN IDEA ANCHOR CHART SONG
www.canyoureadityeswecan.com

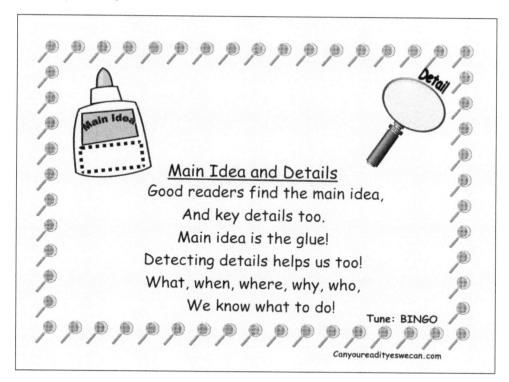

Main Idea and Details

Good readers find the main idea,
And key details too.
Main idea is the glue!
Detecting details helps us too!
What, when, where, why, who,
We know what to do!

Tune: BINGO

Canyoureadityeswecan.com

*Now when we read* I Am a Scientist *let's focus on learning the main idea and details. Remember, the main idea is the big idea that the book is all about. It is the glue that holds the story together. Turn to your turn-and-talk friend, and share what you think the main idea of this book is. Be sure to explain why.* Discuss responses and confirm that being a scientist is the main idea, and we know this from the title, illustrations, and table of contents. *Yes, the main idea of this book is scientists. The glue that connects all of the pages is how scientists learn. That means on each page, the author will share a different detail about how scientists learn about the world around them. Let's be reading detectives and search for facts or details about what scientists do on every page. As I read, I don't want you to just sit and listen. I want you to be discovering new facts about scientists. Who is a superstar reading detective?* Students respond, "I am a superstar reading detective!" *Okay detectives, let's read and discover details about scientists.*

Continue following the reading routine as shown in Figure 3 on page 24. Note, **modeling metacognition** and **discussing guiding questions** requires preparation but both steps can be implemented simultaneously. Examine each page and determine if it is better suited to showcase metacognition or to inspire discussion of a guiding question. Carefully preview the text and post sticky notes on pages where you can intentionally model either metacognition or engage students in discussion. For example, to prepare for metacognition, add a note where you can strategically demonstrate how to use a specific illustration to learn a new fact about a scientist. To prepare for discussing guiding questions, add a note where students can engage in a turn and talk. Turn and talks are a great strategy to use to engage students in **actively interacting with the text and one another.** Prepare open-ended guiding questions on sticky notes on appropriate pages. Encourage students to answer with detail and evidence from the book or from their lives to support their thinking. Don't be afraid to go off script and address the teachable moment. Sometimes the most engaging questions evolve from real-time class conversations.

After students share out, celebrate diversity in responses. Too often learners think there is one right answer. By celebrating different types of answers, you exude enthusiasm and excitement. As teachers, we hold motivation in the palms of our hands. Release reading enthusiasm and **inspire your students to love reading** and to love learning, too. Depending on the text, your grade level, your shared reading time block, and your focus goal, you may need several days to accomplish the first full read. Plan accordingly and be flexible. Be sure to bring closure to the lesson through discussion.

**Reread the story, and listen for something specific in an effort to add a level of engagement.** Provide an opportunity for explicitly practicing the focus skill with a now familiar text. *Yesterday we read the nonfiction book,* I Am a Scientist. *We focused on main idea and details. Let's sing our song.* Refer to the Main Idea Anchor Chart Song. *The main idea in this book was all about what scientists do. Remembering the details can be much more challenging because there are so many of them. I usually have to read an informational book more than one time, so I can remember the details. So let's read the book again, but this time let's play the Grab It Game when we read. To play this game, you will need to quietly grab the details by holding up a finger when you hear a detail.* Model holding up a finger as a detail is read.

This kinesthetic strategy will actively engage students and provide a prompt for remembering details. *As you hear a detail, grab it in your brain and hold up a finger. I hope we can catch two handfuls of details as we read this awesome book. Listen and grab some great details as I read.* Read the book again. Encourage students to share the details they grabbed with their turn-and-talk partner. *I really like the way you grabbed the details. Good readers don't just sit and listen. They are always thinking about the words, and they work hard to remember the details. What details did you grab? When I say go, turn to your partner and share two details that you grabbed. When you are done sharing, turn back to the front and put your hands in your lap. Go!* Provide corrective feedback and scaffolding as needed. Have students share responses with the whole group. *You are fantastic informational readers! You can identify the main idea and the key details when you read. Awesome job!*

Reading and writing go hand in hand. Effective shared reading lessons give students a chance to **respond in writing.** Make a **graphic organizer** part of your reading routine. Beginning readers are learning so much information that they don't know how to keep it organized in their brains. Providing a visual prompt can really help. First, model the graphic organizer. You write on the response sheet while the students share the ideas. Eventually students can use the graphic organizer independently after reading an informational text to showcase what they have learned. Use the same graphics as in the song anchor chart. These symbols will provide consistent visual prompts to help students organize their thoughts.

To be successful with the writing activity, students must talk about the four details they grabbed during shared reading time. Talk is the best rehearsal for writing. Don't skip the turn and talk. Students will be prepared to write if they have previously shared their ideas. Figure 5 shows a kindergarten independent response for the book *I Am a Scientist*. Once this graphic organizer has been modeled, it can be used as a response to any informational text. It is a great tool for students to organize their thinking and for teachers to measure student comprehension and writing skills.

FIGURE 5 MAIN IDEA GRAPHIC ORGANIZER
WRITING RESPONSE
www.canyoureadityeswecan.com

Be sure to get your parents onboard. Most parents want to help, but they don't know what to do beyond just reading with their children. Make **powerful parent take-home letters part of your reading routine.** Send home a parent letter with directions on how to use the anchor chart song and attach a copy of the graphic organizer. Encourage parents to have rich discussions with their children and to explicitly practice the focus skill. Great readers don't just read at school. They read at home, too. Tell your students why you are sending it home, and motivate them to practice the focus skill with their family. This provides powerful parent practice that is authentic and meaningful.

FIGURE 6 PARENT TAKE-HOME LETTER:
MAIN IDEA
www.canyoureadityeswecan.com

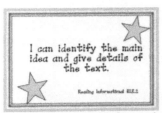

Kindergarten Parents,

It is important that you read and discuss informational
text with your child at home. Learning new facts helps
children build vocabulary and make sense of the world
around them. You can help broaden your child's
background knowledge by exploring nonfiction books at
home. Be sure to pick topics that are interesting. Also it
is very important to stop frequently when reading and discuss what can be learned on each page.
Can your child find evidence in the text and illustrations to prove new learning? We have been
practicing identifying the **main idea** and **details** in informational texts. The kindergartners
know that the main idea is the "glue" that holds the book together and that the details support
the main idea. We have learned the song below sung to the tune of BINGO to help us remember
about these important skills.

Before you read, ask your child to "switch on his or her searchlight" and become a detective for
new facts. You will love the enthusiasm nonfiction reading will bring at home!

**Main Idea and Details**
Good readers find the main idea,
And key details too.
Main idea is the glue!
Detecting details helps us too!
What, when, where, why, who,
We know what to do!
Tune: BINGO
Canyoureadityeswecan.com

Thanks so much for the at home help! The kindergartners will benefit from all of the support!

Please let me know if you have questions! Happy Reading!

_____

**Kindergarten Teacher**

©2013 Canyoureadityeswecan.com

*Your parents will be so proud of you when you share what you learned today about scientists.
You can show them your writing. I am sending home a letter that has our special main idea
song on it, too. Your family will love to hear you sing it. I am also sending home some extra
writing paper. Now when you read nonfiction at home, you can talk and write about the main
idea and details with your family.* (See Figure 6.)

Notice how easy it is to add routines to your shared reading block. Engaging students in
turn-and-talk routines and reading routines will increase their interaction with one another
and with text. Imagine how successful your students will be at identifying the main idea and
details if you use this nonfiction routine every time you read an informational text.

# Lacey Walker, Nonstop Talker
by Christianne C. Jones

**Summary:** Lacey Walker loves to talk. She talks all day and sometimes all night. But when she loses her voice, Lacey learns the importance of listening. In this entertaining **fiction book**, Lacey motivates readers to see the value in listening once in a while, too!

| Focus Skill | I can identify and describe characters in a story. | | |
|---|---|---|---|
| **Supporting Skills** | title/title page/author/illustrator/ front cover/back cover | directionality (top to bottom/left to right) | participates in turn-and-talk conversations |
| | text types (fiction vs. nonfiction) | makes predictions | makes connections |
| | asks questions to gain understanding | actively listens | describes with detail people, places, things, and events |

Display the book. **Warm up** the readers by activating prior knowledge, discussing author's purpose, examining text features, and determining text type. Read the title and ask students about their prior knowledge of the topic. *Class, today we are going to read a book called* Lacey Walker, Nonstop Talker. *Let's think about what we already know about being a nonstop talker. What does that mean?* You can have students share verbally through turn and talks or whole group responses. *Great job readers! It is important to think about the title before we read.*

*Let's look more closely at the book. Good readers always carefully look at the front cover, back cover, and title page before they read to help them predict what the story might be about. It helps them get ready to read and to learn.* Engage students in reviewing the title, author, front cover, back cover, and title page. *Now that we have examined some parts of the book, predict what you think this book might be about? Why do you think so?* Discuss with the whole group or with turn-and-talk partners.

*Illustrations are another important part of a book. The illustrations are the pictures, and they help us understand the story. Looking at the illustrations can help us predict what the story might be about. Let's take a picture walk by flipping through and looking at all the pictures before we read the words.* Take a quick picture walk by turning each page and looking carefully at the illustrations. Stop and discuss targeted pages or wait until the end to discuss them all. Engage students in a turn and talk about their predictions. *Boys and girls, now that we have examined the illustrations, I bet you have an even better idea of what might happen in this book. Thinking about what might happen next is called predicting. Turn to your turn-and-talk partner, and discuss what you predict the book will be about.* Provide feedback as students are engaged in conversations. Discuss several responses with the whole group. *Great job, friends! Wow! You are super-duper predictors. I love the way you used the illustrations and the parts of the book to help you to predict what we might read about in this book.*

*Now we need to get our brains ready for the type of book we are going to read. An author can write a fiction story with characters, a setting, and a plot, or an author can write a nonfiction book that tells real facts and information about a main idea. As readers, we need to know what kind of book we are reading before we begin reading all the words. Discuss with your turn-and-talk partner if you think this is a fiction or a nonfiction book. Be sure to explain why. Discuss responses and explanations. Affirm that it is a fiction book. Yes, the author wrote this book to share a pretend adventure, a story with characters, a setting, and a plot. You can tell it is fiction because owls don't wear clothes, read books, or brush their teeth in real life. We call this type of book a fiction book.*

*Wow! I can't wait to read this book. Let's remember that we read books because it is so fun to read but also to help us learn. So let's make sure we know what important reading skill we are going to learn about as we read our fiction book today.* **Display and discuss the focus standard.** *Our reading learning goal today is: I can identify and describe characters in a story. Have students echo the goal. When we read fiction books we have to get our brains ready to remember details about the characters. Let's make sure we know what characters are. Characters are the people or the animals that the story is all about. They are the stars of the book. Sometimes there is more than one character in a story. I have a song that will help us remember what a character is.* **Display the Character Anchor Chart Song** *at the easel. (See Figure 7.) Have students echo sing the song multiple times to the tune of "Mary Had A Little Lamb." Post the Character Anchor Chart Song in the classroom as a visual prompt to refer to when reading fiction.*

FIGURE 7 CHARACTER ANCHOR CHART SONG
www.canyoureadityeswecan.com

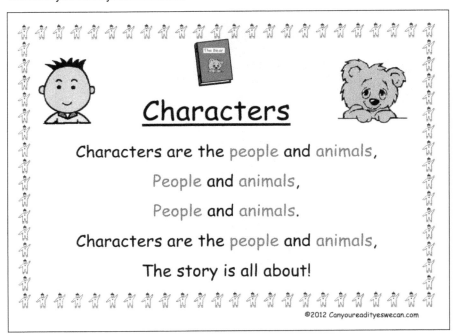

*Now when we read* Lacey Walker, Nonstop Talker *let's focus on learning about the characters. Remember characters are the people and animals the story is about. Turn to your turn-and-talk partner, and share whom you think the main character of this book is, and be sure to explain why. Discuss responses and confirm that Lacey, the owl, is most likely the main character. We know this from the title and illustrations that we have previewed.*

*Let's be reading detectives and search for facts or details about the characters on every page. As I read, I don't want you to just sit and listen. I want you to be discovering new facts about the characters in this book. Who is a superstar reading detective? Students respond, "I am a* superstar reading detective!" *Okay, detectives, let's read and learn about the characters in this book.*

Continue following your reading routine as outlined in Figure 3 on page 24. Be sure you have previewed the book and posted notes at ideal stopping points before reading with the class. For each page choose whether you want to model a reading strategy or engage students in discussing a guiding question. Remember that **modeling metacognition and discussing guiding questions** are best taught in tandem. For example, to model metacognition stop and share how you are using the words and illustrations to remember details about Lacey Walker, the main character. Think out loud and share examples from the book. *I think Lacey Walker is being rude on this page because she is talking while her brother is trying to watch TV. She is not a good listener.* Then engage students in a turn and talk by asking the question, *Can you think of a time when Lacey Walker was not being a good listener. When I say go, share your thoughts with your turn-and-talk partner.* Encourage students to answer with details and evidence from the book or from their lives to support their thinking. Don't be afraid to go off script and address the teachable moment. Sometimes the most engaging questions evolve from real-time class conversations.

Be sure to celebrate ideas and successes. Remember, even the smallest bit of praise can ignite confidence and wonder. This will help to **inspire a love of reading** and a love of learning, too. Depending on the text, your grade level, your shared reading time block, and your focus goal, you may need several days to accomplish the first full read. Plan accordingly and be flexible. Be sure to bring closure to the lesson through discussion.

**Reread the story, and add a level of engagement.** Provide an opportunity for explicitly practicing the focus skill with a now familiar text. Try comparing and contrasting two characters like Lacey and her brother. You could also have students listen for how Lacey changes from the beginning to the end of the story. Try rereading and counting how many times Lacey was not a good listener. Read again and count how many times she was a good listener. Compare and contrast. The rereads should still focus on the concept of character but help engage students in higher-level thinking.

Reading and writing go hand in hand. Effective shared reading lessons give students the foundation to be able to successfully **respond in writing.** Make a **graphic organizer** part of your reading routine. Beginning readers are learning so much information that they don't know how to keep it organized in their brains. Providing a visual prompt can really help. First, model the graphic organizer. (See Figure 8 on the next page.) Explain to students how to use the writing response sheet to write about and draw their favorite character in the story. Have one student share an idea about his or her favorite character while you write it on the response sheet and encourage the student to share details about the character. Eventually all students can use the graphic organizer independently to showcase what they know about characters in fiction texts. Use the same graphics as in the song anchor chart. These symbols will provide consistent visual prompts to help students organize their thoughts.

To be successful writers, students must talk about the characters in the story and their traits. Talk is the best rehearsal for writing. Don't skip the turn and talk. Students will be prepared to write if they have previously shared their ideas. Figure 8 shows a second grade independent response for the book *Lacey Walker, Nonstop Talker.* Once this graphic organizer has been modeled, it can be used for any fiction text. Don't forget, graphic organizers can be great formative assessment tools to measure comprehension and writing.

FIGURE 8 CHARACTER GRAPHIC ORGANIZER WRITING RESPONSE
www.canyoureadityeswecan.com

☺ Trevor

**I can draw and write about the characters in a story!**

Title of Book: Lacy walker nonstop talker

I can draw my favorite character.

I can write to tell who my favorite character is and share a detail about that character.

My favorite character is Lacy.

She leans a very important lesson. She is very talkitive. Kinda like me.

©Canyoureadityeswecan.com 2012

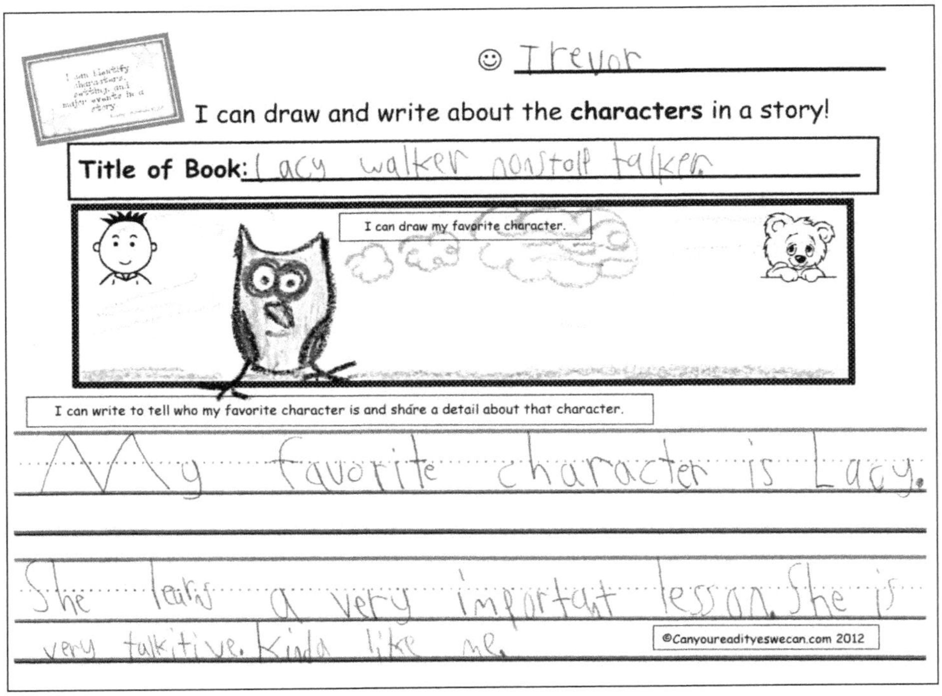

And finally, get your parents on board. Most parents want to help, but they don't know what to do beyond just reading with their children. **Make powerful parent take-home letters part of your reading routine.** Send home a parent letter with directions on how to use the anchor chart song and attach a copy of the graphic organizer. Encourage parents to have rich discussions with their children and to explicitly practice the focus skill. Great readers don't just read at school. They read at home, too. Tell your students why you are sending it home, and motivate them to practice the focus skill with their family. This provides powerful parent practice that is authentic and meaningful.

FIGURE 9 PARENT TAKE-HOME LETTER: CHARACTER

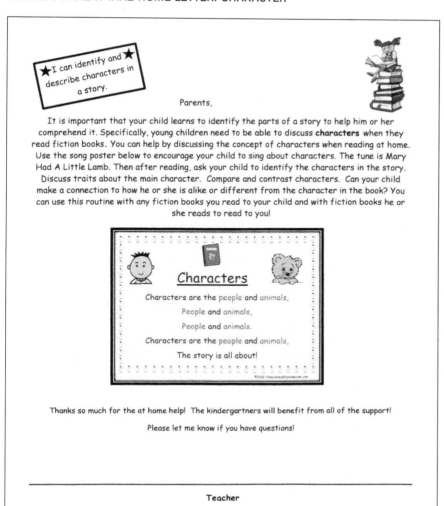

*Your parents will be so proud of you when you share what you learned today about characters. You can show them your writing. I am sending home a letter that has our special character song on it, too. Your family will love to hear you sing it. I am also sending home some extra writing paper. Now when you read fiction at home, you can talk and write about the characters with your family. (See Figure 9.)*

## Conclusion

You can strategically set up your shared reading block for success. Just remember to make your shared reading time intentional with these key points:

- Set a purpose for reading.

- Bundle the benefits of each book by intentionally and explicitly practicing multiple standards.

- Activate thinking by using routines to consistently **engage** your students in discussing literature.

- Build your fiction and nonfiction routine on a similar foundation where your students are encouraged to **interact** with one another and with the text.

- When you build a shared reading routine that creates a community of learners, you **inspire** your students to love reading and learning. You can do it! Just remember to **engage, interact, and inspire!**

. . . . . . . . . . . . . . . . . . . . . . . . . . . . . . . . . . . . . . . . . . . . . . . . . . . . . . . . . . . . .

## References and Resources

A Joint Position Statement of the International Reading Association and the National Association for the Education of Young Children. 1998. "Learning to Read and Write: Developmentally Appropriate Practices for Young Children." Washington, DC: National Association for the Education of Young Children.

Brown, Kathy, and Sarah Martino. 2016. Can You Read It? Yes We Can! Inc. http://www.canyoureadityeswecan.com.

Jones, Christianne C. 2012. *Lacey Walker, Nonstop Talker.* Little Boost. North Mankato, Minnesota: Picture Window Books.

LaCompte, Angela. 2012. *I Am a Scientist.* Wonder Readers. North Mankato, Minnesota: Capstone Publishers.

Fountas, Irene C., and Gay Su Pinnell. 1996. *Guided Reading, Good First Teaching for All Children.* Portsmouth, NH: Heinemann

Holdaway, D. 1979. *The Foundations of Literacy.* New York: Scholastic

# Phonics and Word Recognition Instruction: What Elementary Teachers Need to Know

Sharon Vaughn

## What Is Phonics and Word Recognition Instruction?

Phonics and word recognition instruction addresses the foundational skills included in the Common Core State Standards and is demonstrated through research to be effective in promoting reading proficiency for all students. Phonics is an organized, sequential approach to teaching students the correspondence between the sounds of our language and how they are "mapped" to print. You can think of phonics as the way in which youngsters learn to look at spelling patterns, discern the sounds represented by these spelling patterns, and then blend the sounds to make meaningful words. For example, the word "sat" has 3 sounds /s/, /a/, and /t/. If we know the typical sounds that each of these letters make, we can say those sounds aloud or "in our head" and then blend them to make the word "sat."

Unlike many other languages that have highly consistent sound-to-spelling systems (e.g., Finnish, Spanish), English has numerous exceptions to the sound-letter relationships. Thus, teachers in English-speaking countries have a more complex job when teaching letter combinations and sounds. Some examples of letter-sound combinations include consonant digraphs like "ch" in the word "chat." The /ch/ makes a new sound that is different from blending /c/ and /h/, and students benefit from learning this consonant digraph as well as others. Another example is /sh/ as in "wish" or "shake." These double-letter sound combinations also occur with vowels, such as when the /ea/ makes the long e sound in "eat" and "read." In addition to the rules that help students unlock words, it is critically important in English that students learn to be "on guard" for the many exceptions to the sound-spelling patterns, such as when the "ch" spelling is pronounced as /k/, as in "charisma." Likewise, the exception to the /ea/ spelling pattern would be the word "read" in past tense, such as "Yesterday I read a book." With explicit instruction and extensive practice, students learn the rules and exceptions.

Word recognition involves not only using the sound-spelling rules to decode unknown words but also learning to automatically recognize "sight" words, or high-frequency words, from memory. Many of these sight words do not follow phonics rules and may be thought of as "irregular" words or "outlaw" words. There are many "irregular" words that do not follow the phonics rules, and students need to learn these words without relying solely on their sound-letter correspondence. What are some examples of these irregular words? Well, just look within the sentence asking the question about examples of irregular words and you will see: "What," "are," "some," "of," and "these" are all examples of words with letters that have irregular sounds (i.e., /a/ in "what," /e/ in "are," /o/ and /e/ in "some," /o/ and /f/ in "of," and /s/ in these). This may prompt you to ask the common question, "If there are so many irregular letter-sound correspondences, why do we bother teaching the rules?" The reason is that there is consistent research demonstrating that teaching youngsters the basic rules helps students to unlock words, even if the rules are not applicable 100 percent of the time. We'll come back to these ideas when we discuss instructional routines for teaching phonics.

## Instructional Routines for Teaching Phonics and Word Recognition

Now that you have an overview of phonics, let's discuss instructional routines that promote effective phonics teaching and learning.

1. *Teach letter-sound correspondence, explicitly practicing with real words in isolation and in context.* Some students readily learn how sounds map to print and can unlock words quickly and effortlessly. Most students do not infer this connection and benefit from instruction showing how the sounds of our language map to print and then make words. It is helpful to provide students with multiple opportunities to practice by teaching initially 2–3 consonants and one vowel, so students can make words. A common set of consonants includes "m," "s," and "t" with the short "a"

vowel. After students learn these sounds they can make numerous words. Increase the consonants and vowels they know until they have acquired a successful use of all consonants and short vowels.

2. *Teach students the v/c/e rule.* Another way to describe the v/c/e rule is to say long "e." This rule teaches students that when there is a vowel followed by a consonant that is followed by "e," it is very likely that the vowel is long. For example, in the word "mile," the v/c/e is "ile" and the "i" is a long vowel. In addition to multiple opportunities to practice this rule with words that "play fair," it is also a good idea to teach students that there are many words that do not play fair, so we have to be flexible as we use our phonics rules. For example, students will likely encounter the words "have" and "love," which do not "play fair" but are commonly used. It may be helpful to tell students that when the consonant is a "v" (i.e., v/v/e pattern), the vowel is sometimes not long. Other examples include "move" and "give."

3. *Teach word families.* Word families provide a "pattern" for students to learn a lot of words. It is helpful to teach word families early in the sequence of teaching phonics. As soon as students can blend basic words and learn some of the vowel spelling patterns, teachers can provide practice with word families. Some common word families are listed here. Figure 2 on pages 43–45 provides some common word families and sample words that can be used for teaching.

- VC: -an, -ap, -at, -aw, -et, -in, -ip, -ir, -it, -op, -or, -ot, -ug, -up, -ut
- VCE: -ade, -ake, -ale, -ame, -ate, -ice, -ide, -ike, -ime, -ine, -ope, -ore
- VVC: -ail, -ain, -ait, -eat, -eed, -eek, -eem, -een, -eep, -eet, -oop, -oot
- VCC: -ack, -ank, -ash, -ell, -est, -ick, -ill, -ing, -ink, -ock, -old, -ump, -unk

These are just sample word-building sets that by adding consonants, blends, and digraphs will allow students to learn to both read and write a large number of words. Remember that easier word patterns, such as "an," "it," and "in," are taught first followed by more difficult word patterns, such as "ate," "ore," and "eat" and then by the most difficult, "ank," "oop," and "old" as examples.

4. *Teach inflectional endings.* Inflectional endings, such as "ed" and "s," change the pronunciation and the meaning of the word, so it is helpful to teach them directly to students.

5. *Teach consonant blends.* Consonant blends are when two letters each represent a sound, as in "slip." The /s/ and /l/ each have their own sound. There are many consonant blends including: /b//r/ in "bring"; /b//l/ in "blond"; /c//r/ in "crab"; /s//t/ in "stop"; and /t//r/ in "train."

6. *Teach consonant digraphs.* Consonant digraphs are when two consonant letters are used to make one sound. Examples of consonant digraphs are /sh/ in "ship," /ph/ in "phone," /th/ in "thin," and /ch/ in "champ."

7. *Teach common and tricky syllable patterns.* There are some syllable patterns that occur frequently in English spelling that can be tricky and benefit students to learn explicitly. For example, the /le/ pattern in "little" is an unusual sound-to-spelling pattern as is /ing/ as in "running" and /er/ in "wonder" or "better."

8. *Teach "r" controlled patterns, particularly when "r" follows a vowel and changes the sound.* The letter "r" is powerful and changes the sound of short vowels when it follows the vowel. Some people refer to this as "bossy r" as it is able to tell the vowel what to do. For example, in "ar" words such as "car," "bar," "far," and "tar" the sound of the letter "a" changes when it is followed by "r." This is also true for the other short vowels, for example, "fern," "corn," "burn," "fir," and "torn."

9. *Teach students to read high-frequency words.* English is a magnificent language with lots of words borrowed and adapted from many other languages. This also makes many of the spellings unusual and tricky for mapping the sounds of language to print. For example, many high-frequency words (see Figure 1 on page 42) are also words that we can use only some of our phonics knowledge to read. The most used high-frequency word in English is "the," and we can use our knowledge of the consonant digraph /th/ to help read the word, but our knowledge of vowel sounds does not help us with the letter "e." This is also true for "was," where our knowledge of the /w/ sound is helpful but the vowel sound is irregular. For this reason, it is very important to give students lots of practice with high-frequency words that are not easy to use phonics rules to decode.

10. *Teach students to read both "within" and "around" the word.* What we mean by both "within" and "around" the word is that many words can be partially decoded based on our understanding of phonics but can be more accurately decoded if we use both our knowledge of phonics and the context of the word in the sentence. For words that are completely phonetically regular, reading "around" the word is less important. However, for words that are partially phonetically regular using both phonics skills to read "within" the word and sentence or context to read "around" the word is supportive in more accurately decoding the word.

The most important thing about phonics is to consider these "patterns" as guides to help students unlock new words and read accurately and with comprehension, understanding that with practice, students will learn to be flexible in applying patterns and looking for exceptions. Phonics instruction for typical readers in kindergarten through second grade can take place in a well-organized, sequential, and skillfully taught manner in 20–30 minutes every day. As students reach the older grades, more time is spent on applying phonics and morphological understandings to more complex, multisyllabic words. What about students who are having difficulty learning to read? These youngsters may need more time and intensiveness in phonics instruction; however, in all cases—whether it is typical learners or students with reading difficulties—time to practice reading connected text, such as multiple sentences and paragraphs rather than words or shorter disconnected sentences, and reading for understanding is the critical aim of reading instruction.

## Frequently Asked Questions about Phonics Instruction and Word Recognition

1. *Some students seem to learn to read very easily. Do they need phonics instruction?* Phonics instruction is a tool that helps students unlock words they do not automatically recognize. If you have students who are reading considerably above grade level, it is likely they have already "inferred" the rules of phonics and may not need to be taught them explicitly. I suggest that you observe these students reading and identify word patterns with which they struggle. Then specifically teach the phonics rule that aligns with that word pattern.

2. *Is there an exact order in which students should be taught the sounds and sound combinations?* Many teachers wonder whether students should learn the sound-letter(s) correspondences for particular consonants first (e.g., /s/, /m/, /b/) and also wonder what vowels to teach first (e.g., /a/, /i/, or /o/). There is no research definitively prescribing which letter-sound correspondence should be taught in which particular order, however, there are some guidelines to help with these decisions:

   a. Teach sounds students can readily pronounce. For example, /s/ and /m/ are sounds many students produce early whereas /r/ and /l/ are more difficult sounds to pronounce.

   b. Teach sounds that allow students to readily make words, so they start reading very quickly. For example, if students learn the /a/ sound and the /m/ sound, they can learn the word "am" and then add initial consonant sounds as they learn them ("ham," "jam," "Sam"). Students can readily learn to read the word "I" since it is one letter and the sound it makes is the same as its name. Thus, students can read

"I am" with minimal instruction and begin the reading process.

   c. Teach a few consonants and then one or two vowels, so students can begin to read and form words right away rather than wait until they learn the entire alphabet. If we teach all the consonants first before introducing vowels, it delays unnecessarily word reading and text reading.

3. *When should students be taught irregular words?* Because English has many frequently occurring words that are also irregular, it is necessary for students to learn many irregular words from the very beginning. Some teachers refer to these as "sight" words because we want students to see them and read them automatically without sounding them out. Figure 1 on page 42 provides a list of high-frequency sight words that students need to read automatically because they occur so often in text.

4. *How do you know when to stop teaching phonics?* Typically phonics instruction is reduced considerably as students become more proficient readers. When students can successfully apply the rules of phonics to read words, teach only the phonics rules they need for more complex words. For example, if a student in second grade is reading at or above grade level and is struggling with the word "taught," it is helpful to teach the sound-spelling correspondence for /augh/ and /ough/ since the spellings show up in many words and will help the student in the future. However, if a student is readily reading and understanding text and making few errors, he or she may not need further phonics instruction.

5. *Do students apply their knowledge of phonics to multisyllabic words automatically?* Teachers frequently comment that students are able to apply what they know about phonics to single-syllable words but are less successful at using their phonics knowledge with multisyllabic words. Students benefit from explicit instruction in how to apply the rules they know to multisyllabic words as well as acquire new techniques for decoding multisyllabic words.

For example, students who have good use of short and long vowel rules as well as other common phonetic elements can readily apply them to words like "pancake" and "manipulate." But if they had relatively little practice doing this, they may stumble on words in text. Also students may encounter new uses of phonics rules that occur only in multisyllabic words. For example, words that end in /le/ make a different sound in multisyllabic words than in single-syllable words, and it helps students to learn these rules. For example, note the differences between /sale/ and /candle/ or /mile/ and /middle/. Thus, students need opportunities to apply phonics rules to multisyllabic words as well as learn phonics rules that are applicable for multisyllabic words.

6. *Does comprehension have any role when students are decoding an unknown word in text?* Students benefit from explicit instruction in the application of phonics rules in both single and multisyllabic words and also how to use context to support word reading. For example, in the following sentence a word is underlined and students can learn to use both decoding and comprehension to read the word correctly: *Playing the game well depended on the lucky number that came up on the spinner.* The word "spinner" can be decoded both by using phonics as well as supporting context to understand the word. Often, the context of the sentence will help students confirm a word they have figured out through phonics.

7. *Should phonics instruction occur with nonsense words, real words, or connected text?* Phonics instruction can be effectively done with nonsense words, real words, and connected text depending upon the instructional goal. For the most part, instruction should occur with real words, so students see the decoding process helps them arrive at a word that holds meaning. It is useful to initially teach sound-letter correspondence and then to practice it with real words. After students are proficient applying the sound-letter connection with real words, a fun activity can be mixing real words and nonsense words, asking students to read them, and then asking them to tell you which words are real or fake. For example, after students learn that "e" at the end of a word makes the vowel long, they can practice reading these real and nonsense words and then telling you which ones are real: "made," "bace," "rake," "tile," "fude," "ripe," "pole," "hete."

8. *How do teachers address classroom management issues?* There are several critical ways teachers can address classroom management issues while teaching phonics. First, students who are engaged are far less likely to demonstrate behavior problems. For this reason, make the phonics instruction engaging by demonstrating what you want students to know, giving them an opportunity to respond as a group or class, and then allowing them to practice individually or with a partner. Second, providing specific and ongoing feedback as students are learning new phonics skills increases their engagement and reduces behavior problems. Third, consider providing some instruction to the class as a whole when you are introducing a new phonics rule. Then provide opportunities to practice with more difficult words for more capable readers and with less difficult words for students who are acquiring reading proficiency.

FIGURE 1 COMMON SIGHT WORDS

| | | | |
|---|---|---|---|
| I | first | four | today |
| a | water | girl | order |
| is | called | high | horse |
| on | put | between | color |
| as | off | under | body |
| if | work | story | north |
| of | give | next | south |
| or | where | watch | cried |
| the | any | leave | I'll |
| you | want | it's | fire |
| was | does | every | music |
| for | here | country | question |
| are | only | earth | didn't |
| with | little | eye | friend |
| his | very | always | door |
| this | after | both | become |
| have | great | paper | better |
| one | also | often | during |
| what | large | until | whole |
| were | move | children | himself |
| your | again | river | morning |
| said | point | carry | against |
| use | father | once | table |
| each | sentence | later | pull |
| there | through | without | voice |
| their | following | almost | upon |
| which | even | being | area |
| them | because | example | problem |
| these | different | together | complete |
| some | picture | group | piece |
| her | animal | important | usually |
| has | letter | second | easy |
| two | answer | idea | heard |
| been | study | enough | sure |
| come | learn | really | however |
| from | American | sometimes | product |
| word | world | mountain | happen |
| many | add | young | remember |
| into | city | family | listen |
| number | don't | bird | early |
| people | open | across | cover |
| several | common | present | |

FIGURE 2 EXAMPLES OF WORD FAMILIES AND WORDS THAT FIT THE PATTERNS

## -VC WORD PATTERNS

| -an | -ap | -at | -et |
|------|------|------|------|
| ban | cap | bat | bet |
| can | gap | cat | get |
| Dan | lap | fat | jet |
| fan | map | hat | let |
| man | nap | mat | met |
| Nan | rap | pat | net |
| pan | sap | rat | pet |
| ran | tap | sat | set |
| tan | yap | vat | vet |
| than | snap | brat | yet |
| Stan | trap | chat | |
| bran | clap | scat | |
| | | slat | |

| -in | -ip | -ug | -op |
|------|------|------|------|
| bin | dip | bug | cop |
| fin | hip | dug | hop |
| kin | kip | hug | lop |
| pin | lip | jug | mop |
| tin | nip | lug | pop |
| win | rip | mug | sop |
| shin | sip | pug | top |
| | tip | rug | crop |
| | drip | tug | plop |
| | ship | drug | prop |
| | slip | plug | shop |
| | snip | | stop |
| | trip | | |

## -VCE WORD PATTERNS

| -ake | -ice | -ope | -ale |
|------|------|------|------|
| bake | dice | cope | bale |
| cake | lice | hope | dale |
| fake | mice | lope | gale |
| Jake | nice | mope | hale |
| lake | rice | nope | kale |
| make | vice | pope | male |
| rake | slice | rope | pale |
| sake | | | sale |
| take | | | vale |
| brake | | | Yale |
| flake | | | shale |
| stake | | | whale |

## -VVC WORD PATTERNS

| -ail | -eat | -eep | -ain |
|------|------|------|------|
| bail | beat | beep | gain |
| fail | feat | deep | lain |
| hail | heat | jeep | main |
| jail | meat | keep | pain |
| mail | neat | peep | rain |
| nail | peat | seep | vain |
| pail | seat | sheep | brain |
| rail | bleat | | drain |
| sail | pleat | | grain |
| tail | treat | | plain |
| Braille | wheat | | stain |
| snail | | | train |
| trail | | | |

## -VCC WORD PATTERNS

| -ack | -ell | -ick | -ump |
|------|------|------|------|
| back | bell | kick | bump |
| hack | dell | lick | dump |
| jack | fell | Mick | hump |
| lack | Nell | Nick | jump |
| pack | sell | pick | lump |
| rack | tell | Rick | pump |
| sack | well | sick | chump |
| tack | yell | tick | clump |
| black | shell | brick | grump |
| flack | swell | chick | plump |
| stack | | slick | stump |
| shack | | trick | trump |
| slack | | | |
| smack | | | |
| whack | | | |

## References and Resources

Adams, M. J. 1990. *Beginning to Read: Thinking and Learning about Print.* Cambridge, MA: MIT Press.

Blachman, B., D. Tangel, E. Ball, R. Black, and D. McGraw. 1999. "Developing Phonological Awareness and Word Recognition Skills: A Two-year Intervention with Low-income, Inner-city Children." *Reading and Writing: An Interdisciplinary Journal* 11: 293–273.

de Graaff, S., A. Bosman, F. Hasselman, and L. Verhoeven. 2009. "Benefits of Systematic Phonics Instruction." *Scientific Studies of Reading* 13 (4): 318–333.

Ehri, L. C. 2003. *Systematic Phonics Instruction: Findings of the National Reading Panel.* ERIC Document ED479646.

Ehri, L., S. Nunes, S. Stahl, and D. Willows. 2001. "Systematic Phonics Instruction Helps Students Learn to Read: Evidence from the National Reading Panel's Meta-analysis." *Review of Educational Research* 71 (3): 393–447.

Foorman, B., D. Francis, J. Fletcher, C. Schatschneider, and P. Mehta. 1998. "The Role of Instruction in Learning to Read: Preventing Reading Failure in At-risk Children." *Journal of Educational Psychology* 90: 37–55.

Foorman, B., D. Francis, D. Winikates, P. Mehta, C. Schatschneider, and J. Fletcher. 1997. "Early Interventions for Children with Reading Disabilities." *Scientific Studies of Reading* 1: 255–276.

Jeynes, W. H. 2008. "A Meta-Analysis of the Relationship between Phonics Instruction and Minority Elementary School Student Academic Achievement." *Education and Urban Society* 40 (2): 151–166.

National Governors Association for Best Practices, Council of Chief State School Officers. 2010. *Common Core State Standards for English Language Arts.* Washington, D.C.: National Governors Association for Best Practices, Council of Chief State School Officers.

National Reading Panel (U.S.) and National Institute of Child Health and Human Development (U.S.). 2000. "Report of the National Reading Panel: Teaching Children to Read: An Evidence-based Assessment of the Scientific Research Literature on Reading and Its Implications for Reading Instruction: Reports of the Subgroups." Washington, D.C.: National Institute of Child Health and Human Development, National Institutes of Health.

Shanahan, T. 2015. "What Teachers Should Know about Common Core: A Guide for the Perplexed." *Reading Teacher* 68 (8): 583–588.

Stuebing, Karla K., Amy E. Barth, Paul T. Cirino, David J. Francis, Jack M. Fletcher. 2008. "A Response to Recent Reanalyses of the National Reading Panel Report: Effects of Systematic Phonics Instruction Are Practically Significant." *Journal of Educational Psychology* 100 (1): 123–134.

# Supporting Background Knowledge in a Comprehensive Literacy Program

## Shari Frost

"The snail took so long to get there! I think he must have gone home and forgotten all about that letter," announced first grader Brianna knowingly.

Brianna's group was engaged in a lively book discussion about the story, "The Letter," from the book, *Frog and Toad Are Friends* (Lobel 2003). In the story, Toad is sad because he never gets any mail. Frog, being a good friend, writes him a letter and asks a snail to deliver it to Toad. The snail doesn't arrive with the letter until four days later. (Could this be the origin of the term "snail mail"?)

Clearly, Brianna did not have sufficient background knowledge about snails to truly understand and appreciate the story. Brianna didn't know that snails are very slow-moving creatures, traveling at a rate of about 23 inches (58.4 centimeters) per hour. Lacking that background knowledge, Brianna had found a way to make sense of the story. Why would it take the snail four days to get to Toad's house? She developed a hypothesis and was quite satisfied with it.

With a bit of background knowledge building, Brianna would have not only fully comprehended and enjoyed the story, but also stored away that little nugget of knowledge about snails to be used in future readings.

## Background Knowledge: What Is It, and Why Is It Important?

Background knowledge is the factual information that children already have on a specific topic. This factual information is acquired from various sources, such as their life experiences, what they've read, what has been read to them, conversations they've had with knowledgeable people, what they've seen on television and in films, and even what they've experienced in our classrooms. Children build on their existing background knowledge to support their understanding of new content, concepts, and ideas.

The playing field is not level when it comes to background knowledge. Some children are lucky enough to be born into families where their parents have real conversations with them. These children own books and have a regular bedtime story. Their families take day trips to zoos and museums. They take vacations to more national parks than amusement parks. These children bring lots of background knowledge to their reading. They would surely know what a snail is and understand why it would take a snail four days to deliver a letter. Not all children are so lucky.

The research on background knowledge, also called "schema" or "prior knowledge," is built on Bartlett's work in 1932. This British psychologist proposed that we build on what we already know to help us learn new things. "Schema theory," as it relates to language and reading comprehension, was further developed in a seminal study by the esteemed literacy researcher, Richard Anderson (1977). His study (p. 22) found that ". . . text information is interpreted, organized, and retrieved in terms of high-level schemata. It follows that the student who doesn't possess relevant schemata is going to have trouble learning and remembering the information encountered in stories and textbooks." Marzano (2004, 1) concurs, stating that ". . . what students *already know* about the content is one of the strongest indicators of how well they will learn new information relative to the content."

Background knowledge equips children with vocabulary, idioms, and domain-specific knowledge that support prospective learning. It is also an essential element in applying reading comprehension strategies. Readers must use what they know about the genre and the topic of a text to make valid predictions. Readers use their background knowledge and clues from the text to make inferences.

## Assessing Background Knowledge: Finding Out What They Know

Before you can build children's background knowledge, you have to find out what they know. Engage the children in background knowledge assessment activities when you have little or no information about what they already know on the topic. Here are some strategies to help you assess your students' background knowledge.

### Teacher Questioning

Teacher questioning is a direct, efficient, and effective way of finding out what children know about a certain topic. Brianna's teacher would have been able to immediately identify the gap in her background knowledge if she had posed some simple

questions such as, *What is a snail? What do they look like? How do they move? When you think about snails, what comes to your mind?*

Teacher questioning can be done with the whole class, groups, or individuals before launching a new topic or text. It is quick, taking only a few minutes to prepare and execute, and it gives you pertinent information for moving forward with the lesson.

### Draw and Jot

Draw and jot is a simple, nonthreatening way to find out what children know on a given topic. Most children are willing to draw a picture. Distribute unlined paper and drawing tools (crayons, markers, colored pencils). Ask children to draw a picture and add labels, captions, or even a few sentences about the topic. Brianna's teacher could have asked her group to draw a snail and jot down something they know about snails.

Extend and enrich this activity by pairing the children. Have them share their completed pictures with their partner and read what they have written to their partner. You can circulate among the children and listen in on the conversations for additional information.

Draw and jot makes a wonderful morning bell ringer activity. Have children work on their draw and jot task to provide information for their upcoming guided reading, interactive read-aloud, or content lesson. If you add the date and the name of the topic to the back of the drawings, the draw and jot artifacts can also serve as formative assessment documents.

## Activating Background Knowledge: Helping Them Recall What They Know

We activate children's background knowledge when we think, or hope, that they have at least a little knowledge on a specific topic. These activities support kids in retrieving information, get them to think about that information, and maybe even initiate the process of building more background knowledge through their interactions around these tasks.

## Anticipation Guide

An anticipation guide (Duffelmeyer 1994) is an activity that not only activates children's background knowledge, but can also help to generate enthusiasm and curiosity about the topic. The anticipation guide helps to establish the purpose for reading. When the children finish reading the text, the anticipation guide helps them review and reflect upon the information. Here are the steps for using an anticipation guide:

1. Prepare an anticipation guide, using the template provided on page 50, by writing 5–10 statements based on the information in the text.

2. Distribute copies of the anticipation guide to the children.

3. Have the children read each statement, then mark if it is true or false in the column to the left of the statement (the first column). You can also use "yes" and "no" or a smiley face and a frowning face.

4. Collect the anticipation guides.

5. Have the children read the text and participate in post-reading activities (e.g., discussion, writing).

6. Redistribute the anticipation guides to the children. Ask them to read the statements again and mark if the statements are true or false in the column to the right of the statements.

Name: _____

# **Anticipation Guide**

Before Reading

After Reading

| True | False | Statement | True | False |
|------|-------|-----------|------|-------|
|      |       |           |      |       |
|      |       |           |      |       |
|      |       |           |      |       |
|      |       |           |      |       |
|      |       |           |      |       |
|      |       |           |      |       |
|      |       |           |      |       |
|      |       |           |      |       |
|      |       |           |      |       |

## Gallery Walk

A gallery walk, also called a carousel walk, was developed by Spencer Kagan (1994). It engages the children in self-activating their background knowledge. Small groups of children take two trips through "the gallery" to look at, talk about, and examine images, documents, and artifacts displayed there. On the first trip around, they jot down their thoughts, ideas, and impressions on a sticky note and post it in the space provided near the exhibit. On the second trip around, they read what the other small groups wrote. The whole class reconvenes for a discussion and the generation of a master list of pertinent facts about the topic. Here are the steps for creating a gallery walk:

1. Collect images (photographic if possible), charts and graphs, artifacts, and brief text excerpts related to the topic.

2. Display them around the room, allowing as much space as possible between displays.

3. Affix a sheet of an enlarged (poster size) sticky note near each display item. Or you can also give each small group a stack of smaller sticky notes.

4. Divide the children into small groups. The smaller the size of the group, the better, so try to limit small group size to four at the most.

5. Give each group an appropriate writing implement to record their thoughts, ideas, and questions, such as a marker if you're using an enlarged sticky note or a pen or pencil if you're using smaller sticky notes.

6. Start each group in front of a display. Give them five minutes to discuss the display and record their thoughts, ideas, and questions. After five minutes, have each group rotate.

7. After the first complete rotation, have the groups go through the gallery again. This time, they will read the other groups' notes and discuss them.

8. After two rotations, reconvene the entire classroom. Make a master list of learnings and questions.

## RAN Chart

RAN is an acronym for "reading and analyzing nonfiction." This strategy was developed by Tony Stead (2006). Stead adapted the KWL strategy to address the challenges that K–5 students experience using it. The "What I Know" column is likely to be filled with misconceptions. Children often struggle to identify something that they "Want to Know," especially when they have limited background knowledge on the topic. Here are the steps for creating and using a RAN chart:

1. Prepare a five-column chart on butcher paper or bulletin board paper that is large enough for all of the children to see. The column titles are "What We Think We Know," "Confirmed," "Misconceptions," "New Information," and "Questions."

2. Lead the children in brainstorming *what they think they know* on the topic. Write each of these "facts" on a sticky note, and affix it to the first column of the chart.

3. Provide a reading experience on the topic for the children. It can be an interactive read-aloud, shared reading, or independent reading in a textbook or trade book.

4. When the children find a *confirmation* in the text for a fact in the "What We Think We Know" column, that fact is transferred to the second column—"Confirmed."

5. After reading the text(s), lead the children in reviewing the chart. Discuss the misconceptions among the "facts" in the first column and move them to the third column—"Misconceptions."

6. Revise misconceptions, if possible. Using qualifiers (e.g., "sometimes" instead of "always") might help the process. Add the revised statements to the fourth column—"New Information."

7. Have the children reread the text to discover if there is any additional new information they learned that they would like to add to the fourth column—"New Information."

8. Often, new questions emerge through the reading and discussion. Record the new questions in the final column—"Questions."

## Alphaboxes

Alphaboxes is a graphic organizer used to activate children's background knowledge on a specific topic. This activating strategy was developed by Linda Hoyt (2002) and can be used before, during, and after reading. It supports and encourages children in interacting with text. In addition, Alphaboxes can be instrumental in building vocabulary and increasing comprehension. Here are the steps for using Alphaboxes:

1. Prepare an Alphabox grid of the appropriate size (for a small group or whole class). **An Alphabox grid is a chart, with each letter of the alphabet in a cell.** The grid can be made on chart paper (to preserve it for future use), drawn on the whiteboard, or projected on a screen or smartboard. You can also make standard-sized (8.5 x 11) copies for individuals.

2. Display the Alphabox grid at the children's eye level and within their reach.

3. Ask children to think of "key words" that come to mind when they think of the topic.

4. Distribute sticky notes and have the children record their key words on them using a black or blue writing tool (pencils, pens, markers).

5. Have the children come up and affix their sticky notes to the appropriate boxes on the chart. When multiple children think of the same word, affix them on top of each other, so only one copy of the word is visible.

6. Read the chart together. Select a few critical words to talk about. Using the words from the chart, use shared writing to compose a brief overview of the topic in a few sentences.

7. After distributing additional sticky notes and a red writing tool, engage the children in a reading experience (interactive read-aloud, shared reading, individual reading). Tell them to look in the text for the key words that are currently on the chart. Also tell them to suggest new key words from the text that are not yet on the chart and to record their suggestions on their sticky notes with the red writing tool.

8. When a word that is already on the chart appears during the reading, put an asterisk next to it.

9. After the reading is completed, have the children affix the new key words that they selected and recorded during the reading to the appropriate boxes on the chart. Again, when a word is selected multiple times, stack the copies on top of each other.

10. Review the completed Alphaboxes chart. Acknowledge the new key words from the text that children provided.

11. Have the children write a brief summary on the topic at their level of proficiency. Emergent writers can draw and label.

12. Display the chart to enhance the print-rich environment and to serve as a resource for the children. Children can add more words when they read additional books on the topic.

## Concept Map

A concept map, developed by Joseph D. Novak (1977), is a graphic organizer that supports structured brainstorming by providing specific prompts. It is useful in activating background knowledge because it orients children to new content that they are about to encounter. It gives teachers an idea of children's existing background knowledge and graphically organizes their knowledge and new information. It helps students make meaningful connections between the main idea and key concepts. A concept map supports children in understanding these connections as well as the hierarchy of ideas on a specific topic. A completed concept map becomes a visual representation of the topic. Concept maps are especially supportive to visual learners. Here are the steps for using a concept map:

1. There are a wide variety of concept maps. Taking the text structure into consideration, select a concept map that is most appropriate to the text that will be read. For example, if the text has descriptive text structure, it is a good idea to use a webbing map (circle in the middle with rays extending from the circle).

2. It is advisable to start with a simpler map for your first mapping experiences. Increase the complexity of the maps over time as children become more proficient. You might consider using mapping software such as Kidspiration.

3. The concept map can be projected on a smartboard or a screen, especially if you are using software. You can also draw a map on a whiteboard or chart paper. Eventually, the children will be able to complete maps on a standard-sized sheet.

4. Select the key concept—usually the name of your topic. Record it in the focus space on the map.

5. Follow the prompts provided on the map to fill in the other spaces. Encourage the children to give support for their answers. Expect that you will not be able to complete the map before reading the text.

6. Engage the children in a reading experience (interactive read-aloud, shared reading, individual reading). Include stopping places to verify the information on the map.

7. After the reading, revisit the map to fill in blanks and make appropriate revisions as needed.

8. Display the map to enhance the print-rich environment and serve as a resource to the children.

# Building Background Knowledge

Building background knowledge is certainly worth the time and energy that we devote to it. It allows children to more fully benefit from our carefully prepared lessons. Here are some tried-and-true strategies for building children's background knowledge.

## Direct Experiences

The absolute best way to build children's background knowledge is to engage them in a direct experience. Direct experiences can have a profound impact on their memory because we are engaged with them at multiple levels, including through our senses (sight, hearing, touch, smell) and bodily-kinesthetic interactions. We are more likely to learn from what we do than from what we see, hear, or even read about.

That's why those lucky kids whose families engage them in many rich direct experiences comprehend texts at a higher level of achievement. If Brianna's classroom had contained snails in an aquarium, she would have had the necessary background knowledge to understand the story. Providing direct experiences is also the most time-consuming and undoubtedly the most expensive way to build background knowledge. Therefore, teachers must be thoughtful and purposeful in selecting and planning these experiences.

Provide direct experiences for extended units of study that will involve children in reading multiple texts on the topic over a period of time. If a class is engaged in a six-week unit on plants, it makes sense to have the children plant seeds and document their growth and development. Teachers have brought butterfly eggs, frog eggs, and poultry eggs into their classrooms, so children can directly observe life cycles in action. Some classrooms have worm-composting bins, so children can learn about decomposition.

Some teachers engage their students in direct experiences outside of their classrooms. They participate in projects such as collecting and planting native seeds in forest preserves; participating in local river and pond cleanup projects; or collecting newspapers, cans, and bottles and taking them to a local recycling center. They participate in re-enactments such as medieval fairs and pioneer villages. When children in these classrooms read and write about topics in which they have had direct experiences, they do so with increased comprehension.

## Realia

Realia is the use of concrete objects for teaching purposes. Like direct experiences, they build background knowledge and vocabulary by providing a memorable, multisensory exploration for children. A third grade class was reading *The Lion, the Witch and the Wardrobe* (Lewis 1984), and the children were pondering why it was so easy to convince Edward to betray his sister with the promise of "Turkish delight." The next day, the teacher brought in some Turkish delight for the children to taste. The children agreed that the candy was delicious, but some argued that it is not delicious enough to warrant endangering a sibling.

Bringing in seashells, sand dollars, and sea glass will enhance landlocked children's understanding of a read-aloud of the book, *Out of the Ocean* (Fraser 1998). Bringing in a loom can help children understand the tedious nature of Annie's weaving chores in *Annie and the Old One* (Miles 2005). Bringing in chopsticks and raisins, so children can try them out, can help children understand Liang Suang's pride in his ability to use chopsticks in *Cleversticks* (Ashley 2002). Realia is especially useful in supporting children in reading and understanding multicultural literature. Russian nesting dolls, African masks, Day of the Dead sugar skulls, and Kamishibai story cards all make indispensable teaching tools.

Many museums and libraries have resource lending programs. Teachers can check out cultural toys, flags, musical instruments, fossils, rocks, shells, coral, fossils, mounted butterflies, specimens . . . the list is endless. Make a call to your local library and your science, history, or cultural museum to see what is available to support your next unit of study.

## Field Trips

Federally funded programs to enhance the education of children living in poverty, such as the Elementary and Secondary Educational Act (ESEA) and Headstart, always include a budget line for school field trips. The children who participate in these programs were not born into families that regularly visit zoos, museums, nature centers, or even preschool story time at the local library. The field trip funding in the federal programs is an attempt to address these deficits of experience. It is understood that field trips will help to provide children with needed background knowledge.

Field trips enable teachers to expand children's learning beyond the walls of the classroom. They have an impact on children similar to that of direct experiences—interactive, bodily kinesthetic, memorable, and lived through—contributing immeasurable background knowledge. The learning opportunities in field trips cannot be duplicated by even the very best classroom instruction. Field trips are "living laboratories" in which learning is intensified by authenticity.

After visiting a natural history museum, children will have a deeper understanding of how mummies are made; therefore, they will derive greater benefit from an Ancient Egypt unit in the classroom. After visiting and participating in the simulations in the Pawnee Earth lodge at the Field Museum in Chicago, children will have enhanced comprehension of *The Birchbark House* (Erdrich 2002). Even though the simulations are about Pawnee Indians and the book is about Ojibwa Indians, they were both tribes of the Upper Plains who had very similar lifestyles, so background knowledge about either of them can be transferred to the other as well. Maximize field trip experiences by making use of guides, docents, and special classes for school groups.

## Virtual Field Trips

Field trips can be costly in terms of both money and time. Sometimes, the perfect field trip venue is in another state, another country, or even another planet. Thanks to technology, teachers can take their students on virtual field trips to any place in the world and beyond. An African safari, the Amazon Rainforest, the Great Wall of China, and even Mars are accessible to your students via virtual field trips.

A variety of virtual field trip experiences is available. Some virtual field trips are guided, narrated tours, such as the virtual field trip to Ellis Island. This activity will build needed background knowledge for a unit on immigration or before children read *If Your Name Was Changed at Ellis Island* by Ellen Levine (1994). Some virtual field trips are simply live action webcams like the Giant Panda Cam at the National Zoo. Children can observe giant pandas in action as preparation for a read-aloud of *Mrs. Harkness and the Panda* by Alice Potter (2012).

Virtual field trips can be a whole class experience, done in small groups, or experienced individually. Guided, narrated tours work well for whole class experiences. However, for a webcam experience, you'll probably want to set up a learning station containing a single device connected to the webcam and have children rotate through the station. Webcam experiences require a little patience. The pandas are not always cavorting for the delight of viewers. Sometimes they are sleeping or out of the camera's range.

Do an Internet search to find a virtual field trip that best meets your students' instructional needs. There are many free virtual field trips, but some cost hundreds of dollars. Read the reviews written by other teachers and be sure to watch the whole thing yourself before you show it to children. Previewing the field trip will alert you to any questionable content and confirm that your technology is up to the job.

## Videos

Like virtual field trips, videos are a cost- and time-efficient way to bring the outside world into your classroom. Short video clips from YouTube or full length feature films can be used to activate and build children's background knowledge. Public libraries circulate videos at no cost, provided that you return them in a timely manner. There are also many videos available online, both free and with a paid membership. A full library of videos is offered by respected organizations such as National Geographic, Neo K–12, Edu Tube, and PBS Learning Media.

Make sure children understand that though they are likely to be entertained, the video viewing is not just for recreational purposes. Give children a purpose for viewing the video. Prior to reading *The One and Only Ivan* by Katherine Applegate (2012), children can watch segments featuring the gorilla, Ivan, in National Geographic's video, *The Urban Gorilla*, and video clips of gorillas in their natural habitat (also available through National Geographic). Children will see the gorilla that inspired the book and be able to observe both a gorilla in captivity and gorillas in the wild. Have children look for the differences and think about what would need to be done to make a gorilla comfortable in captivity.

## Picture Book Read-alouds

A simple, effective, and easily accessible way to build background knowledge is to read aloud a picture book. Teachers should read the book aloud, even to children who are capable of reading the book themselves. When you read aloud to them, they can devote all of their attention to the book's content and not expend any energy on processing print.

Picture books build children's background knowledge via a rich blend of both well-chosen words and carefully crafted images. Children's book authors are master wordsmiths. They must relay their message in only about 28 pages, so the words are selected with care. Content-specific vocabulary is presented in the supportive environment of high-quality illustrations or photographs. The recent explosion of picture books, especially informational picture books, offers many options. There is certainly a great picture book for any topic in your curriculum.

Plan for read-alouds to build background knowledge the same way that you plan for any literacy lesson. Give the children a purpose for listening. Plan stopping places for the children to turn and talk. Highlight vocabulary. Include post-reading activities for discussion, writing, and listing questions for inquiry. Make the book available to children after the read-aloud. They can return to the book to closely examine the illustrations and reread it on their own. Read *How to Make a Cherry Pie and See the U.S.A.* by Majorie Priceman (2013) to introduce children to a "regions of the United States" unit. Read aloud *Water Is Water* by Miranda Paul (2015) to launch a unit on the water cycle. Work on building a collection of picture books to support a variety of topics that you teach.

## Background Knowledge: The Key to Successful Reading Experiences

Every minute that we invest in activating and building knowledge will be paid back in dividends for our students. In addition to contributing to successful reading experiences for current lessons, it will also become part of their store of factual information that they can draw on for future reading experiences.

### References and Resources

Anderson, R. C. 1977. "Schema-directed Processes in Language Comprehension (Tech. Rep. No. 50)." Urbana-Champaign, IL: Center for the Study of Reading, University of Illinois.

Applegate, K. 2012. *The One and Only Ivan.* New York: HarperCollins.

Ashley, B. 2002. *Cleversticks.* New York: HarperCollins.

Bartlett, F. C. 1932. *Remembering: A Study in Experimental and Social Psychology.* Cambridge, England: Cambridge University Press.

Duffelmeyer, F. 1994. "Effective Anticipation Guide Statements for Learning from Expository Prose." *Journal of Reading* 37: 452–455.

Erdrich, L. 2002. *The Birchbark House.* New York: Disney-Hyperion.

Fraser, D. 1998. *Out of the Ocean.* New York: Harcourt Children's Books.

Hoyt, L. 2002. *Make It Real: Strategies for Success with Informational Texts.* Portsmouth, NH: Heinemann.

Kagan, S. 1994. *Kagan Cooperative Learning.* San Clemente, CA: Kagan Publishing.

Levine, E. 1994. *If Your Name Was Changed at Ellis Island.* New York: Scholastic.

Lewis, C. S. 1984. *The Lion, the Witch and the Wardrobe.* The Chronicles of Narnia. New York: Scholastic.

Lobel, A. 2003. *Frog and Toad Are Friends.* An I Can Read Book. New York: HarperCollins.

Marzano, R. J. 2004. *Building Background Knowledge for Academic Achievement: Research on What Works in Schools.* Alexandria, VA: Association of Supervision and Curriculum Development.

Miles, M. 2005. *Annie and the Old One.* New York: Little Brown Books for Young Readers.

Novak, J. D. 1977. *A Theory of Education.* Ithaca, NY: Cornell University Press.

Paul, M. 2015. *Water Is Water: A Book About the Water Cycle.* New York: Roaring Brook Press.

Potter, A. 2012. *Mrs. Harkness and the Panda.* New York: Knopf Books for Young Readers.

Priceman, M. 2013. *How to Make a Cherry Pie and See the U.S.A.* New York: Dragonfly Books.

Stead, T. 2006. *Reality Checks: Teaching Reading Comprehension with Nonfiction.* Portland, Maine: Stenhouse Publishers.

*The Urban Gorilla.* 1991. Directed by Allison Argo. National Geographic, DVD.

# Enriched Vocabulary Instruction within a Balanced Literacy Framework

## Charlene Cobb

## Introduction

Many of us can recall vocabulary instruction in elementary school that was less than engaging. If you've ever been given a list of words to look up in the dictionary and then write a sentence using the word, you'll understand. Or you may have had a textbook with daily lessons, which included one page of matching the words to definitions, another page where you selected the correct word to complete a sentence, and then did a word search on the last page. In both of these scenarios, at the end of the week you took a test on those words and then started the process anew the following week. We know now that this is not the most effective way to teach vocabulary.

What we do know is that all students should be active in developing their understanding of words. They also need to personalize their word learning. Students need opportunities to be immersed in words and encounter words repeatedly across multiple sources in order to build their depth of knowledge. What's not always clear is how to provide this instruction in elementary classrooms. This chapter will provide you with information on the value and need for highly effective vocabulary instruction. Additionally, you'll be provided with information on what this looks like in both primary and intermediate classrooms.

The research on vocabulary instruction is robust. Vocabulary is inexplicably tied to understanding, in both verbal and written language. In young learners, we know that vocabulary knowledge contributes to phonological awareness and in turn word recognition (Nagy 2005). A child who hears more words is better able to be aware of the sounds and also recognize the words when seen in print. We also know that vocabulary knowledge in primary grades serves as a predictor of a child's ability to comprehend in the intermediate grades (Cunningham and Stanovich 1997). There is evidence that teaching vocabulary can improve comprehension (Beck, Perfetti, and McKeown 1982).

There are some fundamental understandings about vocabulary. First, how we use words helps to define our depth of word knowledge. Each of us has four types of vocabulary knowledge. See Figure 1 below. We have listening and speaking vocabularies. We also have reading and writing vocabularies.

FIGURE 1 FOUR TYPES OF VOCABULARY

|  | Receptive (Recognition) | Expressive (Productive) |
|---|---|---|
| Speech | Listening vocabulary | Speaking vocabulary |
| Print | Reading vocabulary | Writing vocabulary |

The development of our listening vocabulary is usually a prerequisite to our speaking vocabulary. Similarly, the development of our reading vocabulary is prerequisite to our writing vocabulary. A child's listening and reading vocabulary can be increased by reading aloud to him or her from text with complex vocabulary.

Second, we need to understand that words are merely labels for concepts. These concepts are related to other words and can have multiple meanings and uses. This means that our knowledge of words can deepen. Vocabulary develops over multiple encounters with words across differing contexts. You can't "know" a word after a single encounter or after one week of instruction. Finally, it's estimated that students learn approximately 3,000 new words each year they are in school (Beck and McKeown 1991). It would be impossible to teach that many words, so it's clear that students are learning words through incidental means. This incidental learning comes through listening, wide reading, and discussions. However, we also need to provide intentional instruction through teaching specific words and word learning strategies.

It's also important to understand that words have differing levels of utility. Selecting words for instruction is facilitated by understanding the words' level of utility. Isabel Beck, Margaret McKeown, and Linda Kucan (2002) describe three levels, or tiers, of words. Tier One consists of the most basic words that usually do not need direct instruction. Along with function words such as "in," "out," and "other," examples of other basic words are "house," "mother," and "love."

Tier Two words are those words that can enrich and enlarge a student's reading and writing vocabulary. These are sophisticated words for concepts that students already possess. Examples of Tier Two words are "pretentious," "inquisitive," and "absurd." Finally, Tier Three words are specialized words that are generally found in content areas. The frequency of these words is low, but an understanding of the concept is needed to build the background knowledge essential to future learning. The words that Beck et al. refer to as Tier Three words are generally selected for the teacher by the publishers of content-area textbooks. These words frequently represent concepts that are both complex and abstract.

Michael Graves (2006) has developed a four-pronged approach to vocabulary instruction. Each component is briefly described below. In the following sections, specific information and strategies for integrating this approach in both primary and intermediate classrooms will be shared. The four components include:

- providing rich and varied language experiences
- teaching individual words
- teaching word learning strategies
- fostering word consciousness

*Providing rich and varied language experiences* includes setting up classrooms as print-rich environments. This includes the use of word walls, well-stocked classroom libraries, and access to online print. This also means providing students with opportunities for meaningful discussions with each other and with the teacher. In these classrooms teachers read aloud every day, they write interactively with their students, and they provide time for students to write.

*Teaching individual words* involves strategically selecting words for instruction. This includes instruction that provides both definitional and contextual information. Teaching individual words also provides opportunities for students to actively process their learning.

*Teaching word learning strategies* helps students learn what to do when they approach an unknown word. This calls for teaching roots, prefixes, and suffixes, so students understand the parts of words. This also requires teaching students how to use context to determine word meaning. Students learn to look both inside and outside of a new word they encounter in print. Teaching word learning strategies also involves teaching students how to use vocabulary resources such as dictionaries, a thesaurus, and online tools. However, these resources are not used in the typical "look up the list" format. They are used interactively to support word learning.

*Fostering word consciousness* is simply put as falling in love with words. In word conscious classrooms, students develop an appreciation of how words work to convey ideas and images. They develop an interest in and awareness of the structure and power of words. In word conscious classrooms, students learn how words work in figurative language and participate in wordplay activities to learn that words are interesting and worth learning. Students in word conscious classrooms know that learning words is active, engaging, worthwhile, and fun.

Each of these components is important and using any one of them is better than not using any of them. It's also important to understand that vocabulary instruction must occur beyond language arts and be part of science, social studies, and math instruction. As such, it is the integration of all four components within daily instruction that leads to deep learning and vocabulary growth. This will also look different in a primary classroom as compared to an intermediate classroom. The next sections will provide you with information and strategies for using this approach in all classrooms.

## Vocabulary Instruction in Primary Classrooms

Students in primary classrooms benefit from systematic instruction in phonemic awareness and phonics. In kindergarten and first grade, students need to develop phonological awareness. In grades kindergarten through grade two, students learn how to use phonics to decode unknown words. No one can argue that students need to develop these skills. In fact, these are clearly articulated through the Foundational Skills in the Common Core State Standards (National Governors Association for Best Practices and Council of Chief State School Officers 2010). However, these foundational skills are not enough to ensure adequate vocabulary development. The four-pronged approach to vocabulary instruction

can and should be incorporated into a balanced literacy program in all primary classrooms. Let's explore how to provide rich and varied language experiences, teach individual words, teach word learning strategies, and foster word consciousness in these classrooms.

*Providing rich and varied language experiences* can be easily incorporated into primary classrooms. Using high-quality children's literature and nonfiction text during a teacher read-aloud provides ideal opportunities to engage students with vocabulary. Keep in mind that the first time you read a book aloud, you want students to experience hearing a model of fluent reading. You also want them to enjoy the aesthetic experience through hearing the language and seeing the pictures. These are those rich language experiences. It is through a second, and sometimes third reading, that you provide students with both rich and varied experiences with Tier Two words. These are sophisticated words for which students already know the underlying concept. These types of words are found in complex text that is frequently above the students' reading levels. Here is an example of this type of complex text:

*Martha burst into the room. "Mom," she exclaimed, "look what I discovered on my way home from school!" She could barely contain her excitement. "It's incredible, remarkable, astonishing, and spectacular!"*

During a second reading in a kindergarten classroom you might stop after the word "burst" and say, *I love the way the author describes how Martha came into the room. She didn't say she walked in or came in, instead she said that she "burst into the room."*

Students may already understand the concept of walking or coming into a room. They can learn that "burst" is a more sophisticated way to express those concepts. Engage the students in rich discussion by asking questions such as: *What do you think the word "burst" means? Close your eyes, and imagine what Martha did. Now open your eyes and tell me what you saw.* Have some children act out "burst into." Ask them if it would be appropriate to burst into the lunchroom or when it might be appropriate to burst into their own home.

In a first or second grade classroom you might read the last sentence and say, *I find it very interesting that the author used four words instead of just one to describe what Martha found. The author had Martha say, "It's incredible, remarkable, astonishing, and spectacular!"*

*Why do you think she did that? Sometimes using similar words in a row helps to emphasize an idea or feeling. I think my favorite word here is "astonishing." Using the other words that are around "astonishing," what do you think it means? What is the difference between surprising and astonishing?* In this case, "astonishing" is a Tier Two word that students can explore through their understanding of the word "surprising."

After you've done this type of read-aloud several times, invite students to listen for interesting words during a second or third reading. Creating anchor charts of interesting action or feeling words contributes to the print-rich environment and encourages children to look for words that can be added to the charts. During interactive writing experiences, use the anchor charts and remind students to use the charts when they are writing independently.

The language experience approach (LEA) is another strategy for vocabulary development in primary classrooms (Hall 1977). LEA is built on the concept of developing reading materials based on written versions of students' spoken language. LEA texts can be developed around a shared experience as simple as taking a tour of the school or walking through the school neighborhood. Taking digital photographs during the experience is also a great idea. Use the pictures as prompts and record, either on large chart paper or via an interactive whiteboard, student responses to prompts such as, *What was happening in this picture? What do you notice? How did you feel?* Once the text is created, do a shared choral reading of the text. On chart paper, these become part of the print-rich environment. Printed on regular paper and bound, the texts become part of the classroom library to be read multiple times.

Classroom libraries are another essential element for rich and varied language experiences. Students need access to a wide range of texts in all primary classrooms. Narrative and nonfiction trade books with vivid pictures and illustrations, books of poetry, and magazines should be included. Students should have opportunities each day to spend time exploring books, reading to each other, and discussing books with both the teacher and their peers.

Teaching individual words in primary and intermediate classrooms has some similarities and also some differences. In all primary classrooms, you want to maximize opportunities to increase students' receptive listening vocabularies in order to encourage the development of their expressive speaking vocabularies. Remember that hearing words in multiple contexts will support students' ability to use those words in speech and also help them to recognize those words when they encounter them in print. In primary classrooms, word walls can provide a source for teaching individual words. Patricia Cunningham (2000) explains that in kindergarten classrooms, word walls begin with student names. Each week five words are added to the wall. Each day a student's name is selected, and the entire class spells the name, claps, and cheers each letter. After all student names are placed on the word wall, the words for colors and numbers or shapes might be added. These word wall activities provide multiple opportunities for students to actively process their learning. Cunningham's *Phonics They Use* (2000) has many more activities related to word walls in primary classrooms.

Creating anchor charts with academic vocabulary is another way to teach individual words in primary classrooms. When developing units of instruction in math, science, or social studies providing students with these Tier Three words, a student-friendly definition, and a picture or pictorial representation on a large chart can offer students multiple encounters with the words. For example, if you are studying a unit on geography, you might use the words: "river," "ocean," "lake," "plain," "mountain," and "valley." An anchor chart might look like Figure 2 on the next page.

FIGURE 2 PRIMARY ANCHOR CHART

| Word | Definition | Picture |
|------|------------|---------|
| mountain | land that is very tall and sometimes rocky |  |
| valley | low land between mountains |  |
| plain | flat land covered in grass |  |
| river | water that moves through land |  |
| lake | water with land all around it |  |
| ocean | largest bodies of water on Earth |  |

Many of the activities that would be done in written format in an intermediate classroom can be done orally in primary classrooms. With the above list of words, you might provide students with a set of word cards and ask them to sort the words into two groups, those that are about water and those that are about land. Then ask students to talk to a partner and explain why they put the words into each group. You might also ask them to connect two of the words by saying, *Who can think of a way that at least two of these words are connected? I'll give you an example. Mountains and valleys are connected because a valley is sometimes between mountains. Now you try it.* Give students time to think and then time to talk to a partner before sharing with the entire class. Once students are comfortable connecting two words, ask them to find two words that are NOT connected and explain why. These activities also provide students with those much needed multiple opportunities for engaging with words. Students need time to manipulate, think

about, and talk about words with others. Remember, learning a word is not an all-or-nothing experience. Think of it as the difference between an on-off light switch and a dimmer switch (Cobb and Blachowicz 2014). Words are learned incrementally, over multiple encounters and as students' depth of knowledge grows, their "light" gets stronger.

*Teaching word learning strategies* in primary grades begins by inviting students to use pictures as context. Pictures and illustrations are the starting point for teaching how to use context clues while reading. Reminding students to skip the word and read to the end of the sentence is another word-learning strategy. However, we must remember to teach students that simply skipping the word is not a strategy. Students must go back and reread the sentence. If they are still unable to figure out the word, then they need to use other strategies, such as picture clues or asking someone (either a peer or the teacher) for help.

Another strategy is the ability to identify and use inflectional endings and word parts. In the early primary grades, we begin teaching simple word parts such as inflected ending ("-s," "-es," "-ed," "-ing") and explaining how adding these to a word can change its meaning. By first grade we teach simple compound words to help students understand that two words can be combined to create a new word (sand + box = sandbox).

However, none of these strategies should be taught in isolation or without context. Reading aloud from high-quality literature provides an ideal opportunity to model strategies and have students practice word-learning strategies. This same instruction can then be carried over to small group reading instruction in order to differentiate for the specific needs of students. Having students go on word hunts to find words that end in "-s" and then figure out which of those words are actually plurals is much more meaningful than providing students with a worksheet that asks them to add "-s" or "-es" to an isolated set of words.

*Fostering word consciousness* can occur almost organically in primary grade classrooms through shared reading and writing. As mentioned earlier, the use of high-quality literature during a teacher read-aloud provides ideal opportunities for students to develop an appreciation of how words work. However, a teacher's interest in vocabulary is key. Teachers need to model the joy of discovering new words to convey ideas and images. Also, there are numerous trade books that help to engage students in wordplay. Books such as *Q is for Duck* (Folsom, Etling, and Kent 2005) and *Tomorrow's Alphabet* (Shannon and Crews 1999) allow students to play with the alphabet as they discover new ways of thinking about letters and words. Other books such as *The King Who Rained* and *A Chocolate Moose for Dinner* (Gwynne 1988) provide students with time to play with words and explore figurative language.

There are several ways that teachers in primary classrooms can monitor vocabulary development. Teachers can monitor their students' vocabulary development through their discussions and their writing. Both of these can serve as informal formative assessments. During rich and varied discussions, use a simple checklist to note when students use Tier Two and Tier Three words to pose questions or respond to questions of other students. Focus on 4–5 students each day and over the course of 2–3 weeks, you will have data on your entire class. Figure 3 illustrates a simple checklist to use with the social studies words from the anchor chart.

Student writing provides an opportunity to gather evidence of students' expressive vocabulary development. Encourage students to use the environmental print found on word walls and anchor charts during their writing. Look for their use of Tier Two words in their narrative writing. This type of formative assessment can guide your instruction and support student learning.

### FIGURE 3 CLASS DISCUSSION CHECKLIST

|  | Juan | Celia | May | Omar | Joan |
|---|---|---|---|---|---|
| mountain | P | P R | R |  | R |
| valley |  | R |  | P |  |
| plain | P |  | R | P | P |
| river |  | P | R |  | P R |
| lake | R |  |  | P |  |
| ocean | P R |  | R |  |  |
| P = Posing questions |  |  |  |  |  |
| R = Responding to questions |  |  |  |  |  |

# Vocabulary Instruction in Intermediate Classrooms

Vocabulary instruction in the intermediate grades is a critical component of a balanced literacy program. If students come to grade three with strong foundational skills that include phonics and word recognition of sight words, they are more fluent readers. This fluency supports their efforts in developing strategies to approach new words. This foundation is important as they begin to read more complex texts, both narrative and informational. Also, intermediate grade level students are spending more time involved with content area reading in science and social studies. They encounter Tier Three words, those specialized words whose frequency is low. However, students need to understand these words and their relationships to other words in order to build their background knowledge to support future learning. Let's examine what a four-pronged approach to vocabulary would look like in an intermediate grade classroom.

*Providing rich and varied language experiences* has some similarities to what you would see in a primary classroom, but there are also some differences. Just as in primary classrooms, it's important for intermediate grade teachers to spend time each day reading aloud to students and engaging them in dialogue related to interesting words. However, it's also important for intermediate grade teachers to provide time each day for independent, self-selected reading. Intermediate students also need time to talk about books with their peers and their teachers.

Nagy and Anderson (1984) determined that students learn between 2,700 and 3,000 new words per year. The sheer volume of words learned would make it impossible for any teacher to provide explicit instruction on each new word. So how are students learning so many words? This vocabulary growth is attributed to incidental word learning. One of the primary methods of incidental word learning occurs through both wide and deep reading. By wide reading, we mean providing students with opportunities to explore and select a variety of texts.

Classroom libraries should be filled with narrative and informational texts at a range of reading levels. These libraries should also include books of poetry, how-to manuals, graphic novels, and books with word play such as puns and riddles. Don't forget to provide students with access to online print as well.

Deep reading occurs when a student finds an author, genre, or topic of interest and goes deep with his or her reading. How many of us have a favorite author and read every book we can find? Or perhaps you enjoy baking and have a well-stocked library of specialized cookbooks. This is when we are reading deeply.

Providing a minimum of 15 minutes of daily self-selected reading increases the volume of reading and as such the volume of words students encounter. Wide and deep reading provides students with multiple exposures to numerous words in meaningful contexts. Each time a word is encountered, the student develops a greater understanding of the word's meaning.

Intermediate classrooms should also be print-rich environments that include word walls, anchor charts, and student work on display. The use of word walls in intermediate classrooms will be discussed in the section on teaching individual words. What is important to remember is the print in classrooms should be more than wallpaper that decorates the room. Students must regularly interact with the print in order to support their vocabulary development.

Rich and varied language experiences include opportunities for students to hold meaningful discussions with each other and with the teacher. Some of this discussion can occur naturally during self-selected reading as students share what they are reading. Students should also have opportunities to present and listen to presentations by their peers. They need time to ask meaningful questions and provide feedback to their peers. These experiences can help students to develop and expand their listening, speaking, reading, and writing vocabularies.

*Teaching individual words* in an intermediate classroom can seem overwhelming. If students learn up to 3,000 words each year through incidental learning, which words should teachers select for specific instruction? Many teachers also struggle with the number of words that should be introduced each week. Intermediate teachers should focus on no more than 10–12 words per week for specific instruction. These words should be a combination of both Tier Two words found in high-quality literature and Tier Three domain-specific words discussed earlier. Select words that are essential for students, words that will support academic learning, and words that appear across multiple content areas. Don't be lured into thinking that you have to teach every boldfaced word in a science or social studies unit. Not all words are equal in terms of being essential to students learning and useful in building concepts. As the teacher, you are that critical mediator in deciding which words to teach. For example, the word "current" holds different meanings in science (electrical current), social studies (current events), and geography (ocean current). This is a word worth teaching. When selecting words, think in terms of words that are essential to understanding the main concept of the text and also words that will help students connect words across concepts and content.

Vocabulary frames (Blachowicz, Baumann, Manyak, and Graves 2013), semantic maps, and semantic word sorts are strategies for teaching individual words. These strategies actively engage students in building an understanding of words and concepts. Vocabulary frames create semantically meaningful structures. They provide students with methods to organize vocabulary and tap into their background knowledge. Semantic maps and semantic sorts provide a method for organizing and processing information about new words. Vocabulary frames, semantic maps, and semantic word sorts support comprehension and also provide scaffolds for student writing.

Knowledge Rating is an example of a vocabulary frame that is particularly useful for content area topics (Blachowicz and Fisher 2010). Knowledge Rating frames provide students with an opportunity to preview vocabulary for an upcoming unit and at the same time provide teachers with a diagnostic assessment of students' prior knowledge. These data can help to determine how to group students for instruction and also the level of instruction needed. An example of a Knowledge Rating is shown in Figure 4 on page 65.

Directions for using a Knowledge Rating:

1. Explain to students that they will be starting a new unit with some interesting words.

2. Pass out the Knowledge Rating vocabulary frame.

3. Read each word aloud to the students. (This is important as some of the words may be in the students' listening vocabulary, but not in their reading vocabulary.)

4. Ask them to place an "X" in the box that best explains what they already know about the word.

5. Remind them that they are not expected to know all of the words. If they did, there would be no need to teach the next unit.

6. Give students 5–7 minutes to complete the Knowledge Rating.

7. Have students talk in pairs or groups of four and compare words they already knew and words they were not sure of.

8. Ask the students, *Did anyone have at least one word that you marked, "No clue"?*

9. Briefly discuss student responses.

10. Collect the Knowledge Ratings, and use them to guide instruction.

FIGURE 4 KNOWLEDGE RATING

| Place an X in the box that best describes your understanding of the word. | | | | |
|---|---|---|---|---|
| Word | No clue | Have heard or seen it | Know the word | Know it well and can define it |
| ecosystem | | | | |
| habitat | | | | |
| producer | | | | |
| consumer | | | | |
| decomposer | | | | |
| food chain | | | | |
| herbivore | | | | |
| carnivore | | | | |

Word Squares, sometimes also referred to as the Frayer Model (Frayer, Frederick, and Klausmeier 1969), are a type of semantic map. These can be useful for developing a conceptual understanding of essential vocabulary words. Word Squares should not be done with every vocabulary word. You want to select words that represent essential concepts of the chapter and words for which there are multiple examples. Using the word list from the Knowledge Rating, the words "ecosystem" and "habitat" would be suitable for a Word Square. Students can work on these independently or in pairs. However, first model Word Squares for the class one or more times and also develop some Word Squares interactively before expecting students to work on them independently.

There are four components to a Word Square: the definition, the characteristics, examples and nonexamples, and a drawing or graphic. The definition should include one from the text or glossary and another in the student's own words. Students can draw or find images online or in magazines for the graphic. The Word Square is also a scaffold for students when they are writing about the concept. A Word Square for "ecosystem" is shown in Figure 5.

FIGURE 5 WORD SQUARE

| Definition:<br>a community of living organisms and nonliving things that interact with their environment<br><br>Definition in my own words:<br>plants and animals in a certain area that depend on each other to live | Characteristics of an ecosystem:<br>• aquatic ecosystems are in water<br>• terrestrial ecosystems are on land<br>• can be small, like a puddle, or large, like a lake<br>• living and nonliving parts depend on each other<br>• there is a feeding relationship called a food chain |
|---|---|

| Ecosystems | | |
|---|---|---|
| **Examples**<br>pond<br>forest<br>ocean<br>desert | **Nonexamples**<br>fish<br>rocks<br>sand |  |

Semantic word sorts prompt students to explore the relationship between and among words. They engage students mentally and physically as students manipulate words to develop connections. Semantic word sorts consist of at least 10, and no more than 15, semantically related words from a unit of instruction. Students are given the words in random order. They may either cut them up and physically manipulate them or record them in written form. An example of a math word sort is shown in Figure 6 below. Just as with the Word Square, you will need to model semantic word sorts one or more times before having the students work independently. Directions for using the semantic word sort:

1. Provide students with a set of words. These can be printed as shown in Figure 6, or shown on a whiteboard.

2. Students can cut them out, create a set of word cards, and manipulate them, or organize the words by writing them.

3. As a prereading activity, ask the students to group, or sort, the words to show how they are related.

4. Remind them to try and find at least two words that are related.

5. As the students are working, circulate and notice how they sort words. This will give you an idea of their background knowledge and level of understanding.

6. After several minutes, ask students to turn and talk to a partner about how they decided to organize their words.

7. Then have a class discussion as partners share how they sorted their words and explain their rationale.

8. Remind them to be thinking about how they sorted and organized their words during the next several days of instruction.

As a prereading activity, these are called open sorts. Students may develop any number of different sorts, but you are looking and listening for their explanations as a measure of their conceptual understanding. Open sorts serve as a diagnostic tool to guide instructional decisions and for grouping students based on their level of conceptual knowledge.

The three preceding strategies are designed to support domain-specific, or Tier Three, vocabulary instruction. Domain-specific words can be easily found in curriculum standards and content textbooks. Selecting Tier Two words for intermediate grade students can be a bit more complicated. Many new teachers and also experienced teachers are unsure of exactly which words to select from novels and other narrative texts students read as part of their balanced literacy instruction. This can be an even more daunting task if teachers are using multiple novels in book clubs or literature circles. It's important that the vocabulary tasks do not become disconnected from the primary goal of reading and comprehending the book. One method to address this struggle is through the vocabulary self-collection strategy (VSS) (Haggard 1986).

FIGURE 6 SEMANTIC WORD SORT

| angles | rays | rectangle |
| hexagon | octagon | segments |
| acute | obtuse | lines |
| parallel | perpendicular | right |
| quadrilateral | right | vertex |

VSS engages students in making their own decisions about which words are important to learn. This can be done when all students are reading the same book and can be modified when multiple books are being used within a class. For classes using the same text, students are grouped into teams. After reading one or more chapters, each team selects one word they find interesting and want to learn more about. The teacher also chooses a word. This provides an opportunity for the teacher to model how to select Tier Two words, those words that are sophisticated labels for concepts already held by the students.

Each team shares where the word appears in the book, what they think the word means, and why they believe the class should learn this word. Nominated words are posted, and students enter them into their vocabulary journals. The value of this strategy lies in the rich discussions that take place as words are presented. It is during this time that definitions are refined, word histories are explored, synonyms and antonyms are suggested, and resources such as dictionaries are consulted to confirm word meaning. As this process is completed each week, selected words are posted to anchor charts. Students are encouraged to use these words in their own writing.

Once students are secure in their understanding of VSS, it can be modified for use with multiple texts. For example, a fifth grade class is reading four different novels. During the first week, the teacher asks each group to select a word from their reading that relates to a specific character trait. The next week, they might be asked to select a word that relates to the setting or mood of the story. During some weeks students are free to select any word that they find interesting and believe other students should learn. The teacher also selects a word, and each group of students and the teacher present their words in the same way as the traditional VSS. Words are entered into vocabulary journals and posted to anchor charts. These anchor charts become a part of the print-rich environment of the classroom. The process of self-collection provides students with choices. They are able to take control of their own learning, which supports both motivation and engagement.

Vocabulary journals mentioned in conjunction with VSS can be a useful tool for vocabulary development. Personal vocabulary journals, when used strategically, can help students to expand both their reading and writing vocabularies. There is not a standard format for vocabulary journals. They should be simple to complete and at a minimum have space for the selected word and a definition. Definitions should be written in student-friendly language. Other possible parts to consider include an illustration of the word, the part of speech, and the location of the word in the text. Figures 7 and 8 on the next page provide some sample vocabulary journal pages.

FIGURE 7 VOCABULARY JOURNAL EXAMPLE 1

| Word | Illustration/Picture |
|------|----------------------|
| **Definition** | |
| **Connection** | |

FIGURE 8 VOCABULARY JOURNAL EXAMPLE 2

| Word | Page in text | Part of speech |
|------|--------------|----------------|
| **Definition** | | |
| **Illustration** | | |

Vocabulary journals can contain a combination of words selected by students and the teacher. But don't overuse vocabulary journals. Requiring students to add one or more words daily is a sure way to turn a motivating endeavor into drudgery. Set aside one or possibly two days each week for vocabulary journals. Or ask students to be responsible for selecting one or two words each week. Then at the end of the week have students share their selections with partners and small groups. Students can nominate words for inclusion on anchor charts.

Anchor charts and word walls are two ways of organizing words for display in classrooms. Anchor charts are generally made up of a group of words that are related in some way. As mentioned earlier, you may have anchor charts that provide Tier Two, sophisticated words related to mood, setting, or feelings. So instead of words such as "happy" or "sad," an anchor chart might have the words "ecstatic" or "despondent." These words come from both teacher read-alouds and student self-collections. Anchor charts can also be topically related. When studying a specific unit in science or social studies, displaying the essential words organized to show their relationships provides students with a resource to use while reading and writing about the topic. Anchor charts can be simple lists or words graphically organized in a word web or other type of semantic map. Anchor charts are generally used for a period of time and then taken down to make room for new charts. Previously developed anchor charts can be stored in the classroom for use as reference tools.

Word walls are considered a more permanent structure for organizing words. Frequently in an intermediate classroom, word walls consist of content area words organized by subject. Words are added to the word wall throughout the year as new topics are explored and students increase their word knowledge. Figure 9 below illustrates a content area word wall.

What is important to remember with both anchor charts and word walls is they must be used interactively. If not, then they just become a lovely decoration in the room that does not impact the vocabulary growth of your students. Using words from anchor charts and word walls to develop word sorts or create word frames are just two of the many ways you can bring these words to life in your classroom.

*Teaching word learning strategies* in the intermediate classrooms is primarily about teaching students how to use context to figure out the meaning of an unknown word. Time spent explicitly teaching students how to look both inside and outside of a word for clues to its meaning can provide students with tools that they can use independently during their reading. Looking inside the word includes teaching the parts of words, such as prefixes, suffixes, and root or base words. If a student knows how to search a word for its parts, he or she can use knowledge of "define" to figure out the words "definitely," "indefinite," and "undefined." Teaching common prefixes such as "un-," "re-," "in-," "dis-," and "non-" can help students unlock thousands of words. Anchor charts of prefix "families" can be developed as a shared instructional task. These charts can serve as valuable references for students in both reading and writing.

## FIGURE 9 CONTENT AREA WORD WALL

| Science | Social Studies | Math | English Language Arts |
|---|---|---|---|
| ecosystems | cultural | fraction | simile |
| decomposer | environmental | denominator | metaphor |
| matter | resources | equivalent | idiom |
| interaction | catastrophic | numerator | |
| | | scaling | |

Teaching students to look outside a word provides them with the strategies of reading ahead or going back and reading a previous sentence to look for clues to the word's meaning. Strategies for looking outside a word include understanding connective or cohesive words in text. Intermediate students benefit from learning the most common types of context clues.

1. Definition clues: Sometimes a word is explained directly within the sentence. Commas can be a signal.
   *Joan made an appointment with the endodontist, a dentist who specializes in injuries to the teeth and gums.*

2. Synonym clues: Words are rephrased in simpler language. Signal words can be "such as" and "or."
   *Jonathan was a precocious, or exceptionally smart, child for his age.*

3. Antonym clues: Words are clarified by providing the opposite meaning. Words such as "but" or "unlike" can be signal words.
   *John was loquacious, unlike his brother who barely spoke a word.*

4. Example: Words are found before or after the word and help to explain its meaning.
   *Marcia stamped her feet and pounded the table; she shouted at the top of her lungs. She was furious.*

Teaching word learning strategies also includes providing instruction on how to use various resources such as a dictionary or a thesaurus. However, simply giving students a list of words and asking them to look them up is not a best practice. Consider the word "run." You can run away or get a run in your stocking. You can hit a home run or you can take your pet to the dog run. When given an isolated list of words and sent to look them up in the dictionary, students don't know which definition to use. Typically students will do one of two things, select the first definition or select the shortest. Using a dictionary is a bit like using a GPS system in a car. If you are in a familiar place and have some idea of where you are going, a GPS system can support your navigation. However, if you have no idea where you are and you rely solely on the GPS, you can end up at a dead end street. The same holds true with dictionaries and other word resources. They can provide greater clarity and depth of meaning if the student holds some understanding, but they can confuse and confound students who have no idea what they are trying to discover. This is not to say that these resources should not be used. However, they should be utilized after reading, not before. Having a variety of resources including photo dictionaries, a thesaurus, and access to online dictionaries can be valuable sources of information for students.

*Fostering word consciousness* in an intermediate classroom is dependent upon a teacher's interest and enthusiasm for word learning. Indicators of word consciousness in these classrooms include well-stocked classroom libraries, word games, as well as anchor charts and word walls that are used frequently. Teachers in these classrooms read aloud daily from complex, quality narrative and informational texts. They share examples of well-crafted writing and teach students how figurative language enhances and impacts writing. Students in these classrooms have strategies for unlocking the meaning of new words. They spend at least 15 minutes each day involved in both wide and deep reading. They enjoy word play, riddles, and puns. Word games such as Boggle, Scattergories, and Bananagrams are wise investments in an intermediate classroom. Vocabulary is not something they "do." It is a vital part of their learning, and they have an interest in learning new words and sharing their learning with others.

Formative and summative assessments of vocabulary in an intermediate classroom can occur in a variety of ways. How you assess your students will depend on your goals for instruction. Teacher constructed criterion-referenced assessments such as multiple choice or constructed responses can be used. However, these types of assessment will not provide you with an understanding of the students' depth and breadth of word learning.

A rich source for formatively assessing vocabulary is examining student writing. Questions and prompts that enable students to focus and reflect on their word learning can provide you with useful information. Response journals and quick writes are two examples. Used in conjunction with their vocabulary journals, students can respond to their word learning. Here is an example of a response journal prompt.

*Select a word from our vocabulary journal that you have used at least once this week in your writing or in-class discussions. Explain the situation and why you chose to use that word.*

Don't overuse this strategy. Remember word learning is incremental, and so it is counter-productive to ask students to reflect at this level every week. Asking students to respond every two to three weeks will provide you with multiple observations over the course of a year.

Quick writes can be used more frequently. They work well as both entrance and exit tickets. They should be quick, no more than 5–10 minutes of writing. They can be used with both Tier Two and Tier Three words. Here are two examples.

Quick write with a Tier Two word: *Would you be ecstatic or despondent if you came home and found that your parents had bought you a new bike? Explain why.*

Quick write with a Tier Three word: *What is the relationship between consumers and producers in an ecosystem? Explain the features of each in your response.*

Another way of assessing students is by leveraging some of the strategies used to teach individual words. For example, the use of a Knowledge Rating was explained earlier as a diagnostic, prereading strategy. It can be used as a summative assessment by modifying the form. Provide students with the same list of words and instead of asking them their level of understanding, ask them to explain what they know about the word. Their explanation can be a definition, an example, or a diagram. Figure 10 below provides an example of Knowledge Rating as a summative assessment.

Semantic word sorts can also be leveraged and used as a summative assessment. At the completion of a unit, provide students with the same words used during the open sort, but also include labels for the categories. By organizing the words into specific categories explored through instruction, students will be doing a closed sort. Students must sort the words and provide a brief explanation of why they sorted the words into each category. Figure 11 on the next page provides an example of a closed sort.

FIGURE 10 KNOWLEDGE RATING SUMMATIVE ASSESSMENT

Here are the words we've been learning. For each word, explain what you know. This can include a definition, an example, and/or a diagram with labels.

| Word | What I know about this word |
|---|---|
| ecosystem | |
| habitat | |
| producer | |
| consumer | |
| decomposer | |
| food chain | |
| herbivore | |
| carnivore | |

FIGURE 11 SEMANTIC WORD SORT SUMMATIVE ASSESSMENT

| Sort these words according to the three categories that are below the list of words. After sorting the words, write at least two sentences explaining why you included those words in each category. | | |
|---|---|---|
| angles | rays | rectangle |
| hexagon | octagon | segments |
| acute | obtuse | lines |
| parallel | perpendicular | right |
| quadrilateral | right | vertex |

| Two-dimensional figures | Angles | Lines |
|---|---|---|
| | | |

## Getting Started and Moving Forward

Making the decision to begin systematic vocabulary instruction within a balanced literacy framework is not an all-or-nothing proposition. Just as word learning is incremental and requires repeated exposure to complex words over time, developing a plan of action for vocabulary instruction takes time. Begin by taking stock of your classroom environment. Do you have an adequate classroom library? Can you find ways to enrich your classroom with anchor charts and word walls? If you already read aloud to your students on a daily basis, expand your practice by modeling how to find interesting words in text. Provide students with time for independent reading. Encourage both wide and deep reading. Have a go at one or two of the strategies for teaching individual words.

Seek out additional resources on vocabulary development. Work with a colleague to develop a potential list of domain specific words. Be curious about words. Look for interesting words in your own reading. And don't forget to make some time for play—word play. Use puns and riddles in your classroom. Play word games. Soon you'll find that you are falling in love with words and teaching your students the joy of word learning!

## References and Resources

Beck, I. L., C. A. Perfetti, and M. G. McKeown. 1982. "The Effects of Long-term Vocabulary Instruction on Lexical Access and Reading Comprehension." *Journal of Educational Psychology* 74: 506–521.

Beck, I. and M. McKeown. 1991. "Conditions of Vocabulary Acquisition." In *Handbook of Reading Research Volume II*, edited by R. Barr, M. Kamil, P. Mosenthal, and P. D. Pearson, 789–814. White Plains, NY: Longman.

Beck, I., M. G. McKeown, and L. Kucan. 2002. *Bringing Words to Life: Robust Vocabulary Instruction*. New York: Guilford Press.

Blachowicz, C. L. Z., J. F. Baumann, P. Manyak, and M. Graves. 2013. "Flood, Fast, Focus: Integrating Vocabulary in the Classroom." *IRA E-Essentials-Reading, What's New?*, May. Newark, DE: International Literacy Association. http://rutgersliteracycenter.org/wp-content/uploads/2015/10/Blachowicz-3.pdf.

Blachowicz, C. L. Z. and P. Fisher. 2010. *Teaching Vocabulary in All Classrooms*, 4th Edition. Englewood Cliffs, NJ: Merrill/Prentice Hall.

Cobb, C. and C. L. Z. Blachowicz. 2014. *No More "Look Up the List" Vocabulary Instruction*. Portsmouth, NH: Heinemann.

Cunningham, A. E., and K. E. Stanovich. 1997. "Early Reading Acquisition and Its Relation to Reading Experience and Ability 10 Years Later." *Developmental Psychology* 33: 934–945.

Cunningham, P. M. 2000. *Phonics They Use: Words for Reading and Writing*. New York: Longman.

Folsom, M., M. Etling, and J. K. Kent. 2005. *Q is for Duck*. Boston, MA: Houghton Mifflin Harcourt.

Frayer, D. A., W. C. Frederick, and H. J. Klausmeier. 1969. *A Schema for Testing the Level of Concept Mastery* (working paper no. 16). Madison, WI: University of Wisconsin.

Graves, M. F. 2006. *The Vocabulary Book: Learning and Instruction*. New York: Teachers College Press.

Gwynne, F. 1988. *A Chocolate Moose for Dinner*. New York: Aladdin.

———. 1988. *The King Who Rained*. New York: Aladdin.

Haggard, M. 1986. "The Vocabulary Self-collection Strategy: Using Student Interest and World Knowledge to Enhance Vocabulary Growth." *Journal of Reading* 29 (7): 634–642. http://www.jstor.org/stable/40029691.

Hall, M. 1977. *The Language Experience Approach for Teaching Reading: A Research Perspective*. Newark, DE: International Reading Association.

Nagy, W. E. 2005. "Why Vocabulary Instruction Needs to Be Long-term and Comprehensive." In *Teaching and Learning Vocabulary: Bringing Research to Practice*, edited by E. Hiebert and M. L. Kamil, 27–44. Mahwah, NJ: Erlbaum.

Nagy, W. E. and R. C. Anderson. 1984. "How Many Words Are There in Printed School English?" *Reading Research Quarterly* 19: 303–330.

National Governors Association Center for Best Practices and Council of Chief State School Officers. 2010. *Common Core State Standards for English Language Arts and Literacy in History/Social Studies, Science, and Technical Subjects*. Washington, DC: Authors.

Shannon, G. and D. Crews. 1999. *Tomorrow's Alphabet*. New York: Greenwillow Books.

Steig, William. 1969. *Sylvester and the Magic Pebble*. New York: Windmill Books.

# Learning to Read and Think in an Elementary Classroom

## Elaine M. Weber and Barbara Nelson

> Reading is a basic life skill. It is a cornerstone for a child's success in school and, indeed, throughout life. Without the ability to read well, opportunities for personal fulfillment and job success inevitably will be lost. (Anderson et al. 1985, 1)

Reading is a life skill, and it also creates community. Constructing meaning around a text builds community as students respond to stories that reflect life experiences. Whether it is sharing the menu of the insatiable caterpillar or sharing the strategies a spider uses to save a runt pig or sharing the experiences of a young boy who survives war, blindness, and racial prejudice, the whole class is the best context for building and sharing fictional accounts.

## Building Corporate Knowledge

The whole group is the most effective context for students to read informational text and amass knowledge of the world. This knowledge includes learning how communities expand from the neighborhood to the world, how rules from the classroom to the Constitution define how we live with one another, and how the configuration of our Earth shapes where and how we work and play. Whole group instruction builds understanding of how living things survive, how they reproduce, how they function, and how they support one another. Finally, whole group instruction helps students understand how the tools we use have evolved from sticks to minuscule electronics and how massive tools of exploration help explain Earth's role in the universe.

## Whole Group Instruction

Whole group instruction is the starting point. It is when teachers introduce concepts and strategies efficiently to all students. It is when teachers model strategies with mentor texts. It is when teachers establish a baseline for further content and strategy instruction in small and differentiated groups. During whole group instruction, teachers observe students to determine which ones are exhibiting understanding and need practice and challenge and which ones need further support and scaffolding.

This chapter begins by discussing the role the reader plays in comprehending text and how to teach the reading strategies in the context of whole group instruction. The chapter continues with strategies to teach reading comprehension with both narrative and informational text through close and analytical reading and deep reading that reaches into concepts, generalizations, principles, and life lessons.

## Teaching Reading Strategies in the Context of a Whole Group

The Michigan Department of Education, supported by the International Reading Association, defines reading as ". . . the process of constructing meaning through the dynamic interaction among the reader's existing knowledge, the information suggested by the written language, and the context of the reading situation." (Michigan Department of Education 2002, 2)

This definition came from the 1980s research on reading when it was determined that schema theory/background knowledge contributed significantly to how well a student comprehends text. This led to the identification of what good readers do when they read, and these "good reader strategies" have since been verified by further investigations.

The best researched strategies were compiled in a groundbreaking chapter by David Pearson, Laura Roehler, Jan Dole, and Gerry Duffy, "Developing Expertise in Reading Comprehension: What Should Be Taught? How Should It Be Taught?" (1992). This chapter points out that teachers should model what good readers do and teach students how to use these strategies explicitly in literature-rich learning communities. The list of strategies includes:

- asking questions
- making connections
- visualizing (Keene and Zimmermann 1997, 123–143)
- determining importance
- inferring
- synthesizing
- repairing comprehension

The list is in the developmental order of the strategies. Very young children, as all parents know, can ask questions to gain information. This strategy can easily be applied to reading selections to clarify and make sense of text. Stories read in the early grades also offer students a way to make connections to their own lives. By first grade, students can be guided through a think-aloud to visualize scenes or events in a story. Determining importance along with making inferences need teacher support through fifth grade. Synthesizing and repairing comprehension are strategies done together in a group guided by the teacher well into sixth grade.

To introduce these expert reader comprehension strategies, teachers often model the strategies through a think-aloud. A think-aloud is "making thinking public." A teacher models what an expert reader would be thinking as she or he is reading. The goal of thinking aloud is to explicitly show students what they might do to better understand what they are reading. We've provided an example of this strategy with the narrative selection *Sofia and the Quetzal Bird* (pp. 77 and 88) (Guillain 2016, 16–21):

# Sofia and the Quetzal Bird: "A Rescue"

1     When the quetzal opened its wings, it was clear to both children that one wing was hurt.

2     "The poor bird," Sofia burst out. "We have to help!"

3     She ran to the tree and prepared to climb its thick branches.

4     "Stop!" said Ronny. "The quetzal is a wild bird. If you get too close, it will fly away."

5     "But what if it can't fly?" said Sofia.

6     Ronny thought for a second. "Then it will probably die."

7     "So we must help it right now," said Sofia. She couldn't wait any longer as she climbed up the tree.

8     To Ronny's surprise, the quetzal stayed calm. When Sofia was finally sitting on the branch next to the bird, it hopped into her lap. . . . Carefully placing the bird on her shoulder, Sofia climbed back down. That afternoon, with help from Mrs. Garcia, Sofia fed the quetzal.

9     "I've never seen a quetzal so tame around a person," said Mrs. Garcia. "You appear to have a special way with it. . . ."

10     "I don't think its wing is broken," said Mrs. Garcia, "Although it has clearly been in some sort of fight. The bird will probably be better in the morning."

11     Sofia carefully set the quetzal down to rest in a small box lined with a towel. That night, as Sofia and Mom got ready for bed, the quetzal chirped happily from its new home. . . .

12     But when they woke up early in the morning, the quetzal was gone. It had flown out a window.

To demonstrate how to apply the above strategies to "A Rescue," I would give each student a copy of the selection and refer to sections as I explained and applied each of the strategies to the selection. It is necessary to prepare for this activity, so I have read through the selection and prepared what I would say to demonstrate each strategy. I would say:

- **Asking questions** means stopping while reading to ask questions like, "What will happen next?" or "Why did that character do that?" After reading the title, "A Rescue," I might ask, Who or what is going to be rescued and why? I will read the beginning of the story to find my answer. From reading paragraphs 1 and 2, I think Sofia is trying to rescue a quetzal bird because one of its wings has been hurt.

- **Making connections** means putting things together from what I know, other stories I have read, and what I've experienced and know about the world to help me understand stories better. I can make a connection to what Sofia is trying to do. Just like her, I tried to save injured birds when I was young. It worked sometimes but not always. Sometimes they died. So I am asking another question, "Will Sofia be successful?"

- **Visualizing** means making pictures in your mind about what's going on in the story so you can understand the story better. After reading paragraphs 7 and 8, I can see or visualize Sofia climbing the tree and sitting by the bird. I can also visualize her putting the bird on her shoulder and climbing back down. I can even visualize the surprised look on Ronny's face because he said in paragraph 4 that the bird would fly away.

- **Determining importance** is asking what is most important in the selection. I think the most important information in the selection is Sofia wanted to help the bird (paragraph 2), she was able to rescue it and feed it (paragraph 8), and the bird probably survived (paragraph 12).

- **Synthesizing** means combining new ideas from what I have read with what I already know or have experienced, to learn or understand something new. I read in paragraph 9 that Mrs. Garcia was surprised the quetzal bird was so tame with Sofia, and I know from experience that wild birds are frightened of people, so I can put those things together to figure out that there is something special about Sofia in her relationship with the quetzal bird. I think that means some people have a calming influence on animals like the dog whisperer does.

- **Inferring** means "reading between the lines" or filling in ideas and meaning that the author leaves out. It's using what you know to figure out things the author doesn't tell you. For example, in paragraph 12, it says, "But when they woke up early in the morning, the quetzal was gone. It had flown out a window." I can infer that the bird's wing was not broken and it just needed to eat and rest before it could fly away. It is alive and fine.

- **Repairing comprehension** means using strategies to make sense of something in the story. In paragraph 9 I did not know for sure what the word "tame" meant. I have been told that sometimes if I slow down and stop and think about what I have read so far and what I know, I might be able to figure out what a word means. I remember that in paragraph 4, Ronny said that the quetzal is a wild bird and then Mrs. Garcia was surprised in paragraph 9 that the quetzal was tame around Sofia. That reminded me that the words "wild" and "tame" are opposites, so the word "tame" must mean not afraid and gentle, not wild.

Following is an example of how this might be done using the informational text "Migrating Animals" from *Animal Migration* (on the next page and p. 89) (Krumm 2016, 4–6):

# Animal Migration: "Migrating Animals" (Krumm 2016, 4–6)

1   Every year, birds fly from one part of the world to another. Fish swim across oceans. . . . Each year, many different kinds of animals travel to places that are far away. This is called animal migration. It is the action animals take to move from one area to another at different times of the year.

2   Animals migrate for many reasons. The resources they need to survive, like food or water, change during the year. As seasons change, fewer resources are near them, and more resources can be found far away. Animals must move to where they can find food and water.

3   Animals also have a better chance of finding a partner or giving birth somewhere safe if they migrate. The animals must travel to new areas. They sometimes travel thousands of miles as part of their journey.

4   There is another important reason why animals migrate. Some animals migrate to warmer areas during the winter to survive.

5   Scientists also learned that many of these animals have the instinct to find their way. The animals weren't taught or told where they need to go. Instead, they can find their way as they travel. Animals are born knowing how to do this.

To demonstrate how to apply the above strategies to "Migrating Animals," I would give each student a copy of the selection and refer to sections of it as I explained and applied each of the strategies to the selection. I would say:

- **Asking questions** means stopping while reading to ask questions like, "What will this selection be about?" or "What does that mean?" I would ask, What does "migrating" mean in the title? I will read paragraph 1 to find out what "migrating" means. The last sentence tells me, "It is the action animals take to move from one area to another at different times of the year." So now I know that migrating means moving from one place to another.

- **Making connections** means putting things together from what I know, from other selections I have read, and what I've experienced and know about the world to help me understand selections better. In paragraph 1 it says, "Every year, birds fly from one part of the world to another." I can connect that to something I know about—I see and hear Canada geese flying north in the spring and south in the fall. Could they be migrating?

- **Visualizing** means making pictures in your mind about what's going on in the selection, so you can understand the selection better. I can see or visualize Canada geese flying overhead, and I can hear them, too.

- **Determining importance** is asking what is most important in the selection. I think the most important information in the selection tells me the reasons that animals migrate. Paragraph 2 tells me that animals migrate to find food and water. Paragraph 3 tells me that animals may need to migrate to find partners or a safe place to give birth. Paragraph 4 tells me that some animals may migrate to warmer places so they can survive in the winter.

- **Synthesizing** means combining new ideas from what I have just read with what I already know or have experienced to learn or understand something new. In paragraph 4 I read that some animals migrate south to stay warm and survive in the winter, so now I think about my grandparents who go to Florida in the winter to stay warm. I guess they also migrate.

- **Repairing comprehension** *means to use strategies to make sense of something I don't understand in the selection. I do not understand the first sentence in paragraph 5 because I don't know what the word "instinct" means. I have been told that sometimes if I read further, I might be able to figure out what a word or idea means. I read the last sentence, "Animals are born knowing how to do this." I can figure out that "instinct" is what animals already know without having to learn or without being taught.*

Both of the selections, "A Rescue" and "Migrating Animals," give the teacher opportunities to teach the use of these expert reader strategies. The above think-alouds are examples of how a teacher might use selections to teach all of the strategies, but on the basis of each teacher's knowledge of his or her students' strategy use, teachers will decide how many of the strategies to teach or point out. Once students are aware of the importance of expert reader strategies in comprehending and making sense of what they read, they should be encouraged to use the strategies in conjunction with the focus of close and analytic reading as they extract and analyze different aspects of the text: central ideas, key ideas, or examples; text structure, vocabulary, or author's craft; or concepts, generalizations, principles, or life's lessons.

## Close and Analytic Reading

Close and analytic reading stresses engaging with a text of sufficient complexity directly and examining its meaning thoroughly and methodically, encouraging students to read and reread deliberately. Directing student attention on the text itself empowers students to understand the central ideas and key supporting details. It also enables students to reflect on the meanings of individual words and sentences; the order in which sentences unfold; and the development of ideas over the course of the text, which ultimately leads students to arrive at an understanding of the text as a whole (PARCC 2011, 7).

When students are taught to examine text closely and analytically, it is important to select a short, one-page text that is at the students' independent reading level. Two questions guide students as they read closely and analytically:

- What does the text say? (summary or restatement)
- How does the text say it? (vocabulary, text structure, and author's craft)

The following commentary will help demonstrate how close and analytical reading works. We begin with narrative, *Sofia and the Quetzal Bird* (p. 88) (Guillain 2016, 16–21):

The text is either read by the teacher, choral read, or read independently. The processing of the text is done in a whole class discussion. The questions, *What is this text about?*, *What is the main idea of this text?*, and *What are five key words in this text?* will help students narrow their thinking. Once the summary statement is established, ask students to find support. Are there details? Are there examples? In this case, there are details. Which details support the summary statement? There is an inference that should be noted. The bird left through an open window and had been in a box. The inference would be that there was an open window that the bird had access to from the box.

The final response to, *What does the text say?* is that Sofia saved an injured quetzal bird (summary statement) by (details) rescuing it from a tree, feeding it, and putting it to heal in a box that was near (inference) a window so it could leave when it was ready.

Next the text is read again. This time it is read for the purpose of answering the question, *How does the text say it?* (vocabulary, text structure, and author's craft) The goal of this reading is to learn how the author crafted the text to shape the meaning—text structure, unusual vocabulary, metaphoric devices, foreshadowing, etc. By third grade, students should be familiar with the text structure of problem/solution. The problem is an injured bird up in a tree. The solution is to rescue the bird, feed it, and find a comfortable place to put it so it can heal. Mrs. Garcia provides foreshadowing when she says, "I've never seen a quetzal so tame around a person. You appear to have a special way with it." She also offers more foreshadowing, "The bird will probably be better in the morning."

Now to informational text, "Migrating Animals" from *Animal Migration* (p. 89) (Krumm 2016, 4–6):

Reading informational text to answer the question, *What does the text say?* will need the same support given with the narrative piece to find the summary statement. But in this selection, the summary statement is right in the text, "Animals migrate for many reasons." The supporting details follow in each paragraph—food, safety, and climate.

The text is read again for a description of it or to answer the question, *How does the text say it?* The text structure is informational as it includes statements with facts. The author defines the words, "migration" and "instinct."

Students often need a transition from teacher-led close and analytic reading to independence. Guided highlighted reading (GHR) and other strategies will provide this support.

## Whole Group Close and Analytic Reading: Guided Highlighted Reading

Guided highlighted reading (GHR) is a text-based reading strategy that provides explicit support for close and analytic reading. Teachers choose a short text (from or related to the curriculum) and prepare prompts, generally for one reading purpose at a time. They make the copies available to the students and then read each prompt aloud. Students return to the text to find words or phrases that support their answers. This forces students to attend to text while the teacher's prompts are designed to encourage close and analytic thinking and reading. This strategy engages the reader, making reading interesting and memorable (Weber et al. 2012, 13–21). GHR is a whole class strategy that helps students focus on:

- what the text says, evidence from the text, and possible logical inferences;
- central ideas and themes;

- key ideas and details to be used in summarizing the text;
- vocabulary meaning;
- text structure; and
- author's purpose and point of view.

For the activity, there are two sets of prompts: one set for students to highlight for key ideas, details, and inference; and another set to highlight for text structure and vocabulary. Prompts were developed to call students' attention to salient features of the text: key ideas and details, inference, vocabulary, and text structure. The words in parenthesis are possible responses to the prompts; students do find other logical responses that should be accepted. The words after the parenthesis identify the comprehension skill.

## Close Reading for Key Ideas, Details, and Inference

**Directions: Give each student a copy of a chapter from *Sofia and the Quetzal Bird*: "A Rescue" (p. 88) (Guillain 2016, 16–21) and a highlighter. Read the following prompts, and tell students to highlight as directed:**

In the title, find and highlight the word that tells what will happen in the story. ("Rescue") Key idea

In paragraph #2, find and highlight what Sofia wants to do because the bird's wing was hurt. ("We have to help!") Key idea

In paragraph #6, find and highlight what Ronny thinks might happen to the bird if it can't fly. ("Then it will probably die.") Detail for summary

In paragraph #7, find and highlight what Sofia wants to do right now. ("So we must help it right now.") Detail for summary

In paragraph #8, find and highlight what surprised Ronny. (". . . the quetzal stayed calm.") Detail for summary

In paragraph #10, find and highlight how Mrs. Garcia thinks the bird will feel in the morning.

("The bird will probably be better in the morning.") Detail for summary

In paragraph #12, find and highlight how Sofia knew that the bird was OK. (". . . the quetzal was gone. It had flown out a window.") Inference

## Analytical Reading for Vocabulary, Text Structure, and Author's Craft:

**Directions: Give each student another copy of *Sofia and the Quetzal Bird*: "A Rescue" (p. 88) or a different color highlighter. Read the following prompts, and tell students to highlight as directed:**

This selection is organized by problem and solution. In paragraph #1, find and highlight the problem that the bird had. (". . . one wing was hurt.") Text structure: problem

In paragraph #7, find and highlight what Sofia did first to help the bird and begin to solve the problem. (". . . she climbed up the tree.") Text structure: solution

In paragraph #8, find and highlight two more things Sofia did to help the bird and solve the problem. ("Carefully placing the bird on her shoulder, Sofia climbed back down. That afternoon, with help from Mrs. Garcia, Sofia fed the quetzal.") Text structure: solution

In paragraph #9, find and highlight the word that is the opposite of the word "wild." ("tame") Vocabulary meaning

In paragraph #11, find and highlight a final thing Sofia did to help the bird and solve the problem. ("Sofia carefully set the quetzal down to rest in a small box lined with a towel.") Text structure: solution

GHR offers teachers opportunities to follow up by going over responses to the prompts and clearing up any misunderstandings. Students often come up with perfectly logical responses different from those expected. Students should be asked to explain their responses, and logical responses should be accepted.

Teachers can also use GHR as teachable moments. For example, teachers could teach about the text structure problem/solution by calling attention to the prompts and responses to paragraphs 1, 7, 8, and 11. Teachers also have an opportunity to model or share the writing of a summary using responses to prompts in both sections. In this case, with the teacher's guidance, students would put their highlighted responses into their own words to develop a summary. For example:

> "A Rescue" from *Sofia and the Quetzal Bird* is a story that tells about a girl who saves a bird with a hurt wing. Sofia and her friend Ronny are looking in a tree and see a quetzal bird with an injured wing. Sofia wants to climb the tree and rescue the bird. Ronny warns her that the bird will fly away. He also tells her if the bird cannot fly, it will die. Sofia climbs the tree, rescues the bird, and takes it home. Mrs. Garcia helps Sofia feed the bird. Before going to bed, Sofia prepares a comfortable bed in a box for the bird to sleep in. In the morning, Sofia discovers that the bird has flown out the window. She knows that her rescue is successful.

As students go through the following short strategy instruction with nonfiction text, they will identify the topic of the selection, the central idea or claim, the evidence used to prove the claim, as well as the author's use of description through visualization (birds flying, fish swimming), content-specific vocabulary ("instinct"), and text structure (statement/claim with evidence). Students' attention will be drawn to the details or reasons that animals migrate and, with teacher guidance, students will then be able to summarize the short selection using what they have highlighted. Prompts were developed to call students attention to the salient features of the text: key ideas and details, author's craft, and text structure. The words in parenthesis are possible responses to the prompts; students do find other logical responses that should be accepted. The words after the parenthesis identify the comprehension skill.

## Reading for Key Ideas, Details, and Summary:

**Directions: Give each student a copy of "Migrating Animals" (p. 89) (Krumm 2016, 4–6) and a highlighter. Read the following prompts, and tell students to highlight as directed:**

In the title, highlight the topic of the selection. (*Animal Migration* and/or "Migrating Animals") Topic

The author tells us, "Animals migrate for many reasons." In paragraph #2, find and highlight one reason why animals migrate. ("Animals must move to where they can find food and water.") Central idea, detail for summary

In paragraph #3, find and highlight another reason why animals migrate. ("Animals also have a better chance of finding a partner or giving birth somewhere safe if they migrate.") Detail for summary

In paragraph #4, find and highlight another reason why animals migrate. ("Some animals migrate to warmer areas during the winter to survive.") Detail for summary

## Reading for Vocabulary, Text Structure, and Author's Craft:

**Directions: Give each student another copy of** *Animal Migration:* **"Migrating Animals" or a different color highlighter. Read the following prompts, and tell students to highlight as directed:**

In paragraph #1, find and highlight the two sentences that help the reader visualize or see what certain animals do when they migrate. ("Every year, birds fly from one part of the world to another. Fish swim across oceans.") Author's craft

In paragraph #1, find and highlight the sentence that tells what animals do—the action they take—when they migrate. ("It is the action animals take to move from one area to another at different times of the year.") Vocabulary

This selection is organized by claim/statement and evidence. The author makes a statement and then gives evidence to prove the statement. The author's statement is, "Animals migrate for many reasons." In paragraph #2, find and highlight the evidence or reason animals migrate. ("Animals must move to where they can find food and water.") Central idea, text structure: evidence

In paragraph #3, find and highlight the best piece of evidence or reason why animals migrate. ("Animals also have a better chance of finding a partner or giving birth somewhere safe if they migrate.") Text structure: evidence

In paragraph #4, find and highlight another piece of evidence or reason why animals migrate. ("Some animals migrate to warmer areas during the winter to survive.") Text structure: evidence

In paragraph #5, find and highlight the word that helps animals know where to go when they migrate. ("instinct") Content-specific vocabulary

As with fiction selections, teachers can use GHR to clear up misunderstandings and have students use text evidence to explain their responses. Teachers can also use GHR for teachable moments. For example, teachers could call attention to the text structure statement or claim and evidence by calling attention to the prompts and responses to paragraphs 2, 3, and 4. They might take the opportunity to discuss the meaning of the word "instinct." Teachers also have an opportunity to model or share the writing of a summary using responses to prompts for paragraphs 2, 3, and 4. In this case, with the teacher's guidance, students would put their highlighted responses into their own words to develop a summary. For example:

The selection "Migrating Animals" tells us that there are many reasons why animals migrate, or move from one place to another. Animals migrate to find food and water so they can survive. Some animals migrate because they need to find a partner and a safe place to have babies. Other animals move to places that are warmer in the winter, so they can survive.

## Whole Group Deep Reading Using the Profundity Scales

Reading fiction provides a rich context for students to learn more than the words have to offer. Some stories have such opportunities for students. When reading fiction, students are able to understand what happens literally but often need assistance in understanding the theme(s) or life lesson(s). Profundity is a way to tap into this wisdom through analysis of a character. After closely reading and critically analyzing a piece of fiction, students are ready to look for the wisdom in the narrative. The protocol we have used with kindergartners to adults is called the profundity scales. The scales move from the concrete to the abstract level in layers of planes: physical, mental, moral, physiological, analytical, philosophical, and transformational. The transformations are abstract enough to let students apply them to other situations or even other disciplines. This occurs as students answer questions about a main character's actions and progress to higher levels of thinking in the process. You may wish to refer to the possible answers in the chart on page 91 as you prepare for this activity.

Give each student a copy of *Sofia and the Quetzal Bird* "A Rescue" (p. 88) and a blank profundity chart (p. 90). Have students reread the story and share the reading and completion of the chart using the following:

Have the students select Sofia's **three actions** to save the quetzal bird in the story (**Physical Plane**):

1. Sofia climbed the tree and brought the quetzal bird down.

2. Sofia fed the quetzal bird.

3. Sofia put the quetzal bird in a small box lined with a towel to sleep.

After selecting the actions of the character, discuss with students what the character was thinking when she performed each action. This is the **Mental Plane**:

1. Sofia wanted to save the bird because it seemed to have hurt its wing.

2. She wanted it to get strong.

3. She thought rest would help it heal.

Next, you will discuss with students the answer to the question: Was the character, Sofia, right or wrong in doing each of the actions that she performed? This is the **Moral Plane** of profundity. Have students think and talk about both sides:

1. Right—because she wanted to save its life; wrong—because Ronny said it was wild and would try to fly away.

2. Right—because she thought food would make it strong; wrong—because food might hurt it.

3. Right—because rest might help it; wrong—because not being in the wild might be bad.

Now, you will discuss with students the answer to the question: What did the character get from doing each of the selected actions? This is the **Psychological Plane**:

1. Sofia felt better because she thought she was helping the bird.

2. Sofia felt better because the bird was still alive.

3. Sofia felt better because the bird chirped happily.

In the **Analogical Plane** of profundity, we draw analogies and make connections to ourselves, other texts, and to the world around us. Through oral discussion, have students share how they are like

Sofia and discuss the parallels that they can draw to her life. Have they ever tried to rescue a hurt animal? Chart this information on the profundity chart that you are constructing with your students. Responses might include:

- I was able to get a baby bird back into its nest and it survived.

- We have read articles about successful rescues of wild birds.

- It will be good for hurt animals if people try to help them.

What is the universal theme, principle, or truth in this story? What truths does Sofia learn? What concepts and generalizations are represented in this text? Generalizations are built by connecting two concepts with a verb. This is the **Philosophical Plane** of profundity. Possible answers might include:

- Survival depends on change. (The quetzal could only have survived if it had been moved to a safe place where it could heal.)

- Advocacy requires responsibility. (Taking care of the bird requires removing it from the tree, feeding it, and providing a safe place where it can heal.)

What is the lesson learned from this story? How has my thinking changed because of this story? How am I a different person because of my reading and discussing this story? This is the **Transformational Plane** of profundity. This is taking the story to the highest level where not only do we learn a lesson from the story, but also the story has transformed us or changed us in some identifiable way. The story has allowed us to identify with the character, discover the lesson or theme, and make a plan to apply the lesson or theme to our own lives. The story has helped us solve problems in our life or find answers to situations in our own lives. Possible answers might include:

- The golden rule, "Do unto others as you would have them do unto you."

- Helping others makes you feel good.

These possible answers appear in the completed profundity chart on page 91. It is our experience that students respond enthusiastically to this activity and come up with their own logical and thoughtful ideas that show they are engaged and thinking critically.

## Whole Group Deep Reading Using Levels of Meaning

Another protocol for helping students discover the wisdom in a piece of informational text is "levels of meaning." Again students are scaffolded from the concrete to the abstract, moving from the ideas and facts in the selection to topics, concepts, generalizations or principles, and finally to theories. (Erickson and Lanning 2014, 97–113)

This activity is to be done in a whole group setting. Each student should have a copy of *Animal Migration*: "Migrating Animals" (p. 89) and access to a blank Levels of Meaning chart (p. 92). The first two columns of the chart are to include information drawn directly from the text. Students can find the facts or arguments and generate that list. Usually small groups of students think of topics first and then share.

Concepts are too difficult for students to generate. The teacher needs to generate the list in advance, then present it to the class and ask for additions, *Are there any other concepts that you can think of that fit here?* and verification, *Do you think these concepts fit?* Students can be guided to build generalizations. Generalizations are two concepts joined by a verb: adaptation promotes survival, actions cause consequences, and change challenges tradition. Ask students to together generate a list of verbs that could link concepts (for example: creates, causes, defines, drives, promotes, etc.) All students must be able to see the list. Students can practice making generalizations in small groups, and these can be added to the list. The theory will probably come from the teacher. The application of the theory comes from a class discussion of "When have you or someone you know instinctively moved from where there is scarcity to where there is abundance." (For example: Fishing with your father.

Family moving because of a new job. Returning to the buffet table with an empty plate.) You may wish to refer to possible answers below and on page 93 as you complete the chart with students. Again, students' logical and thoughtful responses should be considered and accepted.

At the elementary level, students are able to find examples of generalizations in a text. The concepts in the generalization must be at the level of their understanding. An activity for identifying examples of the generalizations follows. With a copy of the text, *Animal Migration*: "Migrating Animals," (Krumm 2016, 4–6) (p. 89) and a highlighting pen, students are to look through the text and highlight any example of one of the generalizations. For example, the teacher asks students to find an example in the text that suggests migration supports survival: ("Animals must move to where they can find food and water." "Animals also have a better chance of finding a partner or giving birth somewhere safe if they migrate.") Students are encouraged to explain their selection(s).

The students can continue to find and highlight support for other generalizations. They can use a different color highlighting pen. The teacher would ask students to find and highlight an example of the generalization, "abundance causes movement" ("As seasons change, fewer resources are near them, and more resources can be found far away.") The inference is that the scarcity of resources causes the migration or movement from fewer resources to more. This activity can continue with all possible generalizations. With more sophisticated students or after more experience with this kind of thinking, finding and highlighting support for the theory could be pursued. This activity is intended to teach students how they can use information to build generalizable knowledge. Remember, we all have easy access to information, but knowledge must be built.

## Conclusion

In this chapter we have shared activities and strategies intended to create an active, engaged, reflective, and critical reader in the context of a whole group learning environment. Over time, the plan is students will independently use the strategies of expert readers to construct the meaning of text, they will read closely and analytically using evidence from the text, and they will synthesize and generalize information to apply it to different disciplines. Finally, students will use text to arrive at new insights, create new solutions, and generate new knowledge.

### Levels of Meaning

| Facts/Argument/Evidence | Topics | Concepts | Principles/Generalizations | Theory |
|---|---|---|---|---|
| Different kinds of animals migrate each year.<br><br>Migration is moving from one area to another.<br><br>Animals migrate to find food to survive.<br><br>Animals migrate to find a partner or give birth.<br><br>Animals migrate to a better climate to survive.<br><br>Animals migrate by instinct, no one teaches them. | Different animals migrate.<br><br>Animals migrate to survive: find food, better weather, and give birth.<br><br>Animals migrate by instinct. | Movement<br><br>Survival<br><br>Migration<br><br>Instinct<br><br>Scarcity<br><br>Abundance | Migration promotes survival.<br><br>Instinct drives migration.<br><br>Scarcity causes migration.<br><br>Abundance causes movement. | Instinct drives movement from scarcity to abundance. |

## References and Resources

Anderson, Richard C., Elfrieda H. Hiebert, Judith A. Scott, and Ian A. G. Wilkinson. 1985. "Becoming a Nation of Readers: The Report of the Commission on Reading." Washington, DC: The National Institute of Education.

Erickson, H. Lynn, and Lois A. Lanning. 2014. *Transitioning to Concept-based Curriculum and Instruction: How to Bring Content and Process Together.* Thousand Oaks, CA: Corwin.

Guillain, Adam. 2016. *Sofia and the Quetzal Bird.* North Mankato, MN: Capstone.

Krumm, Brian. 2016. *Animal Migration.* North Mankato, MN: Capstone.

Keene, Ellin Oliver, and Susan Zimmermann. 1997. *Mosaic of Thought.* Portsmouth, NH: Heinemann.

Michigan Department of Education. 2002. *Certification Standards for the Preparation of All Elementary Teachers.* Lansing, MI: Michigan Board of Education.

Partnership for Assessment of Readiness for College and Careers. 2011. "PARCC Model Content Frameworks: English Language Arts/Literacy Grades 3–11." http://parcconline.org/resources/educator-resources/model-content-frameworks.

Pearson, P. D., L. R. Roehler, J. A. Dole, and G. G. Duffy. 1992. "Developing Expertise in Reading Comprehension: What Should Be Taught? How Should It Be Taught?" In *What Research Has to Say to the Teacher of Reading* Second edition, edited by A. Farstrup and S. J. Samuels. Newark, DE: International Reading Association.

Weber, E., B. Nelson, and C. L. Schofield. 2012. *Guided Highlighted Reading: A Close Reading Strategy for Navigating Complex Text.* North Mankato, Minnesota: Capstone Professional.

# *Sofia and the Quetzal Bird*: "A Rescue" (Guillain 2016, 16–21)

1    When the quetzal opened its wings, it was clear to both children that one wing was hurt.

2    "The poor bird," Sofia burst out. "We have to help!"

3    She ran to the tree and prepared to climb its thick branches.

4    "Stop!" said Ronny. "The quetzal is a wild bird. If you get too close, it will fly away."

5    "But what if it can't fly?" said Sofia.

6    Ronny thought for a second. "Then it will probably die."

7    "So we must help it right now," said Sofia. She couldn't wait any longer as she climbed up the tree.

8    To Ronny's surprise, the quetzal stayed calm. When Sofia was finally sitting on the branch next to the bird, it hopped into her lap. . . . Carefully placing the bird on her shoulder, Sofia climbed back down. That afternoon, with help from Mrs. Garcia, Sofia fed the quetzal.

9    "I've never seen a quetzal so tame around a person," said Mrs. Garcia. "You appear to have a special way with it. . . ."

10   "I don't think its wing is broken," said Mrs. Garcia, "Although it has clearly been in some sort of fight. The bird will probably be better in the morning."

11   Sofia carefully set the quetzal down to rest in a small box lined with a towel. That night, as Sofia and Mom got ready for bed, the quetzal chirped happily from its new home. . . .

12   But when they woke up early in the morning, the quetzal was gone. It had flown out a window.

# Animal Migration: "Migrating Animals" (Krumm 2016, 4–6)

1    Every year, birds fly from one part of the world to another. Fish swim across oceans. . . . Each year, many different kinds of animals travel to places that are far away. This is called animal *migration*. It is the action animals take to move from one area to another at different times of the year.

2    Animals migrate for many reasons. The *resources* they need to survive, like food or water, change during the year. As seasons change, fewer resources are near them, and more resources can be found far away. Animals must move to where they can find food and water.

3    Animals also have a better chance of finding a partner or giving birth somewhere safe if they migrate. The animals must travel to new areas. They sometimes travel thousands of miles as part of their journey.

4    There is another important reason why animals migrate. Some animals migrate to warmer areas during the winter to survive.

5    Scientists also learned that many of these animals have the *instinct* to find their way. The animals weren't taught or told where they need to go. Instead, they can find their way as they travel. Animals are born knowing how to do this.

**Blank Narrative Profundity Chart**

| Physical: What did the character do? (Action—Do) | Mental: What was the character thinking or feeling when s/he did it? (Intention—Do/Think) | Moral: What was right and wrong with what the character did? (Judgment — Judge What They Do/Think) | Psychological: What did the character get from doing what s/he did? (Benefit—Reasons Behind What They Do/Think) | Analogical: What links are there to me, to what I have read, and to my world? (Comparison—Where Else Have I Seen This?) | Philosophical: What is the lesson or principle that I can learn from this story? (Abstraction—Lessons Learned About the World) | Transformational: How can this lesson, insight, or wisdom change my life? (Transformation—Reading Changes and Helps Me) |
|---|---|---|---|---|---|---|
| | | | | | | |
| | | | | | | |
| | | | | | | |

Narrative Profundity Chart—*Sofia and the Quetzal Bird*— "The Rescue"

| Physical: | Mental: | Moral: | Psychological: | Analogical: | Philosophical: | Transformational: |
|---|---|---|---|---|---|---|
| What did the character do? (Action—Do) | What was the character thinking or feeling when s/he did it? (Intention—Do/Think) | What was right and wrong with what the character did? (Judgment—Judge What They Do/Think) | What did the character get from doing what s/he did? (Benefit—Reasons Behind What They Do/Think) | What links are there to me, to what I have read and to my world? (Comparison—Where Else Have I Seen This?) | What is the lesson or principle that I can learn from this story? (Abstraction—Lessons Learned About the World) | How can this lesson, insight, or wisdom change my life? (Transformation—Reading Changes and Helps Me) |
| Sofia climbed a tree and brought the quetzal bird down. | Sofia wanted to save the bird because it seemed to have hurt its wing. | Right—because she wanted to save its life.  Wrong—because Ronny said it was wild and would try to fly away. | Sofia felt better because she thought she was helping the bird. | I was able to get a baby bird back into its nest, and it lived.  We have read articles about successful rescues of wild birds. | Survival depends on change.  Advocacy requires responsibility. | The golden rule: Do unto others as you would have them do unto you.  Helping others makes you feel good. |
| Sofia fed the quetzal bird. | She wanted it to get strong. | Right—because she thought food would make it strong.  Wrong—because food might hurt it. | Sofia felt better because the bird was still alive. | It will be good for hurt animals if people try to help them. | | |
| Sofia put the quetzal bird in a small box lined with a towel to sleep. | She thought rest would help it heal. | Right—because rest might help it.  Wrong—because not being in the wild might have been bad. | Sofia felt better because the bird chirped happily. | | | |

| Facts/Argument/Evidence | Topics | Concepts | Principles/Generalizations | Theory |
|---|---|---|---|---|
| | | | | |

Chart constructed by Weber and Nelson using information from Erickson and Lanning 2014, 97–113

Levels of Meaning—*Animal Migration:* "Migrating Animals"

| Facts/Argument/Evidence | Topics | Concepts | Principles/Generalizations | Theory |
|---|---|---|---|---|
| Different kinds of animals migrate each year. | Different animals migrate. | Movement | Migration promotes survival. | Instinct drives movement from scarcity to abundance. |
| Migration is moving from one area to another. | Animals migrate to survive: find food, better weather, and give birth. | Survival | Instinct drives migration. | |
| Animals migrate to find food to survive. | Animals migrate by instinct. | Migration | Scarcity causes migration. | |
| Animals migrate to find a partner or give birth. | | Instinct | Abundance causes movement. | |
| Animals migrate to a better climate to survive. | | Scarcity | | |
| Animals migrate by instinct, no one teaches them. | | Abundance | | |

Chart constructed by Weber and Nelson using information from Erickson and Lanning 2014, 97–113

# Why Reading Fluency Matters

## Chase Young and Timothy V. Rasinski

Tommy posed a bit of a dilemma for Mrs. Carson. Clearly, Tommy was a bright second grader, but his reading development was just not coming along the way she thought it should. He had a large vocabulary and was able to comprehend very well when stories and other texts were read aloud to him. And when he read on his own, he was able to decode nearly all the words correctly after spending time using work attack strategies, such as sounding out the words. Yet when he was asked to retell what he read, he had little to say; and when he was asked questions about what he had just read, his most common response was that he didn't know.

Although Mrs. Carson had heard of reading fluency, it was most often in the context of making students read quickly. Mrs. Carson did not sense that reading quickly should be an appropriate goal for her reading instruction, and so she dismissed fluency as nothing important.

Later, Mrs. Carson participated in a webinar on reading fluency and wondered if fluency may be the concern. Reading fluency was described as the ability to read words accurately and effortlessly, so the reader could give his or her attention to comprehending the text and reading with expression that reflected the meaning of the text.

The lack of effortless, expressive, and meaningful reading seemed to characterize Tommy as well as several other students in her class. Although Tommy was able to accurately read the words he encountered in a text, his reading of the words was very labored. He would often have to stop for a second or two to analyze the word, and then grudgingly, almost, decode the word sound by sound. Moreover, the extreme effort he put into the word reading resulted in an oral reading that was halting, monotone, excessively slow, and not showing any indication that he was taking in the meaning of the text. "Could it be," Mrs. Carson thought to herself as she observed the second grader struggle, "that Tommy's problem was in reading fluency?"

## What Is Reading Fluency, and Why Is It Important?

Although the concept of reading fluency has been mentioned in the professional literature on literacy for years, there is not complete agreement as to what constitutes fluency. The most common misconception about reading fluency is that reading fluency is reading quickly. Research has demonstrated that reading speed is strongly correlated with overall reading proficiency. Thus, increasing reading speed (i.e., fluency) will result in increasing overall reading proficiency.

The problem with this line of thinking is that correlation does not imply causation—increasing reading speed is not necessarily the cause of improved reading proficiency. We feel that accurate and automatic word recognition will help enhance reading speed, but reading speed should not be the goal. As students grow as readers, their ability to recognize words accurately improves. However, something else happens as well. Students also become more automatic and effortless in their word recognition. The significance of automaticity in word recognition lies in the notion that all readers have a limited amount of cognitive energy. If this cognitive energy has to be used for lower level reading tasks, such as word recognition, the reader will have less energy available for the more important task of making meaning from the print. Readers who are accurate but not automatic are able to decode the words in print. However, in order to do so they have to use an excessive amount of their cognitive resources, and the result is poor comprehension as fewer resources can be devoted to this task. Tommy appears to be one of those children.

Automaticity in word recognition is achieved when the reader is able to recognize words accurately and effortlessly, or automatically. Automatized word recognition means the reader can devote a maximum amount of her or his cognitive resources to the more important task of reading comprehension. Perhaps the best example of an automatic reader is you. If you are a proficient reader, chances are you do not have to stop and analyze or apply your phonics knowledge to the words you are encountering in text. Rather, the words on this page are recognized instantly and accurately as they come into your visual field. Because of this automatic word recognition, you are able to devote your cognitive energy to understanding the message we are attempting to embed in this text.

We have often said the goal of phonics instruction is to get students to not use phonics. Phonics is needed to decode unknown words. However, once a word is encountered multiple times, it becomes embedded in our memories and automatically recognized upon sight—essentially the words become

sight words. Fluent readers have large sight-word vocabularies that allow them to use their cognitive energy to comprehend the text.

So accurate and automatic word recognition results in better comprehension. As mentioned above, there is another consequence of automatic word recognition: speed in reading. Automatic recognition of words takes less time than analyzed recognition of words. Thus, as readers improve in automaticity, comprehension and speed will increase. Word recognition automaticity leads to improved comprehension and faster reading. Focusing on increasing reading speed through timed readings may help students to read more quickly; however, it might not improve word recognition automaticity or comprehension. We see students all the time who have been drilled on quick reading. Their purpose for reading becomes getting from point A to point B in a text as quickly as possible. When this happens, reading becomes a race as students no longer attend to punctuation or making meaning. Comprehension suffers.

Word recognition accuracy and automaticity are only one of two parts of reading fluency. The second element in fluency is prosody, or expression, in oral reading. If you think about someone who is a fluent speaker or fluent oral reader, you are likely to think about someone who speaks with confidence and who has good posture and volume, good expression that enhances the meaning of the words and emphasizes key words, and appropriate phrasing and attention to punctuation. Research has demonstrated that students who read orally with these prosodic features are more likely to be proficient readers (even while reading silently), while students whose reading lacks good prosody, reading in a word-by-word monotone and disinterested manner, are more likely to be less proficient readers (Rasinski, Reutzel, Chard, and Linan-Thompson 2011, 286).

Word recognition automaticity, prosody, and comprehension go hand in hand. As readers become more automatic in their word recognition, they can attend to the prosodic elements of their reading.

Reading with good prosody enhances the meaning of the text so comprehension improves. Think about when you have had to listen to a lecture delivered in a less-than-prosodic manner. Now think of a time when you listened to a lecture that was presented in an enthusiastic and expressive manner. Which lecture was easier to engage in and understand?

So, you see, reading fluency is made up of these key components: word recognition accuracy and automaticity and prosodic reading. The reasons these fluency components are important are simple—they lead to improved comprehension and more proficient overall reading. Research has demonstrated that among students who are not proficient readers, fluency is a major concern (Duke, Pressley, and Hilden 2004, 451; Valencia and Buly 2004, 522). Moreover, other research has found that difficulties in reading fluency can manifest themselves into high school if not appropriately addressed through instruction (Paige, Rasinski, and Magpuri-Lavell 2012, 67).

## Elements of Effective Fluency Instruction

How can we teach fluency in reading? There are several building blocks that can help you design instruction that will meet the fluency needs of your students (Rasinski 1989, 690).

### Model Fluent Reading

If we want students to become fluent readers, they need a good understanding of what is meant by fluency. We think the best way to help students understand fluency is to see it in action. This means reading to our students in ways that demonstrate fluent reading. We all know that reading to students is a great way to improve reading comprehension, build vocabulary, and increase students' motivation for reading. However, it also allows us to show students how they should read when they engage in reading. After reading to students, we might draw their attention to various fluency features of our reading: Did they notice that we read with automatic recognition of words, and did they notice our expression, our phrasing, our emphasis, and our volume? We might occasionally read in a less-than-fluent manner to help students notice what happens when reading is not fluent: Engagement and comprehension suffer.

### Assisted Reading

For students who are not fluent readers, reading a text on their own may be a frustrating experience. Assisted reading is a good alternative to independent reading. During assisted reading the reader reads while simultaneously listening to an oral reading of the same text in a fluent manner. The assist may be in the form of an adult or classmate who reads with the student; or it may be in the form of reading a text while listening to a prerecorded version of the same text. Whether the assist is a live person or recording, the text is read in an appropriately expressive manner, so the student is receiving help with word recognition as well as an expressive reading that reflects the meaning of the text. A good body of research supports assisted reading in all its various forms (Rasinski, Reutzel, Chard, and Linan-Thompson 2011, 286).

### Practice Wide Reading

Clearly, to become fluent at any task, whether it is making a jump shot in basketball, preparing a delicious dinner, driving a car, or reading, it requires practice. Most often we think of practice in reading in terms of wide reading—reading as much as possible, one text after another. Moving from one passage to another is the type of reading that most readers engage in. So it should be encouraged among all readers, including those who struggle and those who don't. The importance of wide reading practice is intuitively appealing, and a compelling body of research also supports wide reading for improving reading fluency (Kuhn, Schwanenflugel, Morris, Morrow, Woo, and Meisinger 2006, 380; Rasinski, Reutzel, Chard, and Linan-Thompson 2011, 286).

## Practice Repeated Reading

For less-than-fluent readers, reading a text one time may not be sufficient to achieve fluency. For these students, practice reading of the same text two, three, or even four times or more may be required to achieve some degree of fluency. The repeated practice should be aimed at both improving the automatic recognition of words and the expressive oral interpretation of the text. Research has shown that students who engage in repeated reading not only improve their fluency and comprehension on the texts they practice repeatedly, there is also a transfer or generalization effect as students demonstrate improved fluency and comprehension on new texts not previously encountered (Samuels 1979, 758).

We should note that the purpose of repeated reading should be made authentic and clear for students. In some approaches the purpose of repeated reading is to get students to increase their reading speed with each new reading of the same text.

We think a more appropriate purpose for repeated reading is the performance of a text. If students know they will be performing a text for an audience, they will engage in rehearsal (repeated reading) with the goal of delivering an oral performance of a text that is effortless and expressive. Of course, if performance is the aim of repeated reading, it is important that we find texts that are meant to be performed. Poetry, song lyrics, scripts, monologues, dialogues, and the like are good examples of texts that fit this bill.

## Practice Text Phrasing

One of the hallmark characteristics of disfluency in reading is word-by-word reading. Each word in a text seems to be read as an independent unit of meaning. Fluent readers, on the other hand, tend to read in syntactically appropriate phrases: noun phrases, verb phrases, and prepositional phrases. Helping students read in phrases is a direct way to improve fluency and, because good phrasing reflects meaning, also improve comprehension (Rasinski 2010, 14). Help with phrasing can take two major approaches. First, students can practice reading short

phrases or sentences, such as "We the people," "I have a dream," "Four score and seven years ago," "near the woods," and "my little brother." A second approach / is to mark phrase boundaries / on texts / that students / will be reading, / as shown / in these sentences. / In doing so, / we are making visible / for students / phrase boundaries / that are often not marked / in text. / Practice with such marked texts should eventually move to practice reading of the same texts without the phrase markings (Rasinski, Yildirim, and Nageldinger 2011, 254).

## Tiered Fluency Instruction

By using the building blocks of fluency just described, alone and in combination, we can create authentic fluency instruction that meets the various and differentiated needs of our students. In this section we describe what we call the three tiers of fluency instruction—instruction for large groups of students, focused instruction for smaller groups of students with similar needs, and intensive fluency instruction for small groups and individual students (Young and Rasinski 2017, 8).

### Tier 1 Fluency Instruction

All students, particularly those in the primary grades, need some degree of instruction in and nurturance of fluent reading. Tier 1 fluency instruction is instruction that can be delivered to an entire classroom of students in relatively short periods of time. Done consistently, Tier 1 instruction can help all students move toward the goal of fluent and meaningful reading.

A very common example of Tier 1 fluency instruction is choral reading (Paige 2011, 435). In choral reading a group of students (possibly an entire classroom) orally read a short text multiple times with the teacher. Choral reading can be done as a beginning of the day activity for which the intent is not only to build fluency, but also create group cohesion. The text needs to be relatively short. Poems and songs work particularly well. The text is often displayed in a large format for all students to see.

Each day or two a new text is presented for choral reading.

A typical choral reading scenario begins with the teacher presenting a challenging text to the students and providing some background information about it. Then the teacher reads the text orally, asking students to follow along silently and pointing to the text as it is read. Next, the teacher invites the students to join in with him or her in reading the text. This is followed by continued oral reading by the large group or other readings of the text by smaller subgroups (e.g., girls, boys, front of the class, back of the class, etc.). Throughout these readings the teacher or a student points to the text as it is read to ensure that students are tracking the text visually as it is read. The teacher can call attention to the text again before recess, after recess, before lunch, after lunch, before the end of the school day, and other transition times. Near the end of the day the teacher might ask for individuals, pairs, or small groups of students to read and perform the text. On subsequent days a similar routine is followed with new texts chosen by the teacher or students.

As you can see, choral reading incorporates several of the building blocks of fluency. Because choral reading is a group experience, assisted reading is a primary characteristic. The students who are disfluent are assisted by more fluent readers in the form of their peers and the teacher. The teacher modeling expressive reading at the beginning of the choral reading lesson is another building block. Modeling also occurs toward the end of the day when individual students are invited to read. Repeated reading clearly is part of choral reading because the text is read over and over again throughout the day. And, because each day brings a new text for choral reading, wide reading is embedded in the lesson over time. Phrasing could easily be embedded into the choral reading lesson if the teacher marks phrase boundaries on the display text.

## Tier 2 Fluency Instruction

Tier 2 fluency instruction is intended for students who may need a bit of a boost in fluency. Tier 2 instruction can be implemented in small groups or on a one-to-one basis. It is a bit more informal than the more intensive Tier 3 instruction and can easily be implemented in a variety of settings from classroom to intervention clinic to home (Young and Rasinski 2017, 48).

Paired Reading (Topping 1987, 604; Topping 1989, 488) is a fine example of Tier 2 fluency instruction. Paired reading is a 10–15 reading session in which a less-fluent reader (tutee) is matched with a more-fluent reader (tutor). The more-fluent reader can be a teacher, parent, classroom volunteer, older student, or even a same-age classmate. The 10–15 minute paired reading lesson begins with the tutee selecting a text to be read together. The text can be a book read for pleasure or an assigned reading from school. It is important that the tutee has some ownership of the activity.

Sitting side by side, the tutor and tutee begin together by reading aloud the selected text. The tutor adjusts his or her reading pace to match or gently pull the tutee along. The tutee has control of Paired Reading in an important way. During Paired Reading, if the tutee feels that he or she can read successfully on his or her own, a signal is given to the tutor. The signal can be a tap on the wrist or a thumbs-up. When this happens, the tutor switches from oral to silent reading, tracking the reading of the tutee. This continues until the tutee signals the tutor to rejoin the oral reading. If the tutee experiences some difficulty, the tutor can automatically come to the rescue of the tutee by going back to oral reading. When difficulties occur, it is important for the tutor to join in and lead the reading without stopping the reading, disrupting the fluency, or turning the difficulty into a "teachable moment." Paired Reading is about building fluent, meaningful reading. Stopping the reading disrupts this goal. At the end of the oral reading, it is often good for the tutor and tutee to discuss the reading.

How did it go? The tutor should also discuss difficulties and check comprehension.

Topping's (1987, 610) research has demonstrated remarkable gains in fluency and comprehension by students who do Paired Reading on a regular basis. Although we describe Paired Reading as a one-to-one activity, it can be adapted easily for groups of two or even three tutees and one tutor. In Paired Reading we can see elements of modeling, assisted, and wide reading. If the same text were read on a subsequent day, repeated reading would also be an embedded element.

The Fluency Development Lesson (FDL) (Rasinski 2014, 26; Zimmerman and Rasinski 2012, 172; Zimmerman, Rasinski, and Melewski 2013, 137) is another Tier 2 lesson that is usually implemented in small groups, but it can easily be adapted for whole class or individual instruction. Disfluent students rarely experience the satisfaction of being able to read a text well. The goal of the FDL is for students to end each lesson with the ability to read a text fluently and meaningfully, so that they, too, can have the sense of success that more fluent readers experience on a regular basis.

The FDL is a daily lesson that takes approximately 15–20 minutes. Each lesson has a short text, usually a poem or a brief segment of a story, to master. Individual copies of the text are made for students as well as a display copy that could be put on the classroom whiteboard.

Each FDL begins with the teacher reading the text aloud to students several times while the students follow along silently. The teacher will vary his or her fluency with each reading. Following the teacher readings, the teacher and students discuss the content of the text as well as the teacher's various readings. They might focus on which of the teacher's readings was the most fluent and why. Next, the teacher has the students join in as they read the text two or three more times chorally. Variety in the oral reading can be achieved by reading the text in different ways and/or having different groups of students read the text. After the choral reading, the teacher will group students into pairs or threes, so they can continue practice reading the text multiple times in their group. The teacher acts as a coach, listening to the children read and offering advice and constructive feedback. A natural outcome of the repeated readings is performance. After the groups practice, the teacher invites individuals and small groups of students to perform the text for the class or other audiences. Often a parent may be asked to sit in the hallway with the students, so they do not disturb the class with the oral reading. Parents listen to each student read, and provide positive feedback to each reader.

After the performance, the students and teacher regroup, choose interesting words from the text, and engage in a brief word study. They may be examining word families, prefixes and suffixes, or word derivations, or they may engage in word sorts or word games. Although the formal lesson ends with word study, the students are encouraged to take a copy of the text home and read it repeatedly for family members and friends. The lesson is then repeated on the following days with each day bringing a new text to be mastered.

Research on the FDL indicates that not only do students improve in their fluency and overall reading achievement, their confidence as readers increases (Rasinski, Padak, Linek, and Sturtevant 1994, 163; Zimmerman and Rasinski 2012, 180; Zimmerman, Rasinski, and Malewski 2013, 154). The FDL gives proof to the old adage: Nothing succeeds like success. When students see themselves as competent and confident readers, they will drive themselves to ever higher levels of proficiency in reading.

## Tier 3 Fluency Instruction

Some students need intensive, intentional, and direct instruction in fluency. These are the students who are candidates for Tier 3 fluency instruction. Like Tier 2 instruction, Tier 3 instruction can be implemented with individual students or as small group instruction. The focus of the instruction is improvement in fluency, with the assumption that overall reading achievement will also improve.

Read Two Impress (R2I) is a one-on-one fluency intervention that can increase students' reading fluency, including rate and expression, but it also promotes reading comprehension and overall reading achievement. This is a good strategy for disfluent readers who also struggle with reading comprehension (Young, Mohr, and Rasinski 2015, 9; Young, Rasinski, and Mohr 2015, 635). The strategy combines two previously researched fluency methods—the Neurological Impress Method (NIM) (Heckelman 1969, 277) and repeated readings (Samuels 1979, 757)—and essentially requires a more fluent reader to read aloud slightly ahead of the student and then listen to the student as he or she rereads the text.

Before the intervention, choose a text that is approximately one year above the student's independent reading level. This first part of R2I is similar to NIM. However, instead of reading the entire book, you will need to chunk the text. For picture books, you can usually read the entire page, but we recommend chunking novels into paragraphs. The duration of chunks can be adjusted later to meet the need of the student. For example, if a student can handle reading more, then plan for that in the future. Conversely, if a student seems to struggle during the strategy, you may need to reduce the length of the chunks, or perhaps even choose an easier text.

Sit next to your student, and begin reading aloud together. As soon as you begin, adjust your rate so you are reading slightly ahead of the student. By "slightly" we mean reading one or two syllables ahead. In most cases, you will need to constantly adjust your rate because the student's pace often varies throughout the text. In addition, read with good expression. Thus, while you are providing strong support for your student as you read slightly ahead, you are also serving as a model for fluent oral reading.

After you read a chunk of text, stop and ask the student to reread the text aloud. Because of the assisted approach, students should be able to reread the text with sufficient accuracy and at a decent pace. Also, you will likely hear expressive reading similar to your own. R2I has a tendency to "etch" the tutor's expression into the mind of the student, a phenomenon that you can actually hear as the student rereads the text. After the student rereads, move on to the next chunk and repeat the strategy. We recommend you continue the strategy for 20 minutes at least three times per week.

Sufficient research indicates that NIM (Eldredge 1990, 75; Eldredge and Butterfield 1986, 33; Hollingsworth 1970, 113; Hollingsworth 1978, 625) and repeated readings (Mathes and Fuchs 1993, 239; Mercer, Campbell, Miller, Mercer, and Lane 2000, 186; Samuels 1979, 758; Vadasy and Sanders 2008, 955) are effective methods for increasing students' reading fluency. Research on R2I also indicates the method has significant positive effects on reading fluency and can increase overall reading achievement (Young, Mohr, and Rasinski 2015, 9). Like many Tier 3 interventions, the method calls for a one-on-one environment conducive for strengthening relationships while accelerating reading development.

## Back to Mrs. Carson and Tommy

Thinking about fluency in this new way was an epiphany for Mrs. Carson. She decided to create a small fluency group that included Tommy and five other students who exhibited a similar lack of fluency. She had 20 minutes before the beginning of the school day and asked the six students to come to the classroom each day for the next five weeks. During this time, Mrs. Carson implemented the FDL. Each day her students learned to read a poem or other short text fluently. They engaged in listening to Mrs. Carson read fluently, assisted reading, and repeated reading on their own. Then, on the final day, Mrs. Carson had her six students perform the text for the entire class, the school principal, and other classrooms.

"I couldn't believe the results. These were students who didn't see themselves as good readers. Yet, because every day they learned to read something well, they began to develop confidence in their ability to read. They also gained skills in word recognition accuracy, automaticity, and expression that they transferred to texts they had not seen before. Not only did they gain in fluency and confidence, their reading comprehension also improved—and quite dramatically in a couple cases. Oh, and I found the lesson so easy to implement. All I had to do was find a different poem or text for each day. I didn't even have to worry too much about the difficulty of the text. If the text was challenging, they just have to practice a bit more, often at home. And the payoff was when they were allowed to 'show off' by performing their text for others. I am a believer in authentic fluency instruction."

Reading fluency is not the answer to all reading problems. Nothing is. However, we know that many students struggle in reading because of their difficulties in reading fluency. When we can implement real fluency instruction that focuses on automaticity in word recognition and prosodic reading, rather than on making students read faster, we will be helping many students make the transition from struggling to proficient and engaged readers.

## References and Resources

Duke, Nell, M. Pressley, and K. Hilden. 2004. "Difficulties in Reading Comprehension," in *Handbook of Language and Literacy; Development and Disorders*, edited by C. A. Stone, E. R. Silliman, B. J. Ehren, and K. Apel, 501–520. New York: Guilford.

Eldredge, J. Lloyd. 1990. "Increasing Reading Performance of Poor Readers in the Third Grade by Using a Group Assisted Strategy." *Journal of Educational Research* 84: 69–77.

Eldredge, J. Lloyd, and D. D. Butterfield. 1986. "Alternatives to Traditional Reading Instruction." *The Reading Teacher* 40: 32–37.

Kuhn, Melanie R., P. J. Schwanenflugel, R. D. Morris, L. M. Morrow, D. Woo, and B. Meisinger. 2006. "Teaching Children to Become Fluent and Automatic Readers." *Journal of Literacy Research* 38 (4): 357–387.

Heckelman, R. G. 1969. "A Neurological-impress Method of Remedial-reading Instruction." *Academic Therapy* 4: 277–282.

Hollingsworth, Paul. 1970. "An Experiment with the Impress Method of Teaching Reading." *The Reading Teacher* 24: 112–114.

———. 1978. "An Experimental Approach to the Impress Method of Teaching Reading." *The Reading Teacher* 31: 624–626.

Mathes, Patricia, and L. Fuchs. 1993. "Peer-mediated Reading Instruction in Special Education Resource Rooms." *Learning Disability Research and Practice* 8 (4): 233–243.

Mercer, Cecil, K. U. Campbell, M. D. Miller, K. D. Mercer, and H. B. Lane. 2000. "Effects of a Reading Fluency Intervention for Middle Schoolers with Specific Learning Disabilities." *Learning Disability Research and Practice* 15 (4): 179–189.

Paige, David. 2011. "'That sounded good!' Using Whole-class Choral Reading to Improve Fluency." *The Reading Teacher* 64 (6): 435–438

Paige, David, T. Rasinski, and T. Magpuri-Lavell (2012). "Is Fluent, Expressive Reading Important for High School Readers?" *Journal of Adolescent & Adult Literacy* 56 (1): 67–76.

Rasinski, Timothy. 1989. "Fluency for Everyone: Incorporating Fluency in the Classroom." *The Reading Teacher* 42: 690–693.

———. 2010. *The Fluent Reader: Oral and Silent Reading Strategies for Building Word Recognition, Fluency, and Comprehension*. New York: Scholastic.

———. 2014. "Delivering Supportive Fluency Instruction—Especially for Students Who Struggle." *Reading Today* 31 (5): 26–28

Rasinski, Timothy, D. R. Reutzel, D. Chard, and S. Linan-Thompson. 2011. "Reading Fluency," in *Handbook of Reading Research, Volume IV*, edited by M. L. Kamil, P. D. Pearson, B. Moje, and P. Afflerbach, 286–319. New York: Routledge.

Rasinski, Timothy, N. D. Padak, W. L. Linek, and E. Sturtevant. 1994. "Effects of Fluency Development on Urban Second Grade Readers." *Journal of Educational Research* 87 (3): 158–165.

Rasinski, Timothy, K. Yildirim, and J. Nageldinger. 2011. "Building Fluency Through the Phrased Text Lesson." *The Reading Teacher* 65: 252–255.

Samuels, S. Jay. 1979. "The Method of Repeated Readings." *The Reading Teacher* 32: 756–760.

Topping, Keith. 1987. "Paired Reading: A Powerful Technique for Parent Use." *The Reading Teacher* 40: 604–614.

———. 1989. "Peer Tutoring and Paired Reading. Combining Two Powerful Techniques." *The Reading Teacher* 42: 488–494.

Vadasy, Patricia and E. A. Sanders. 2008. "Code-oriented Instruction for Kindergarten Students at Risk for Reading Difficulties: A Replication and Comparison of Instructional Grouping." *Reading and Writing: An Interdisciplinary Journal* 21 (9): 929–963.

Valencia, Sheila, and M. R. Buly. 2004. "Behind Test Scores: What Struggling Readers Really Need." *The Reading Teacher* 57: 520–531.

Young, Chase, K. A. J. Mohr, and T. Rasinski. 2015. "Reading Together: A Successful Reading Fluency Intervention." *Literacy Research and Instruction,* 54 (1): 67–81.

Young, Chase, and T. Rasinski. 2017. *Tiered Fluency Instruction: Supporting Diverse Learners in Grades 2–5.* North Mankato, MN: Capstone.

Young, Chase, T. Rasinski, and K. A. J. Mohr. 2015. "Read Two Impress: An Intervention for Disfluent Readers." *Reading Teacher,* 69 (6): 633–636.

Zimmerman, Belinda, and T. V. Rasinski. 2012. "The Fluency Development Lesson: A Model of Authentic and Effective Fluency Instruction," in *Fluency Instruction: Research-based Best Practices,* edited by T. Rasinski, C. Blachowicz, and K. Lems. New York, NY: The Guilford Press.

Zimmerman, Belinda, T. V. Rasinski, and M. Malewski. 2013. "When Kids Can't Read, What a Focus on Fluency Can Do: The Reading Clinic Experience at Kent State University," in *Advanced Literacy Practices: From the clinic to the classroom,* edited by E. Ortleib, E. Cheek, 137–160. United Kingdom: Emerald Group Publishing Limited.

# Writing Is Back! How to Start and Maintain the Conversation about Writing

## Hillary Wolfe

With the introduction of national Standards, writing instruction in the elementary classroom has become an integrated component of a rigorous literacy program. What does this mean for the elementary classroom teacher? Think of writing as an ongoing conversation that you and your students should be having almost every day. Share with your students how writing connects to reading, speaking and listening, and language; and address writing within whole group instruction, across all content areas. Once the silence is broken, stand back and listen—chances are, your students have a lot to say.

This chapter will offer guidance to best practices for writing instruction in the K–2 and 3–5 classrooms, based on the best practices and research. According to numerous studies on effective literacy practices, there are five key components to strategic writing instruction (Troia and Graham 2003; Zumbrunn and Krause 2012; Graham, Bollinger, et al. 2012; Troia 2014). These include setting up your classroom for writing success by:

- **building a culture that supports the writing process** and active collaboration;

- making sure to **include writing in your instruction every day**, in small ways or as larger assignments and across content areas, so students become comfortable with writing as part of the learning experience;

- **tying writing to reading by incorporating a wide range of texts,** including fiction and nonfiction, media, art, primary sources, and more;

- **modeling (a lot!) and providing explicit strategy instruction** using a gradual release of responsibility to introduce steps in the writing process, offer guided practice, and give students opportunities to practice independently; and

- using **assessment practices that foster student growth** by encouraging feedback at every step in the process, and by having students reflect on their own work and the work of their peers with precise and constructive critiques.

This chapter provides information on each of these key components with ideas that will jump-start the dialogue and build excitement for writing into your classroom culture.

# Build a Culture that Supports the Writing Process

Writing is risky business. It involves feeling vulnerable, as students reveal deep thoughts they may have never shared before. It is imperative that the environment is writing-friendly. Academically, this means immersing students in language through word walls, interactive vocabulary lessons, and word games. In terms of classroom management, it means having designated spaces for writing, time carved out intentionally for writing, and an expectation that writing will be an ongoing part of instruction. Behaviorally, it means fostering a collaborative culture where students learn to express their views, disagree respectfully, or build upon the ideas of others without discrediting them. All of these activities help create an environment that supports student writers. As Troia and Graham (2003, 79) state, "Make writing motivating by setting an exciting mood, creating a risk-free environment, [allowing students choice], specifying the goal, and promoting an 'I can' attitude."

An important part of the classroom culture involves a print-rich environment that supports reading. When students are surrounded by words, they get more experience with vocabulary and see reading as an integral part of learning. But a print-rich environment also supports writing. Students are immersed in the great words of other authors, including their peers, and come to cherish writing as an attainable art form. When they have the tools, and when they are given the time, students can give voice to their thoughts in spectacular ways.

## Supplies

The most obvious way to support writing is by having plenty of writing utensils. Cups filled with pencils, crayons, markers, and chalk should be readily available and utilized frequently. In K–2 start with chalk, finger paint, and even shaving cream with food coloring as writing tools, and use butcher paper, the pavement, or a canvas.

Show students the fun of forming letters or even squiggles as a way to express themselves. As they get better at managing the tools, raise the discourse by having partners play 20 questions with vocabulary words or create cryptic messages to be deciphered by riddles or poems. Include poetry with nonsense words to build phonemic skills, or show students how to label a diagram or use cloze sentences to contribute to a story. Students can add captions or dialogue to pictures to foster their storytelling proficiency.

In upper grades, take every opportunity to encourage writing by having paper at the ready and by dedicating time at the end of lessons to reflect. Even if it is never graded, free writing should always be an option for students. Some will enjoy the creativity of being able to write a story or make a card for a friend or family member. Set up a mailbox system where students can post notes to classmates, or even to you! Parents and visitors can also be encouraged to leave mail. When students have options to write for fun, they are more likely to be receptive to assigned writing. And, according to research, "If students know they will receive adequate support to be successful with writing assignments, feel writing is exciting and important, and believe that their teachers and peers value their writing contributions, they are more likely to be motivated to write" (Troia 2014, 13).

## Organization

Portfolios for each student that either stay in a desk or are stored in a special box elevate the status of writing in the classroom as something to be cared for and carefully maintained. Graphic organizers that are used during instruction to aid and organize thinking should be kept in the folders and be revisited during drafting, so students understand their role in the writing process. In grades K–2, students can keep a journal in their portfolio, where they draw or reflect on an assignment on a daily or weekly basis. Use a portfolio to capture important information about text, and tie English language arts reading to a social studies or science unit, such as Communities or

Weather. Each day, students use writing to respond to the topic and begin to integrate ideas across content areas. For example, students can draw and journal about the life cycle of a silk moth. Reading materials support the science, and students use their own observations to build background knowledge. These integrated experiences expand the conversation and open new avenues for discussion.

In upper grades, a portfolio can serve as a way to support process writing. Research indicates that when students learn writing skills and strategies in small increments, it can minimize their feelings of being overwhelmed by an assignment. "[E]ncourage flash drafting, a technique in which smaller segments of text (e.g., the climax of a story) are drafted, examined through conferencing, and revised to help students feel less invested in a completed draft of the whole paper" (Troia 2014, 34).

Use the portfolio at least two to three times each week to capture students' practice attempts and their revisions as well as to communicate your feedback. The portfolio is a tool for keeping work consolidated and a reflection tool for students. When the unit or assignment is complete, empty the portfolio to signal the start of a new unit, but remember to save or upload the final products for publishing.

Another option for upper grades is to use the portfolio all year as a living text. Use a composition book or even a spiral notebook. Create a routine where students record modeled and guided practice of a specific writing strategy, like using a graphic organizer or revising simple sentences into complex ones. Students record your examples on the right-side pages of the book and use the left-side pages for their own independent practice. Have students number the pages and build a table of contents on the first page or inside the cover, so they can always have access to your examples and their attempts.

## Classroom Management and Scheduling Time for Writing

Contrary to intuition, writing can be a social activity. Structure ways for partners or small groups to co-construct paragraphs, complete graphic organizers, or collaborate on research. When students share in the process, they benefit from the language and ideas of their peers. For language learners, collaborative activities provide safe exposure to academic vocabulary, which will encourage risk-taking and foster trust. "Collaboration can increase the sense of community in a classroom, as well as encourage students to become engaged in the writing process with their peers. When students feel connected to one another and to the teacher, they may feel safe participating in the writing process and sharing their writing with peers" (Graham, Bollinger, et al. 2012, 34).

For younger students, assign pairs or table groups a poster, a presentation, or a short story. For older students, use reader's theater as a way to practice fluency and to support presentation skills. Students of any age can follow the rules of collaboration, including how to have respectful dialogue, how to share responsibility, and how to advocate for an idea. Create posters that reflect their rules, or make table tents to remind them as they work. Fisher, Frey, et al. (2008, 19) explain how a partner or group assignment improves discussions, especially for English learners or shy students, by giving them access to "language brokers," who help by providing model sentences and talking points. "[P]urposefully [organize] . . . groups such that students at the beginning levels of English proficiency had access to language brokers who could support their participation." Rather than stifle the voices of some students, a more outspoken student can provide an entryway into a conversation.

Many classrooms include writer's workshop, a mirror of the reader's workshop based on the work of Lucy Calkins (1994). During writer's workshop, students gather on the rug for a 10-minute mini-lesson on a specific writing strategy, followed by 30 minutes of guided and independent practice. Writer's workshop is an effective and strategic way to incorporate writing into the schedule two or three days each week, or even daily.

But there are more ways to bring writing into daily instruction.

- Start the day with a quick journal write to focus the students.
- Use writing as an anticipatory activity that lays the groundwork for an upcoming unit.
- Spark students' creativity by providing a few quiet minutes with a prompt that inspires out-of-the-box thinking such as, "Imagine if the character in yesterday's story lived in a different time in history. How would the story have been different?"
- Schedule a short written response to a lesson or a unit as a ticket-out-the-door, so students can demonstrate what they've learned, reflect on their progress, or synthesize information.
- Build in five to 10 minutes of writing at the end of each content-area block of instruction. The insight you will gain about students' understanding will be worth the few minutes of instruction you sacrifice. Later you can show students how their thinking changed over time, and they can feel proud of how much more they understand as the year progresses.
- Encourage students to give you feedback on your writing. What could you have done differently to better present the information? When students see you are open to constructive criticism, they take ownership of their own learning and see the value of open and transparent conversation.
- And finally, when it comes to scheduling time for writing, include creative writing that allows students choice of topics. The freedom will promote writing as a fun and challenging activity they will anticipate, especially if there is time to share and present their writing for the entertainment of the class or during a literacy night for parents.

These steps in scheduling writing time align with the research. Per Zumbrunn and Krause (2012, 349), "Set the stage by recognizing student interests and experiences and creating a context in which students are excited to write in meaningful ways." In this way, writing becomes an organic part of classroom time that students look forward to.

## Include Writing in Your Instruction Every Day

Research supports the inclusion of writing in daily instruction. Graham, Bollinger, et al., recommend up to an hour each day of writing instruction and practice, in all subjects, to help students gain confidence and competence, and also to learn how to write for different purposes and audiences (2012). Troia and Graham (2003, 79) also encourage "daily writing on a wide range of tasks . . . ." as effective writing practice.

Writing daily will teach students how to write in multiple genres and help them learn to write for a variety of reasons. Some of these reasons include:

- writing to learn, such as when taking notes and summarizing information.
- writing to explain, such as when presenting a step-by-step process or showing cause-and-effect relationships.
- writing to understand, such as when comparing two pieces of literature or different perspectives of one event.
- writing to prove, such as when stating a claim and citing evidence to support your claim.
- writing to be creative, such as when telling a story, writing a play, or inventing a game.

The Anchor Standards for writing explicitly require students to write for a variety of reasons and over various time spans: "Write routinely over extended time frames (time for research, reflection, and revision) and shorter time frames (a single sitting or a day or two) for a range of discipline-specific tasks, purposes, and audiences" (CCSS.ELA-LITERACY. CCRA.W.10). Let's examine what those various purposes might be, starting with the different text types: argumentative, explanatory, and narrative.

*Argumentative text* is presented first in the Standards because it is possibly the most important type of writing, and *thinking*, that students need to learn to master. CCSS ELA Appendix A includes the following quote: "While all three text types are important, the Standards put particular emphasis on students' ability to write sound arguments on substantive topics and issues, as this ability is critical to college and career readiness. English and education professor Gerald Graff (2003) writes that 'argument literacy' is fundamental to being educated. The university is largely an 'argument culture,' Graff contends; therefore, K–12 schools should 'teach the conflicts' so that students are adept at understanding and engaging in argument (both oral and written) when they enter college" (National Governors Association Center for Best Practices and the Council of Chief State School Officers 2010, 24). Argumentative text presents a claim and uses evidence to support that claim. In language arts, that may look like an editorial, an advertisement, a speech, or a position paper. But the skills involved in crafting a valid argument are the skills that will allow students to advocate for themselves, think critically when they go online, ask for a raise, or fight injustice.

*Explanatory writing* is meant to explain (e.g., explain how to build something, explain the differences between two ecosystems), and *informational writing* is meant to inform or give facts about something (e.g., what happened on this date in history, who was Harriet Tubman, and information about calories). These are the most common types of writing students will encounter, both as writers and readers. Directions for conducting an experiment or filling out a test booklet are explanatory texts. A news article that describes two sides of a story and a description of a healthy way to eat are examples of informational text. Writing these types of texts requires a strong understanding of facts, research, and credibility.

*Narrative writing* is about telling a story, but it is not limited to fiction. Biographies are narratives. Narrative structures can be effective and creative strategies to bring a historical figure to life. Teachers use storytelling to invest students in a lesson. Asking,

"What if . . ." is a great way to spark creative thinking about a complex subject. Television commercials use narrative structures to sell products. They are often mini-movies, and they make the viewer feel he or she could be "in the story" if only that person had the product being advertised.

Students need to learn about each of these text types and how to use details, language, and examples to add richness to their writing. But they also ultimately need to learn how to artfully combine these text types for greatest effect, since that is what complex text offers and what skilled writers know how to do. Per Appendix A, "Skilled writers many times use a blend of these three text types to accomplish their purposes" (National Governors Association for Best Practices and the Council of Chief State School Officers 2010, 24). This is where CCSS.ELA-Literacy-CCRA.W.4 comes in: writing in which the development and organization are appropriate to task, purpose, and audience. First, students need to identify the task—what is the format my writing will take? Will it be a brochure? A report? A story? Understanding the task helps students choose the structure and organize their ideas.

Once the format is understood, students need to know the goal of the writing. "In teaching a particular genre, teachers should emphasize the purpose of that genre and how its features are related to the purpose" (Graham, Bollinger, et al. 2012, 20). Have students identify the purpose: Is it to inform? Persuade? Entertain? Knowing the purpose of the writing helps students choose the right language and the appropriate examples and pinpoint the exact type of evidence that will best support the writing.

Then, students need to know who their reader will be, so they can choose the appropriate tone, insert the right amount of emotion, or rely more on data and logic. "Familiarity and facility with these conventional patterns, or genres, will position students to attempt writing assignments with confidence, explore hybrid patterns of writing, or even invent new types of writing" (Troia 2014, 19).

Finally, when it comes to integrating more writing into daily ELA instruction, look at ways to make writing a more collaborative activity. Start with Speaking and Listening activities that encourage conversation. Have students work in pairs, trios, and small groups intermittently, and include reflection, summary, and goal setting in independent writing activities. In K–2 have students practice taking turns in conversations, and teach them how to ask a question or to build upon another person's ideas. Highlight examples in literature of effective communication, and use props such as talking chips to ensure everyone gets a chance to share an idea. Play word games with students as a whole class or in small groups, so they practice playfully using language and benefit from hearing how others think.

To begin a collaborative writing activity, provide sentence starters, sentence frames, and word banks to ensure that students are incorporating complex sentence structures, academic language, and key vocabulary in their responses. Use activities like Four Corners, where students go to a location in the room if they Agree, Strongly Agree, Disagree, or Strongly Disagree. They talk among their peers, then choose a delegate to share out their rationale. Students can then switch groups, as long as they articulate which evidence changed their mind.

Once students can comfortably express their thoughts orally, and practice explaining their thinking with their peers in a safe setting, it will be easier to put their thoughts to paper. The verbal interaction they have with their peers will translate to high-quality writing on paper.

Older students can co-construct paragraphs or whole projects and check each other's work with specific rubrics. "Students improve their writing quality when they use explicit criteria (e.g., rubric traits) to self-evaluate their writing performance" (Troia 2014, 11).

## Tie Writing to Reading by Incorporating a Wide Range of Texts

When students are exposed to a wide variety of texts and print materials, they hear words and phrases used in multiple contexts that extend beyond literal meanings and vocabulary that is beyond their traditional repertoire. They also stretch themselves to understand text that may be more challenging than they have experienced. Students may not be exposed to a wide variety of texts at home, so the classroom setting needs to present rich and diverse options. It may seem that nuanced language is too challenging for young students to master, but when the task is motivating and fun, students will push themselves to understand texts that may seem above their reading levels. (For example, many video games have extremely complicated story lines, but students will immerse themselves and master the complexities because the game is fun.) This speaks to two important elements in writing instruction:

- use mentor texts that can be models for a wide variety of writing styles, and

- plan fun activities that will engage students and motivate them to try something challenging.

You can recognize a good mentor text by looking at how the author used structure, word choice, crafting choices, and literary devices. A rich text will offer nuances of language, encourage students to dig deeper into the topic to gain a more comprehensive understanding of it, use structure artfully and thoughtfully, and present shades of meaning that allow the student to gain a new or different understanding with every reading. "Exemplary texts can illustrate a number of features, including text structure; use of graphs, charts, and pictures; effective word choice; and varied sentence structure. . . . Students will then be prepared to emulate characteristics of exemplary texts at the word, sentence, and/or text level" (Graham, Bollinger, et al. 2012, 22).

Wide reading means including a combination of fiction and nonfiction, posters, ads, visual texts such as videos or artwork, primary source documents, poems, songs, and performances. Highlight the choices the authors of these texts made, and ask students to practice using some of these techniques in their own writing. Encourage students to engage with texts multiple times, until they are comfortable with different styles and formats. Show how two different text types (a poster and a song) can still present the same idea, or how two poems about the same subject can be very different. Each text that diversifies their reading adds another model that students can turn to as they are building their confidence as writers.

As you read together, highlight a key detail, a choice the author made, or a thematic idea. Ask students to practice finding these elements in their own independent reading. During writer's workshop, revisit a text they have been reading, and ask students to try their hand mirroring an author's style, a specific structure, or use of language in their independent writing.

In K–2 picture books can be a perfect introduction to wide reading. When you show how the illustrations contain clues that will help make predictions about the story, or small details that will tell a lot about the characters, students are actually learning about text features and the importance of descriptive details. Having students retell a wordless or nearly wordless story forces them to pay attention to these details, underscoring the importance of pictures, illustrations, charts, and even the way a text is laid out on the page. Then ask students to cite evidence from the pictures to support their summaries. Finally, they could explain what the author might have been thinking when choosing pictures to include. When it's their turn to write, you can encourage students to include some of these types of details and text features, so their writing can be as clear as the texts they've read.

In grades 3–5 integrate nonfiction texts and primary sources into language arts for more opportunities to examine ways to enrich writing. For example, include a news story about stray animals when reading *Because of Winn Dixie* (DiCamillo 2000).

Discuss the differences between the two texts. Which is a narrative, and which is explanatory? How did you know? When students are making decisions about their own writing, remind them about these differences. How did the news story help their understanding of the fiction book? This is where wide reading is most important—by encouraging them to expand their understanding through the integration of a variety of texts. Finally, ask them to write a news article of their own about India Opal and her dog. Who were the important characters that should be interviewed? Why did they make those choices? That is a fun way to get them to summarize the story and to demonstrate their understanding of the characters and themes. And don't underestimate your youngest learners—even wordless books offer plenty of evidence that can spur a discussion or prompt an imaginary interview.

## Model (a Lot!), and Provide Explicit Strategy Instruction

Writing may not come naturally to students. You need to offer **step-by-step strategy instruction** using a gradual release of responsibility. **Model** for your students with **think-alouds**, engage in **guided practice** with **scaffolds and sentence frames**, and celebrate students' **independent writing** by **publishing** and displaying their work.

Modeling may be one of the most challenging aspects for teachers. Modeling writing takes a certain amount of confidence, and teachers may not feel like they are good writers. What they don't realize is their discomfort is exactly what their students need to see. Young children are not confident either. Imagine how empowering it is to see their teacher struggling and feeling unsure! "Guided writing instruction, in which teachers guide students through the writing process with a combination of modeling, direct instruction, and guided and independent practice, is one such way that teachers can provide appropriate scaffolding for individual students to improve writing proficiency (Gibson, 2008)" (Zumbrunn and Keegan 2012, 352).

The first step is to let students into your thought process by modeling with think-alouds. "Model how to use the targeted strategy and then provide students with as much support as they need to progress toward independent use of the strategy" (Troia 2014, 16). How do you start to write? Do you brainstorm and jot down all kinds of ideas on paper? Show your students and have them try that, too. Maybe you create maps and use graphic organizers, or you use sticky notes to move ideas around. Perhaps you like to make an outline or do your brainstorming on the computer where you can edit and revise with ease. Whatever your preferred method is, show your students, and encourage them to try something else that might work for them. Let them know there is no right or wrong way to get your ideas out, as long as you start somewhere.

Once you've modeled and checked that your students are mirroring one or more of your strategies, start with guided practice (Troia and Graham 2003, 76). Take your ideas and start organizing, then drafting. Think aloud again, revealing how you make choices about what is most important, or how you want to order information. These think-alouds can be done with the whole class or in small groups, but after each example, have students work with a partner to try to revise their work. "Although guided instruction is teacher led, this does not mean that students are not talking. They use talk to ask questions—of the teacher, of peers, and of themselves—as well as to clarify understanding, provide feedback to a partner, and reflect once more on their learning" (Fisher, Frey, et al. 2008, 17).

This is prime time for quick conferencing. While students are engaged with their partner, walk around and listen in on their conversations; glance over their shoulders at what they're writing; and offer a quick comment, encouraging suggestion, or a provocative question. Then stand back and let the students grapple with what you said. Have students share out, or collect their drafts for quick formative assessments. For K–2 students, you may need to use word banks, picture cards, or sentence strips to scaffold the drafting process. "Younger writers

and those who struggle with writing will require greater explicitness, more practice, and enhanced scaffolding (e.g., repetitive modeling, graphic aids, checklists, incremental goals, expectations)" (Troia 2014, 10). For grades 3–5, use sentence frames and graphic organizers again, and explicitly show how to structure sentences by introducing grammar and spelling concepts in the context of drafting and revising.

Help students construct longer pieces of writing in small increments so you have a chance to offer constructive feedback that students can act on right away. Plan to revisit writing over several days, or for a longer piece and older students, over two to four weeks. Not only are you fostering perseverance, your final assessment will be so much easier since the extended time allows students to revise their writing for specific product goals while identifying structural or grammatical errors. "Goals can focus on a writing process or aspect of the product. For writing product goals, quality and quantity goals can be established and explicitly linked" (Troia 2014, 31). By the time students are ready to engage in independent writing, they should have a full portfolio of organizers, drafts, and edits. Have them turn in a pre-final draft so you can add your final comments, then let them publish their very best work, using your comments as a base! Their final piece should represent a full body of work, with many thoughtful revisions and justifiable choices. That piece should be proudly displayed as a testament to both process and product. "Publishing student work in this manner celebrates writing and helps create a physical environment that is conducive to learning" (Graham, Bollinger, et al. 2012, 38).

## Assessment Practices that Foster Student Growth

Because good writing consists of many attempts, assessment must be varied and multipurpose. Combine **peer editing**, **checklists**, **rubrics**, and **portfolios** to monitor students' progress, and give them meaningful **feedback** to continuously improve their writing skills.

Peer editing gets a bad rap mostly because students often don't know how to offer constructive feedback. How could they? They are still learning themselves, so to ask them to offer informed criticism is unfair. However, peer editing can be a great way to get eyes on a paper before grading happens. And a rubric that specifies the skills focused upon will make the purpose of the writing clear and will help students to focus their attention and feedback. "Concrete and discrete feedback provided through the rubric will help students improve their writing" (Troia 2014, 23).

Here's how to make peer editing meaningful and productive. First, it's imperative that the classroom is a safe environment. This is accomplished through lots of classroom practice and by fostering an attitude of acceptance and support. In this environment, students feel comfortable if you model peer editing using one of their papers. Cover up the name and display the paper on an overhead projector or use a document camera. Choose a paper that has examples of good writing techniques as well as some areas that could be improved. Only edit one paragraph (or even one sentence) at a time. Walk through the paper word by word or line by line, and think aloud with questions like, "Is this the best word choice? Is this the correct punctuation? What would make this clearer?" Have the students make suggestions and explain their reasons. Then ask students to trade papers with a partner and peer edit one sentence or paragraph using the same questions to guide their thinking. By asking questions, the students are able to impress upon each other the need to clarify their writing, be more specific, and make careful choices about their writing, without really offering judgment.

Another form of peer editing is through the use of checklists. As your students progress through the writing process, include specific checklists for each step along the way. For an introductory paragraph, the checklist could include things like:

- ☐ opening line grabs attention (like a question or startling statistic)
- ☐ introduces the topic
- ☐ states an opinion about the topic

- ☐ describes the main ideas that will support the topic

As the teacher, you can tell how much each student understands about the components of an opening paragraph by seeing if they can recognize those parts in a friend's work.

A rubric is another kind of checklist, but it is more comprehensive because it distinguishes gradients of proficiency. The trick to creating an effective rubric is to have a clear idea of what an ideal paper should look like, and then work backward from there. Break down the grading into categories, like organization, ideas, and so on. If the assignment covers specific content, include a category for the vocabulary and explicit concept understanding that is demonstrated in the writing as well. It may be helpful to actually write your own paper first to see exactly what you want included. That will help you as you teach, too, since you'll be emphasizing those characteristics. Once you've described all the elements of an ideal paper, consider which elements would be sufficient to demonstrate proficiency, then which elements, if they were missing, would lower the quality of a paper to the point where it is nearly proficient, but not quite, and finally, describe a paper that just meets the most basic, minimum requirements. Writing rubrics is challenging. Work with your grade-level colleagues to share the load and to provide consistency for students. Most of all, remember that rubrics require ongoing refinement, just like good writing.

To truly see a student's progress over time, maintain a portfolio of their work. There are different ways to use portfolios. A portfolio can be a way for students to keep notes, research, organizers, and drafts in one place. All can be used as reference when students write their final published work. This use of a portfolio allows students to revisit their own work, make decisions about revising, and crystallize their thinking. "Students should eventually be taught to use the writing process in an iterative and recursive fashion in which all elements occur multiple times and with a great deal of overlap among the elements"

(Troia 2014, 10). Plus, this kind of system allows a place for ongoing feedback between you and the student by collecting and commenting on work as it progresses. That way, the final product represents the culmination of a large body of work, and can be honored and respected as the finest piece of writing the student could offer.

Another kind of portfolio is one where the student saves the final products for reflection later in the year. The student can choose his or her favorite pieces to include, you can make the selections, or both you and the student choose the pieces together—but the pieces should demonstrate how the student has grown over time. Display or share the final portfolio at an open house, and pass it on to the teacher in the next grade. What a treasured memento for the student to carry forward to upper grades and middle school!

Finally, HAVE FUN! Rigorous standards and creative fun writing projects are not mutually exclusive. We can have high expectations for our students and still foster their sense of individuality and voice. We want our students to see writing as a creative outlet, something at which they can be successful, and as an effective means of communication. They will feel more confident if they are enjoying the process as much as the product!

## References and Resources

Calfee, R. C., and R. G. Miller. 2013. "Best Practices in Writing Assessment for Instruction." In *Best Practices in Writing Instruction*. 2nd Edition. Edited by S. Graham, C. MacArthur, and J. Fitzgerald, 351–380. New York: Guilford.

Calkins, Lucy M. 1994. *The Art of Teaching Writing*. Portsmouth, New Hampshire: Heinemann.

DiCamillo, Kate. 2000. *Because of Winn Dixie*. Somerville, Massachusetts: Candlewick Press.

Fisher, Doug, Nancy Frey, and Carol Rothenberg. 2008. *Content-Area Conversations: How to Plan Discussion-Based Lessons for Diverse Language Learners*. Alexandria, VA: ASCD.

Graham, S., A. Bollinger, C. Booth Olson, C. D'Aoust, C. MacArthur, D. McCutchen, and N. Olinghouse. 2012. *Teaching Elementary School Students to Be Effective Writers: A Practice Guide* (NCEE 2012-4058). Washington, DC: National Center for Education Evaluation and Regional Assistance, Institute of Education Sciences, U.S. Department of Education. Retrieved from http://ies.ed.gov/ncee/wwc/publications_reviews.aspx#pubsearch.

National Governors Association Center for Best Practices and the Council of Chief State School Officers. 2010. *Common Core State Standards for English Language Arts and Literacy in History/Social Studies, Science, and Technical Subjects*. Washington, DC: Authors.

———. 2010. *Common Core State Standards for English Language Arts and Literacy in History/Social Studies, Science, and Technical Subjects: Appendix A: Research Supporting Key Elements of the Standards Glossary of Key Terms*. Washington, DC: Authors.

Olinghouse. 2012. *Teaching Elementary School Students to Be Effective Writers: A Practice Guide* (NCEE 2012-4058). Washington, DC: National Center for Education Evaluation and Regional Assistance, Institute of Education Sciences, U.S. Department of Education. Retrieved from http://ies.ed.gov/ncee/wwc/publications_reviews.aspx#pubsearch.

Troia, Gary. 2014. "Evidence-based Practices for Writing Instruction" (Document No. IC-5). Retrieved from University of Florida, Collaboration for Effective Educator, Development, Accountability, and Reform Center website: http://ceedar.education.ufl.edu/tools/innovation-configuration/.

Troia, Gary, and S. Graham. 2003. "Effective Writing Instruction Across the Grades: What Every Educational Consultant Should Know." *Journal of Educational and Psychological Consultation* 14 (1): 75–89.

Whitaker, Charles. (n.d.). "Best Practices in Teaching Writing." www.learner.org/workshops/middlewriting/images/pdf/HomeBestPrac.pdf. 1–8.

Zumbrunn, Sharon, and Keegan Krause. 2012. "Conversations with Leaders: Principles of Effective Writing Instruction." *The Reading Teacher* 65 (5): 346–353.

# The Rigor of Independent Close Reading: Teaching Students to Think Deeply—on Their Own

Nancy Boyles

. . . . . . . . . . . . . . . . . . . . . . . . . . . . . . . . . . . . . . . . . . . . . . . . . . . . . . . . . . . . . . . . . . .

One of the greatest challenges teachers face is getting kids to produce the same quality work on their own as they do with step-by-step guidance. This is especially true for close reading where the expectation is for deep thinking and the texts are complex. Is it realistic to think that students in the elementary grades beyond the primary level can manage the rigor of close reading independently? Yes, if we understand what rigor really is, choose resources that require students to flex their mental muscles sufficiently, and engage in an instructional process that integrates thoughtfully selected best practices.

## What Is Rigor, Anyway?

"Rigor" is one of those terms that we toss about with abandon, like we know exactly what it means. But I suspect that if we asked 10 people for its definition, we'd get 10 quite different answers. There may be some agreement over probable synonyms: "deep thinking," "high expectations," "complexity." But the part that people might miss is rigor is more about the *result*, the outcome of learning, than the learning process itself. The outcome that educators commonly align with rigor is a student's capacity to demonstrate insight into a challenging problem or situation:

> Rigor is the result of work that challenges students' thinking in new and interesting ways. It occurs when they are encouraged toward a sophisticated understanding of fundamental ideas and are driven by curiosity to discover what they don't know. (Sztabnik, 2015)

It is this "sophisticated understanding of fundamental ideas" that we hope our close reading instruction will accomplish. However, close reading itself is not synonymous with rigor. Close reading is a *process*. We teach the process of close reading so students will develop the skills and strategies to understand a text deeply. But until students actually *produce* something for us in response to reading, either orally or in writing, we don't really know how effective their close reading has been. Reread the first line of the definition above: "Rigor is the *result* of work that challenges students' thinking . . . ." Close reading is the process we will teach so students can respond with rigor.

Rigorous response is a challenge for close reading in general, and an even greater challenge as we pursue students' independent close reading. To reach this lofty goal we will need to put into place practices and principles that maximize our students' potential to think deeply. Let's begin by considering where we will position close reading within our literacy block.

## How Can We Go Beyond Whole Class Instruction to Maximize Students' Potential as Close Readers?

I love the idea of introducing the rigor of close reading through whole class shared lessons. The teacher models the thinking processes of serious text analysis and asks the kinds of text-dependent questions that demonstrate to students that they, too, can comprehend text in deep ways. I often use picture books for this purpose. There are so many beautiful and highly complex picture books available for children of all ages that launching close reading in this manner yields great results. Students are engaged. They get to witness close reading in action, and since the teacher is typically reading the book aloud, they are not sidelined by having to read the text themselves. This is especially helpful for students whose decoding skills are not as well developed as their capacity to comprehend.

What a positive way to introduce kids to the promise of close reading! Still, we can't stop here; students must also participate in the discussion. If our goal is independent close reading, there needs to be more monitoring and accountability than whole class instruction allows. Let's be honest: When you're teaching any kind of whole class lesson, there are too many of "them" and not enough of "you" to go around. If children participate, you know what they're thinking and have a general idea of how well they are doing with whatever the lesson is. If they sit silently, even when they appear to be tuned in, you can't know for sure what they are absorbing. Even when students turn and talk, it's hard to get around to every partnership.

Moreover, at some point students will need to read a text themselves if they are to qualify as *independent* close readers. We could hand them a book after we've modeled the process with those fabulous picture books and ask students to have a go on their own. But that would be a giant leap when what most students need is a sequence of smaller steps with monitoring and support as they wobble forward, tentatively

at first, and then with more confidence and skill. Students need to practice the work of close reading while supported by their teacher. Small group instruction is the perfect setting for this to take place.

Typically, in small groups, there are a half dozen or so students gathered with you at a table, or maybe you're sitting shoulder to shoulder on a rug or carpet squares. Everyone has a copy of the text, and they can all read it. There may be some disparity in reading levels, but the range is close enough that a bit more or less teacher scaffolding makes the text accessible to all. Perhaps most significant is the "feel" of the small group: cozy, low risk, a place where thoughts can be shared respectfully and without reprisal. This is a place where everyone sitting around that table can feel extra special. In many ways, small group time is my favorite time of the literacy block because it's not about teachers and students; it's about friends coming together to share their thinking and what's important to them about something they've read. Now they need something to read worthy of this small group time.

## What Kind of Literacy Resources Will Help Students Flex Their Mental Muscles for Independent Close Reading?

### Consider Text Complexity

With a few of their peers sitting with you around a table, let the serious close reading work begin. First, we need the right text. We hear a lot about the need for complex text for close reading. But too often when people refer to "text complexity," they view it very narrowly, simply as a Lexile score that just relates to sentence length and how often a particular word is likely to appear in print. There's more to complexity than that! There are the qualitative features to keep in mind, too, and these are especially important when students are reading a text closely themselves.

Take into account the background knowledge required by a text. We don't want students to read text totally beyond their realm of experience or capacity to comprehend, but a little stretching is a good thing for close reading. Without their own background to fall back on, students have to rely on the text itself to get meaning—one of the key criteria for close reading.

What contributes to complex meaning? **Meaning**, **language**, and **structure** are all different complexities:

What contributes to **meaning** complexity?

- lots of inferential thinking
- multiple themes or big ideas
- intricate plot or sequence of events
- complicated relationships between characters or people

What contributes to **language** complexity?

- lots of unknown words
- figurative phrases
- archaic terms
- long sentences

What contributes to **structural** complexity?

- dialogue and other author's crafts
- flashback
- foreshadowing
- parallel plots
- "busy" page layout with text boxes and other graphics

We don't want *all* of these complexities to be present in any one text, but we do want a balanced diet of complexities over time: If today's story is complex in its meaning, maybe tomorrow's news article will feature language complexities.

Exactly what will students read in their small groups to become adept close readers who demonstrate rigor? First, think short! It's not that we want to eliminate longer texts from the literacy curriculum. But when we want to teach a process (such as close reading) and when the text is challenging, *short* works better than *long*. Struggling students will be able to maintain the stamina to persevere through a few paragraphs where a lengthy chapter book, or even a picture book read alone, might be overwhelming. Shorter selections also allow more opportunities for different kinds of texts, both informational and literary.

## Keep Your Options Open for Informational Text

We need to think outside the box when choosing texts for small group close reading. The Common Core reminded us that there should be significantly more informational text in our curriculum than we may have included in the past—a valid expectation. But too often I see a very narrow view of nonfiction. Go-to resources typically have a main idea/detail format with headings and subheadings, bolded words, and accompanying photographs, charts, maps, and the like. These are useful tools, and we need them. But we also need other things. We need primary sources like speeches and songs, diary and journal accounts, personal narratives, and biographies. This can get a little tricky because most speechwriters do not write with an audience of 10 year olds in mind. Still, informational text is a diverse field, and students need to experience its full range. With a little sleuthing, there's some great stuff out there. Some of it is even free!

Many patriotic songs like "America the Beautiful" and "The Star-Spangled Banner" are out of copyright and can be downloaded from online sites. There are also sites with speeches, some of which are manageable for elementary students. I especially like Lou Gehrig's Farewell Speech, which is heartfelt and a perfect example of a well-constructed argument.

Capstone offers an array of informational options, some of which have become personal favorites. I love the Primary Source History series. These small books include titles such as *Westward Expansion* (Otfinoski 2015), *The American Revolution* (Powers Webb 2016), and *Slavery in the United States* (Kimmel 2015) and can be purchased in sets of six for individual titles.

They show what it was like to live through these historic periods through the voices of people who were actually there—with quotes, photos, captions, and more. I especially appreciate that they give young readers a context for those complicated quotes to make the language and big ideas more accessible. Here is an example from *A Primary Source History of Slavery in the United States* (Crotzer Kimmel 2015, 10):

> Many Northern citizens objected to slavery and wanted it abolished in the new country. New York lawmaker John Jay wrote, "The honour of the States, as well as justice and humanity . . . loudly call upon them to emancipate these unhappy people."

Different color print, fonts, and bolded words contribute to the clarity of the message. Still, my top pick for historical content in a unique format is Capstone's You Choose Interactive History Adventure series. Reminiscent of the "choose your own adventure" books we may remember from our own youth, these small volumes (also sold as sets) make history come alive. Students can choose among three story paths, making about 40 choices along the way, with three possible endings.

For example, in *The Underground Railroad: An Interactive History Adventure Revised Edition* (Lassieur 2016), students can choose to be a slave, a slave catcher, or an abolitionist. Faced with the decision of whether or not you (a slave) should talk to a stranger along the road, the stakes are high: If the person turns out to be an abolitionist, all is well. But if he's a slave catcher, you will pay dearly with a severe punishment. I've had kids yell at each other for the choice they made: "I *told* you we shouldn't have talked to that guy."

Yelling aside, I love to see this kind of passion toward close reading. Why are these books so popular? Typically, when students read historical content they're reading about choices others have made. The event is over. But here *they* are the history makers. When you make a decision that matters, you are invested in the outcome. You reason as logically and as strategically as possible because a lot is at stake. If you're playing the role of a slave, the best use of evidence might even save your life! Reasoning logically and strategically are true indicators of rigor.

With regard to informational text, try to find attention-grabbing topics. Some animals are winners every time: pandas, sharks, sea turtles, penguins. Older students love speed and daring feats (roller coasters and extreme sports). Even better: something gross. I recently had the "opportunity" to model a close reading lesson in a sixth grade science class last period on a hot, muggy Friday afternoon in a building with no air conditioning. What worked? Rats!

In an especially descriptive sentence in *Oh Rats! The Story of Rats and People* by Albert Marrin (2006), readers learn that rats in India can fill a freight train 3,000 miles long with the food they eat for the year. That train would stretch from this school in Massachusetts all the way to Los Angeles, California, I told my incredulous group of 12 year olds. I had no trouble keeping their attention from that point forward.

## Literary Text Is Important, Too

While informational text is important, we can't neglect literature. Nonfiction tends to be complex in the same ways over and over: a lot of facts compacted into a short space with many unfamiliar words, accompanied by a host of text features. Literature presents the increased likelihood of an even broader range of complexities with the inclusion of author's crafts such as imagery, dialect, and metaphor.

Again, focus on short pieces and consider a greater emphasis on the classics. Traditional literature like fables, folktales, fairy tales, myths, and legends are mostly a click away at Project Gutenberg. This mammoth-size digital archive of sources is a treasure trove of texts. Choose something nice and short. Or take an excerpt from a longer work such as *The Velveteen Rabbit* by Margery Williams (1922).

> For a long time he lived in the toy cupboard or on the nursery floor, and no one thought very much about him. He was naturally shy, and being only made of velveteen, some of the more expensive toys quite snubbed him. The mechanical toys were very superior, and looked down upon every one else; they were full of modern ideas, and pretended they were real.

Now there's an opening paragraph for close readers to sink their teeth into!

Beginning with what you're going to teach with is critical to any close reading lesson. But teaching that text well is nonnegotiable if your goal is rigor.

## How Do We Design Instruction for Independent Close Reading so Students Can Demonstrate Rigor?

A three-step process will go far in achieving this goal. Step 1 asks students to get as much from the text on their own as they reasonably can on a first close read. In Step 2 the teacher is tasked with asking text-dependent questions that probe students' thinking beyond what they are likely to do by themselves. In Step 3 the teacher identifies a component of the text that is particularly complex or challenging for students and teaches a lesson specific to that skill.

Before any "close" reading, you might want students to read through the whole passage one time, just for the gist. This is especially effective with poetry because students will lose the sense of the rhyme and rhythm once they begin pulling the piece apart line by line. This can be an effective approach to other texts as well. I typically ask, "What's *one* thing you got from this passage?" Or "What's your first impression?" Although low-risk and low-stakes, reading for the gist provides a quick estimate of just how difficult the close reading of a passage is likely to be.

## Step 1: Read the Text Closely Independently, Monitoring Understanding and Reflecting on Meaning

Imagine that you have a short informational text, one of the out-of-the-box variety. *The Diary of Sallie Hester: A Covered Wagon Girl* (Hester 2014) is the diary account of a 14-year-old girl named Sallie Hester who is traveling west with her family by covered wagon in the mid 1800s. Imagine as well that you are teaching this text to a small group of fourth graders reading approximately on grade level. Today's portion of the text is a single entry from May 21, early in the trip. It contains a mere 350 words. Note that this limited amount of reading would not be appropriate every day of the year as students also need to engage with longer texts. But when the charge is close reading, text that can fit onto a single page is just fine.

On the first day with this diary you'll want to introduce it. But keep your introduction brief— less than five minutes is good. Omit lots of the standard prereading fare such as predictions, personal connections, and even vocabulary because we want readers to learn to get their information from the text, not the teacher. In particular, skip the background building as the author builds all the knowledge needed for comprehension right within the diary.

Now how will we proceed? Students need a few manageable strategies to check their comprehension all by themselves. I begin by having them monitor their understanding as they proceed through the text, one short chunk at a time: What words need clarification? What details are worth noticing? They ponder these questions after each chunk, typically a paragraph or two, though even a lone sentence can be a "chunk" if the text is extra challenging. If they're reading the text alone, these are silent reflections. If they're reading the text in their small group, they can share their observations orally. Either way, students quickly discern whether they have succeeded in constructing meaning adequately—or if they've gotten a little lost along the way. A chunk from the Sallie Hester passage appears on the next page.

> We are in the **Pawnee Nation**, a dangerous and hostile tribe. We are **obliged** to watch them closely and double our guards at night. They never make their appearance during the day, but skulk around at night, steal cattle and do all the mischief they can.

Words that might need clarification here are "Pawnee Nation," "obliged," and "skulk." Sallie believed the Pawnees were a dangerous tribe, a detail worth noticing. Then at the end of the passage, students ask themselves four Good Reader questions: What are the key words? Can I summarize what I just read? What are the central ideas? What author's crafts and text features add to meaning? The words from each chunk needing clarification might, or might not, make the final list of key words for the full passage. The Pawnee Nation detail would likely find its way into the summary and contribute to the central idea.

I suggest an annotation sheet containing these four questions to help students clarify their thinking in these areas. I also suggest that these strategies be taught individually before students attempt to use them together. The mini-lessons could be taught early in the school year, or as the need arises when you identify an area where students demonstrate difficulty. You might want to have students practice the strategies below, one at a time, before expecting them to respond to all of the questions together.

## Teach Students to Identify Key Words

Close reading isn't about the hard words; it's about the important words. While this may represent a shift from our vocabulary focus in the past, which emphasized unfamiliar words, we now need to recognize that for close reading the word challenge is different: What words will we absolutely need in order to talk and write about this text? Although there may be some challenging language sprinkled throughout this list, a simple way to explain this to students is: What words will you need for your summary? The rigor is in selecting the most essential

words. For Sallie's May 21 diary entry I might choose "May 21," "Sallie," "good health," "wagons," "death," "cholera," "west," "beautiful," "Pawnee Nation," and "hostile." Notice that this is not a long list. Important words often include characters' names, dates, and places. There are a few lesser-known or new words here: "cholera," "Pawnee Nation," "hostile." But I've also left out some other words from the entry that are hard, and perhaps interesting, but not really needed for meaning: "We are *obliged* to watch them closely." "They *skulk* around at night." I might return to the text to talk about "oblige" and "skulk" later, but for a first close read, go with the basics.

"What words did you find?" I ask the group. The discussion gets pretty animated as students defend their own choices and challenge those of their peers. "Why do you think 'feather beds' is important?" one student questioned. "It's just a little detail." This dialogue helps children refine their thinking. Sometimes it's hard for me to believe that we haven't focused more on key words in the past, even before the Common Core, for without a solid understanding of the important language in a text, how can students express their thinking about its meaning? This is especially crucial for English language learners and other low language students. Insufficient word knowledge can spell disaster for comprehension.

## Teach Students to Summarize Critical Details

Identifying key words also positions students well for fashioning a summary. Students need to recognize how the most important words fit together to create a coherent idea of what the text was about. With less savvy readers I sometimes settle for individual details, and we put them together into a summary collaboratively. But most often I want to confirm that readers recognize how the details fit together on their own. A short paragraph, stanza, or passage can be paraphrased in a sentence or two. Longer chunks need to be abbreviated in a more traditional summary. Either way, the goal is accuracy—without spinning the details into a personal opinion. Just the facts, please. There will be time for interpretation of the facts later.

Here's the kind of summary we would like students to write about Sallie's May 21 entry:

> On May 21 Sallie and her family were heading west in a wagon train for a better life. At first her mother was really sick. Now she was back to good health, but some people making the trip died of cholera. Although the Plains were beautiful, Sallie worried they were in the Pawnee Nation because the tribe was hostile.

Notice that lots of the key words identified above found their way into this summary, along with other words from the text. The summary is only four sentences and is a reasonable synthesis of basic content, without drilling down to those tiny details that may add intrigue, but aren't essential to meaning. For example, there's no mention of the cooking stove that was made of sheet iron or that they buried the dead on the banks of the Blue River.

I often ask students to write their quick summary for sharing, though these are not graded. I want students to hear each other's summaries so we can decide together what works and what doesn't. Rigor in summarizing is defined by accuracy.

## Teach Students to Infer the Central Ideas

A glance at a good summary should help readers determine the central ideas, those understandings an author wants readers to recognize without stating them outright. "What is the author *showing* us but not *telling* us?" I often ask. In the case of Sallie's diary entry, sometimes I get incomplete or not quite accurate responses:

"A trip west in a covered wagon." (This is barely a phrase and doesn't respond to the meaning of the trip.)

"Sallie and her family had a hard time on their trip west." (This is only part of the message.)

1. Sallie and her family had some good times and some hard times on their trip west.

2. Sallie was afraid of the Pawnees because they were hostile.

3. The Pawnees weren't really hostile; they were helpful.

Now we've got it! A central idea isn't an individual word or even a quick phrase; it's a brief statement. In fact, as above, there could be multiple central ideas. Before expecting students to generate their own central idea statements, show them some examples such as those above. Talk about why some statements are effective and others are not. Here the rigor lies in the capacity to synthesize information into a brief, coherent thought that captures general meaning.

## Teach Students to Recognize Author's Craft

To be truthful, students new to close reading may not recognize much in the way of author's craft. In past practice, we've focused primarily on *what* an author says in a text, not *how* the author says it. This is the difference between content and craft. Begin with the most obvious craft elements like page layout and text features.

Page 21 of *The Diary of Sallie Hester* includes a date at the top of the page, an illustration, and a text box with additional information. Why would the author include these features? How might they support readers' understanding? Students might also notice some archaic words and phrases: "Our family all in good health." "We are obliged to watch them safely." How does this phrasing contribute to the message?

Beyond page layout and text features, teach students to look for figurative language such as personification, idioms, metaphors, and similes. Teach them to examine the structure of the text: Did the author organize it as a series of events, main ideas with supporting details, a problem and its solution, or something else? How does one paragraph fit into the passage as a whole? What is the genre, and what genre characteristics can be found within the passage? Students will need to focus on author's craft and text features in the close reading of many texts before they become adept at reading like a writer. Where's the rigor in author's craft and text features? Students who are good at identifying these features not only recognize them, but also interpret how a particular craft or feature is significant to a text's meaning.

Remember that author's craft as well as theme, summarizing, and even key words can also be addressed in Steps 2 and 3 of moving toward independence in close reading: responding to text-dependent questions and skill instruction.

## Step 2: Respond to Text-dependent Questions that Model Deeper Thinking about a Text

It's tempting to jump right to text-dependent questions as the strategy-of-choice when teaching students to read closely. As teachers, we're good at asking questions, and we know if we ask the right questions, we can push students thinking beyond superficial meaning to more rigor.

But wait (literally)! Resist this temptation because your students will not always have you by their side to coax them toward deeper understanding. At some point they'll need to struggle through on their own, quite likely this year on an assessment in your class, a state test, and subsequently in assigned readings in a later grade. So honor all of the messiness of Step 1. But don't expect repeated practice with those four Good Reader questions to transform your students' thinking completely. For some of the deepest insights, you will need to lead the way—at least initially.

Take stock of what your students are able to do well and not so well in their initial day with a text. Follow that lesson with a return to the passage to respond to carefully selected text-dependent questions. This will propel students back into the text and will get them to the rigor you yearn for them to achieve.

For the most impact, make sure your questions address a full range of standards and your questions go beyond evidence.

## A Full Range of Standards that Lead to Greater Rigor

For states that continue to subscribe to the Common Core State Standards, and even for those that follow different standards, expectations are similar to what we've always required of readers: Find the main idea, understand characters, determine word meanings, sequence the events of a story, and so on. But while we may have given a nod to other standards in the curriculum maps, there honestly wasn't much persistent attention to elements such as text structure, author's purpose, critiquing a text, and connections between texts.

When we examine the Standards-based assessments, such as those designed by the Smarter Balanced Assessment Consortium (SBAC) and the Partnership for the Assessment of Readiness for College and Careers (PARCC), it is evident that our reading instruction must embrace *all* standards more fully. And here's the double whammy. Not only do we now need to incorporate *all* standards, we also need to measure them at a deeper level. When teachers and students stress that these new assessments are "hard," they are referring as much to the rigor required by these assessments as they are to the Standards themselves. We need to better prepare students for this rigor through the text-dependent questions we ask during instruction.

## Examples of Rigorous Standards-based Questions

Remembering that rigor is a *result*, an outcome of learning, what will be expected of students now as they demonstrate "a sophisticated understanding of fundamental ideas"? Here are a few examples of the rigor on elementary grade assessments for those sometimes underrepresented Standards:

- Language and vocabulary: Which words in [stanza 2] reveal the poet's feelings about _____?

In the past: We would have asked about the meaning of words, but not so much about the tone the author creates with the choice of words.

- Text structure: How is the [second paragraph] different from the ones that come [after it] in the passage?

  In the past: We would have asked how the text was organized (problem/solution, main idea/details), but not so much about how parts of a text fit together.

- Purpose and Point of view: What is the most likely reason the author included [the information in paragraph _____]?

  In the past: We would have asked about the general purpose of a text—to entertain, inform, or persuade, but probably not about the role of particular details or portions of a text.

- Use of nonprint texts: How does the [chart] add to your understanding of _____?

  In the past: We would have asked students to identify the text feature, but were less inclined to analyze the way that feature informed meaning.

- Critiquing text: Which details in [paragraph 3] are most relevant to the author's claim?

  In the past: We may have asked students their opinion about a text, but we didn't regularly pursue a deeper analysis of the sufficiency and relevance of specific information.

- Text connections: How do the authors of Source #1 and Source #2 each develop the theme of _____?

  In the past: We overemphasized text-to-self connections, and spent too little time on connections between texts.

## Let's Talk

In order for students to become more proficient at responding to questions such as these, we not only need to *ask* these questions, we need to get students *talking* about them. Yes, talking. Our ultimate goal may be for students to respond in writing. After all, that's the way reading performance is measured. But

these are places we haven't ventured before in our literacy instruction, and few kids will feel confident enough to publish their thinking for the world to evaluate without first trying out that thinking in a lower-risk situation. A discussion that you facilitate and guide with a small group of peers to confirm or critique will help students to clarify their thinking as they grapple with big ideas.

## Digging Deep into the Diary Account of Sallie Hester

Remember that students have read a passage of a mere 350 words for this lesson, so we don't want to overdo it with an extensive list of questions. I suggest two or three that could get students thinking in new directions:

1. How does Sallie help you picture the camp, both during the day and at night? What words help you create a picture in your mind? (Hint: Look for really great descriptive words. Do these words create a happy, positive tone or a sad, negative tone? Or both?)

2. Why is the information in the text box about the Pawnees important to your understanding of this passage? Why do you think the author included the information in this text box? (Hint: Think about what you would have thought about the Pawnees if you had read *only* Sallie's account.)

Imagine the interaction that these questions might generate. I saw this firsthand with my group of fourth graders. The first question (about visualizing) took metacognitive strategies to a new level. Instead of simply asking what students could picture in their mind, this question asked them to examine how the author crafted the text to support their mental images. The group had fun with this, choosing and explaining the details that were the most vivid to them, and why. But it was the second question about the Pawnees that produced the most conversation and yielded the best insights.

On this second instructional day I asked everyone to read the information in the text box as they had not done so previously. I asked, *In your own words, what is the author telling us here?*

Maeve: "The information says the Pawnees were actually helpful to the pioneers and kept other tribes from attacking them."

Another student countered, supported by the nodding heads of her peers: "Wait. In her diary, Sallie said the Pawnees were dangerous and hostile."

At this point all five students were looking at me, like it was my job to straighten this out. Instead I asked a question, *Who do you think wrote the information in this text box?*

Not Sallie, they all concurred.

Alex: "Someone who studied about the Pawnees? Someone who checked the facts?" It was more of an inquiry than an assertion, but it led us in the right direction.

Another question from me: *When you read something from someone's point of view, like a diary or a story written in the first person, do you always get facts?*

Luis: "You get feelings."

Maeve again: "And opinions. So maybe Sallie just *thought* she knew about the Pawnees because she'd heard about them and that's why she was afraid. Not because she knew the real facts."

Me: *So why is the information in the text box important to your understanding of this passage? Why do you think the author included this information?*

Elena: "If we just read Sallie's words, we wouldn't have known the truth. The diary shows Sallie's opinion and feelings about the Pawnees, but not the facts. There's another side of the story."

One last question from me: *Can we learn something from this?*

Luis: "Sometimes it's hard to tell if something is an opinion. You have to be careful. You have to check."

When we say that "rigor is the result of work that challenges students' thinking in new and interesting ways," we should keep this kind of discourse in mind. It's the kind of discourse that leads to "aha" moments that may resonate with students long after they've finished reading Sallie Hester's diary and have moved on to other texts to read closely.

Students have now read this diary account independently and they have returned to it to reread and respond to a couple of text-dependent questions. Are we done with Sallie? That depends. For Sallie's Diary, I might move on to one or two additional passages using the same sequence of independent close reading followed by text-dependent questions. Meanwhile, when I work with a small group, I'm always on the lookout for something they're on the verge of understanding, some text-connected skill or concept I could strengthen with a wee bit of explicit attention.

## Step 3: Skill Lessons Aligned with a Standard and Text Complexity

On the surface, skill lessons sound sort of "old school" and not something we associate with close reading. Close reading is more about the integration of all text elements to make meaning, whereas skill instruction isolates one element and teaches solely to that specific point. High-quality close reading that focuses on deep meaning through both independence and text-dependent questions should result in the need for fewer lessons on individual skills. But let's be practical here. We could wait for weeks or months for students to finally have enough textual evidence for them to build their own theory about something new—or we could teach a lesson on the skill and build the necessary understanding in a day or two.

In this instructional sequence, students were genuinely surprised that some of Sallie's words in her diary were more opinion than fact, which helped me recognize their limited understanding of this genre. I decided that a skill lesson on the characteristics of a diary would give them a more powerful lens for viewing this genre. Now how do we teach a skill well? Honor all of the steps of the gradual release model. This not only leads students to skill mastery, but to skill independence.

## Explain the Skill

For students to succeed with a skill, there's more to a good explanation than we sometimes realize. Giving a good explanation is not simply giving instructions: "Today we will look for genre characteristics in Sallie's diary." This identifies the "what"—*what* students need to do, but fails to clarify the "how"—*how* students will go about meeting this goal. *How* to proceed through the steps of a skill to identify the best evidence is the part that confuses kids. Unless we can offer up some tips for getting the right evidence, our strugglers will continue to struggle.

I like the image of a target to make the explanation visible to students. How will they "hit the target" as they're looking for evidence of a diary entry—or the evidence for any skill? My target for diary characteristics might look like this:

---

 **Skill target: What characteristics of a diary do you find in the diary entry of _____.**

**How to hit the target:**

1. Understand what a person might write in a diary:
   - an event in the person's life
   - something good or bad that happened to the person
   - the person's thoughts or feelings about something in his or her life
   - hopes, fears, joys, sorrows, and other emotions
   - vivid descriptions of something the person has seen or done

2. Identify what *this* person is writing about.

3. Find one or more details in the text to support your thinking.

4. Think about what this shows about this person: What was important to him or her?

---

It's just a few straightforward, cut-to-the-chase steps: Do these things and you'll succeed with this skill! My target sheet goes right in the middle of our small group instruction table where I can use it to explain the skill initially, and then return to it as a reference point throughout the lesson.

## Model the Skill

If you've explained your skill well, the rest of the lesson will fall into place easily; just follow the points on your target:

Me (pointing to a sentence in the passage): *I see right here that Sallie is telling about something good in her life: Her mom is healthy now. And here* (pointing to a different sentence) *she's explaining her fear of the Pawnee tribe, an emotion.*

I minimize modeling, just an example or two, because children quickly lose interest with too much teacher talk. In fact, though modeling means we are sharing our own thinking, we want to incorporate kid thinking into our lesson as soon as we can. This begins the release of responsibility from teacher-in-charge to students-in-charge.

## Prompted Practice

Now rather than me showing my thinking, I ask students for *their* thinking:

Me: *Sallie says two people died of cholera. What kind of detail is that?*

And after students respond, a bit more release:

Me: *What is Sallie telling us right here? What diary characteristic is this?*

Elena: "She's telling us about the beauty of the plains. It's something that's happening in her life, and it's also an emotion because she's happy. Those are both diary characteristics."

## Guided Practice

When students have gained enough confidence and proficiency through teacher prompting, they're ready to try the skill on their own, or possibly with a buddy from the group.

Me: *Today we learned the characteristics of a diary entry, and you found some of those characteristics in one of Sallie's entries. Now I want you to go back to your seats and find three more examples in a different entry. Please jot some notes, so you can share them tomorrow with our group. You can choose to work with a partner, or alone.*

## How Will You Move Forward with Independent Close Reading in Your Classroom?

A single lesson won't result in complete skill independence for students. But taking the opportunity to reinforce a concept, such as genre characteristics, when it fits naturally into the close reading conversation will move students systematically toward this goal.

In fact, for young readers, none of these instructional components alone will produce the rigor we seek: the four Good Reader questions, high-level text dependent questions, or skill lessons. But they offer a powerful package of instructional strategies when taken together. Meeting the expectations of rigor that new Standards and assessments represent—a sophisticated understanding of fundamental ideas—means implementing a mosaic of best practices in the best possible way.

### Reflecting on the Rigor of Independent Close Reading

1. Think about the four Good Reader questions. Which one(s) do your students need more practice with to maximize their initial comprehension of a text?

2. What kind of text-dependent questions might you ask about literary or informational text that would provide opportunities for students to demonstrate their capacity for rigor—insights into the content and craft of a text, rather than just basic evidence?

3. What standards-based comprehension skills would benefit your students in their quest for deeper understanding of complex texts?

## Action Steps to Get Started on Rigorous Independent Close Reading

1. Select a small group for independent close reading. This should be a group that is reading beyond the primary level, where the main focus has shifted from fluency to comprehension.

2. Select a short informational or literary text that you consider complex, but within reach for your students with regard to meaning, language, and structure.

3. Select one or two of the Good Reader questions and ask students to read the text, jotting notes in response to the one or two selected questions. Discuss their responses when you meet. (You can then determine if students need a mini-lesson on those Good Reader questions, or if you can move on to add other questions.)

4. Create some text-dependent questions that will inspire your students to analyze the text for greater insights. In your next group session, use these questions to generate conversation: How much rigor do students demonstrate as they discuss?

5. Identify a standards-based skill that would help your students dig even deeper. Create a target for this skill: How will you explain step-by-step how to find the best evidence? Teach your skill lesson in a way that gradually releases responsibility, concluding with follow-up practice of the skill.

## References and Resources

Hester, S. 2014. *Diary of Sallie Hester: A Covered Wagon Girl*. First-Person Histories. North Mankato, MN: Capstone.

Kimmel, A. 2015. *A Primary Source History of Slavery in the United States*. Primary Source History. North Mankato, MN: Capstone.

Lassieur, A. 2016. *The Underground Railroad: An Interactive History Adventure Revised Edition*. You Choose: History. Mankato: MN: Capstone.

Marrin, A. 2006. *Oh, Rats! The Story of Rats and People*. New York: Dutton.

Sztabnik, B. 2015. "A New Definition of Rigor." *Edutopia*, May 7. http://www.edutopia.org/blog/a-new-definition-of-rigor-brian-sztabnik.

Williams, M. 1922. *The Velveteen Rabbit*. New York: Doubleday, Doran and Company.

# Guided Reading in a Comprehensive Literacy Program

Michael P. Ford

## Introduction

In 2014 I was invited to present for a professional development conference that attracted more than 6,000 educators. While I was asked to present on what I thought were three contemporary hot topics (complex texts, integrating nonfiction, and using accessible assessments), a session I conducted entitled "Guided Reading: What's New?" drew the largest number of educators—almost four times more than the others. Should I have been surprised that so many educators were still interested in learning more about guided reading? I thought the role of guided reading in a comprehensive literacy program was well established. Guided reading hadn't received much recent scholarly attention, but the practice still dominated literacy programs. In fact, forms of guided reading were now carrying responsibility to meet the increasing demands from Response to Intervention (RtI) frameworks and College and Career Readiness Standards. For many teachers, guided reading plays a critical role in their classrooms especially in working with readers who need help the most. Perhaps that is one reason why teachers are still interested in improving the role of guided reading.

Models of guided reading have existed for many decades (Ford and Opitz 2011, 225–226). Current models gained traction with the popular embrace of Fountas and Pinnell's (1996) text *Guided Reading: Good First Teaching for All Children*. Their book was followed by a number of how-to resource books that emerged to support teachers. One was a text I co-authored called *Reaching Readers*. This book was written to expand the vision of guided reading models and encourage teachers to break out of a "one right way" orthodoxy that had quickly developed around the practice (Opitz and Ford 2001, 1–2). Since that early flood of resources, fewer books have been written about guided reading until the Capstone text *Guided Reading: What's New, and What's Next?* was published in 2016. Before that, one of the last resources to focus attention on this topic was *Preventing Misguided Reading*. It offered a more critical view and warned:

> Education is littered with the remains of educational trends lost in translation. Often, the reality is that we compromised the fidelity of their implementation. So, critics assemble and declare that the approach doesn't work, as researchers and publishers line up to set a new program in place. We see this trend surfacing with guided reading, and we lament the energy and resources that districts may expend in totally revamping literacy instruction that may simply need adjusting (Burkins and Croft 2010, xv).

This chapter will help us refocus needed attention on key basics to ensure teachers are getting the most out of their time with guided reading.

## Basic #1 Remember the History of Guided Reading

Like many of the practices examined in this book, guided reading has a significant history in classroom literacy programs. When something has been around a long time, it is important to look at its history. Examining its original intent and subsequent evolution is a reminder of what is "basic" about the practice. The history of guided reading has always been entangled with the history of grouping practices. For many years, small group reading instruction dominated most classroom programs. Reading instruction was often exclusively carried out in homogenous small groups. Typically there were three groups: one at, below, and above grade level. They were often labeled in subtle or not too subtle ways to reflect the perceived level of the group. The structure was so pervasive that it was often seen in most elementary classroom reading programs (Caldwell and Ford 2002, 1). It should be pointed out that it was not the use of small groups that was problematic. It was the exclusive use of small groups without the balance of other grouping formats and the static nature of those small groups. Once students were assigned to those small groups, the group assignment rarely changed throughout a student's school experience.

Then *Becoming a Nation of Readers* (BANOR) was published in 1985. BANOR revealed what many already knew: There was no positive research base for the exclusive use of homogenous small groups in reading programs (Anderson et. al. 1985, 71). The widespread embrace of BANOR led to many shifts in reading practices, including rethinking the exclusive use of homogenous small groups.

After BANOR was published, small group instruction disappeared from many classrooms. Whole class instruction began to be the main component of many literacy programs. Most teachers marched all students through the same instruction with the same text at the same time (Caldwell and Ford 2002, 13–14). The inherent flaws of whole group instruction became magnified when it was used exclusively in reading programs. Teachers quickly became frustrated because they were unable to meet the needs of diverse students. Concerns related to the exclusive use of static homogenous small groups were just replaced with new concerns related to the exclusive use of heterogeneous whole class instruction (Ford and Opitz 2011, 230).

Within a few years, educators were looking for yet another alternative to less than satisfying grouping practices. They needed a model of instruction that targeted learners more effectively. Suddenly small groups reemerged in literacy programs.

Guided reading evolved as an alternative to the past exclusive use of static homogeneous small groups or heterogeneous whole class instruction. The goals of guided reading reflected a vision and direction that was different from these previous grouping models. Guided reading was proposed as an important part but not the only component of a flexible grouping model. Guided reading groups would be more dynamic than those of the past with ongoing assessment informing decisions about students' group assignments. Transforming small group reading instruction as guided reading was informed significantly by individual and small group intervention programs, including what had been seen in New Zealand classrooms (Fountas and Pinnell 2012, 263). Classrooms Down Under had been promoting the use of guided reading years before its widespread use in the states (Holdaway 1979, 142; Mooney 1990, 46–47). Guided reading should provide *good first teaching for all children* to reduce the number of children who would need individual interventions or at least provide instruction that could support and build on the work done in intervention programs.

## Basic #2 Stay Focused on the Purpose of Guided Reading

Another critical basic for effective guided reading is the importance of honoring its intended purpose. A clear definition of guided reading helps define its purpose. Guided reading is defined as "an instructional context for supporting each reader's development of effective strategies for processing novel texts at increasingly challenging levels of difficulty" (Fountas and Pinnell 1996, 25). It includes these essential elements:

- Teacher works with small groups of students who are similar in their development and ability to read about the same level of text,

- Teacher introduces the texts and assists students in developing strategies that reach the goal of being able to read independently and silently,

- Each student reads whole texts with an emphasis on reading increasingly challenging texts over time, and

- Students are grouped and regrouped in a dynamic process that involves ongoing observation and assessment.

"Guided reading has shifted the lens in the teaching of reading to a focus on a deeper understanding of how readers build effective processing systems over time and an examination of the critical role of texts and expert teaching in the process" (Fountas and Pinnell 1996, 4). Most researchers who have defined essential elements tend to agree that guided reading is planned, intentional, focused instruction where the teacher helps students, usually in small groups, learn more about the reading process (Ford and Opitz 2011, 229). In defining guided reading, it is also important to remember what guided reading is and what it is not. See Figure 1 below.

FIGURE 1  THE ACRONYM GR IS USED TO REPRESENT "GUIDED READING" IN THIS CHART.

| What Guided Reading IS NOT | What Guided Reading IS |
|---|---|
| GR IS NOT an end in and of itself. Its intent is NOT to make good guided readers. | GR IS a means to an end. The end is always to develop independent readers. |
| GR IS NOT the entire reading program; GR IS NOT the only time during the day that the teacher is teaching reading. | GR IS part of a comprehensive literacy program that focuses on teaching reading and writing throughout the school day. It works best when it is connected to other aspects of the classroom literacy program, including read-alouds, shared reading, content instruction, and independent reading. |
| GR IS NOT something you do by following a script or a program outline. | GR IS an opportunity for targeted, responsive teaching in which we teach to the needs of the students. It includes different models to meet these needs. |
| GR IS NOT exclusively taught with leveled texts. | GR IS a time to use a wide variety of appealing and high-quality texts in lessons for readers. |
| GR IS NOT instruction focused exclusively on word-level strategies and accurate oral reading. | GR IS focused on both word-level and text-level strategies (i.e., accuracy with meaning making). |
| GR IS NOT an intervention. | GR IS an essential element of universal instruction made available to all learners within high-quality, regular classroom instruction. Varying the frequency, duration, intensity, or focus of GR can reposition it as an intervention. |

Modified from Ford 2016, 34

The purpose of guided reading is informed by transactional rather than transmission-oriented models of learning. Transactional models of reading suggest an interaction between the reader and text. Meaning is constructed based on both reader and text factors. Transmission models of reading suggest more of a one-right meaning inherent in the text that has to be discovered by the reader. In the past transmission models defined a teacher's purpose often as covering materials–teaching texts. The basic purpose of guided reading changes that. Transaction models remind teachers to consider *learner* factors, not just *text* demands when teaching reading. A critical and basic point to remember is the intentional use of the term "guided" to describe instruction in these groups. Distinguishing guided reading from past small group instruction is the role of the teacher. Teachers "coach" the students during their guided reading. Results from one study indicated that coaching during reading was so critical, it was the frequency of that one practice that separated the most effective schools from others (Taylor et al. 1999, 156–157). Coaching requires scaffolded instruction. Teachers need to learn where their students are at, where they need to be, and then build scaffolds to support the students as they move from one point to the other. Scaffolding requires targeted, responsive instruction to provide that bridge. This is what shifts teachers from just covering materials to teaching learners. In other words, teachers should use *guided reading sessions* not just teach *guided reading lessons* (Burkins and Croft 2010, 22). Bottom line—guided reading sessions need to be more focused on helping learners make growth and be less concerned with just completing lessons.

Fountas and Pinnell remind us that guided reading "gives children the opportunity to develop as individual readers while participating in a socially supportive activity (1996, 1)." When used effectively, guided reading:

✓ targets both similar needs across learners and specific needs for individuals,

✓ scaffolds learning to accelerate the growth of similar learners while attending to the growth of individual learners,

✓ provides opportunities for teachers to observe learners' similarities and variations to provide responsive instruction, and

✓ should be positioned for greater intensity and impact by adjusting frequency, duration, focus, membership, and monitoring of the small group.

Students arrive with different needs, and our responsibility is to meet those specific needs. All teachers need tools, structures, and resources to help them meet those needs. The purpose of guided reading is to bring differentiated, responsive instruction into those classrooms. That is why guided reading matters.

## Basic #3 Guided Reading Grows in Power When It Is Integrated with Other Elements

This book clearly presents the importance of looking at many different dimensions of a comprehensive literacy program. The stronger each dimension is, the stronger the overall program will be. No matter how powerful guided reading is, it is just one element of a comprehensive literacy program and no one component of a comprehensive literacy program can carry the burden of accelerating the growth of all readers (Routman 2000, 151–152). Teaching and learning happen all day in a classroom, not just during guided reading (Mere 2005, 13–15). While this seems so basic, a common misunderstanding about guided reading is that it is often seen as the only time reading is taught (Burkins and Croft 2010, 11). It is important to remember that what a teacher does during guided reading shouldn't be any more important than what a teacher does during read-alouds, shared readings, independent reading, and other components of a comprehensive literacy program.

I often tell the teachers with whom I work that a comprehensive literacy program can be summed up in three words: *to*, *with*, and *by* (Mooney 1990, 9–12). You need to read *to* your students, *with* your students, and get your students to read *by* themselves. A comprehensive program recognizes that all are critical because they have different purposes, levels of support, and literacy goals. When we look at what happens in a typical day in an elementary literacy program, learners still spend significant time in the large group setting (Kelly and Turner 2009, 1673). This shouldn't be surprising since the most efficient use of time and resources is using a whole group setting—working with all children at the same time using the same materials. It makes the most sense for modeling and demonstrating skills and strategies during components like read-alouds and shared readings. If teachers do not intentionally consider how to support all learners during whole group instruction, this part of the literacy program may be less successful in reaching those students who may need the instruction the most.

With guided reading, there is more intentionality about how to support all learners. The teacher schedules time to meet with guided reading groups. The teacher carefully selects texts and targets instruction to meet the needs of learners in the group. This part of the literacy block is important for reaching students who may need the most support, but it can't carry the entire burden. In fact, the small group work is only part of guided reading. The teacher must also be very intentional in supporting learners who are working on their own as he or she works with other groups. If guided reading is to reach all students, the teacher must carefully consider how to structure this independent work time.

With the content areas, the teacher often returns to whole class instruction with the same text for all students. Students in need of the most support spend even more time with texts that are often not within their levels. By the end of the day, those students in need of the most support often receive the least amount of instruction within their levels. Clearly while guided reading is critical for accelerating the growth of all readers, it is only as strong as the other elements that surround it. Guided

reading acknowledges the basic understanding that accelerating the growth of all readers must be a focus throughout the literacy program. (Note: Other chapters in this book will address other elements more completely.)

## Basic #4 Selecting Appropriate Texts for Guided Reading Is Critical

Much attention is given to the leveled texts used in guided reading; however, it is important to remember that attention needs to be given to the student reading the texts during guided reading. Remember, a basic understanding of guided reading is we are not just teaching texts, we are teaching learners. Text selection is still critical, however, because specific texts may better allow the teacher to zero in on what an individual needs to develop as a strategic reader.

Most models of guided reading suggest that texts selected should be at the instructional level of the reader. If the model for guided reading is scaffolding, then those texts become the bridge between what readers are capable of doing on their own (independent level) and what readers are unable to do even with support (frustrational level). So how are instructional level texts determined? The formula to determine instructional level texts is rooted in work done 70 years ago by Betts and has been relatively unchanged since then (Halladay 2012, 53–54). For Betts (1946), a 95 percent accuracy rate with comprehension is what distinguishes an instructional level text from frustrational. [For Clay (1993, 23), a 90 percent accuracy rate was the mark of the same distinction.] In his review of the research, Allington (2012, 72–73) advocates for higher levels of accuracy, suggesting that instruction with texts of high success rates (low error rates) often lead to greater gains. Allington suggests Betts' criteria are best for guided reading sessions. He points out however, that no matter what criteria are used, levels need to be used with flexibility.

Why flexibility? Leveling systems both simplify the complex interaction between the reader and text, as well as often add a cumbersome layer of complexity by developing multiple discrete levels (Glasswell and Ford 2011, 208–211). First, leveling systems simplify the interactions of readers and texts. For a reader to be successful with a text, a number of factors must be in play. And a change in any one of those factors can make the text easier or harder for the reader. Most factors used to determine levels relate to the texts themselves since they are the most stable components and easy to count (e.g., sentence length, word frequency). Variations of readers and contexts are virtually impossible to capture in these formulas and rubrics. In the end, leveling systems over-promise a magical match between a text and a reader, suggesting the best way to secure a successful interaction is to match the learner to a text at his or her level. Teachers need to be aware of these limitations and be allowed to use their judgment in effectively choosing leveled materials. Lists and numbers should not replace teacher judgment (Worthy and Sailors 2001, 228–229).

A second problem with leveling systems is their use of criteria per level that can be perceived as lacking in objectivity. One leveling system, with 26 levels of texts and readers, suggested that J level texts were determined by reviewing 66 specific criteria. In contrast the next level up—K—used 71 specific criteria. Twenty-one of the criteria were the same for both levels and others were only distinguishable by qualitative degrees (i.e., *some* vs. *many*). In the end, books assigned to the J and K baskets are labeled as such but often indistinguishable. Practically speaking, the differences do not seem meaningful enough to use a book with one group while withholding it from another group.

Outsourcing decisions to leveling systems can be too rigid and should not replace professional judgment. When the level is the exclusive focus in selecting texts, unintended consequences can occur. It can compromise opportunities for those who need the most practice. In a second grade class, a teacher was working with a group using a 16-page level G text that contained about 80 words (5 of which were multisyllabic). Then the teacher moved to her N level group, who were reading 10 pages from a short chapter book. The selection had 87 words (11 multisyllabic) on the first page alone. By the time the N group had read their chapter, they had received 10 times more practice than the G group who had the greater needs. With the focus on teaching a text at a specific level, guided reading carried out in this manner does little to close the gap between readers.

One way to close the gap when selecting texts for readers with the greatest needs is to be more intentional about the number of words students are asked to read. That leads to the basic concept of reading mileage, which starts with increasing awareness about the word counts of texts. Establish a baseline on the number of words practiced by guided reading groups. Since same-level texts often vary in word count, pick texts that provide the most practice. During your planning, also consider how rereading can increase the practice of a low word count text. Purposeful repeated reading can also flow from the guided reading table into independent routines. To practice even more words, include at the table additional related texts at the same level. Reading a variety of texts at the same level offers practice with a greater variety of words.

Systems with multiple discrete levels often cause teachers to focus on students making progress through the levels rather than on students achieving proficiency. I was involved in a project to map out the trajectory of three different groups of learners using a popular guided reading program. Progress was plotted following the pacing recommendations suggested by the materials. Each group of readers was put on a path that would lead to making progress. But the paths laid out in the pacing guide for above, at, and below grade level readers raised a confounding issue. If teachers followed the guide, they would leave below grade level readers far short of proficiency. What's more, if teachers in a school used the materials for multiple years, the gap between readers would actually widen. If teachers get comfortable seeing progress, they can lose sight of the fact that proficiency is the end goal. An important goal of guided reading is that end points or accepted benchmarks need to be very clear. Therefore, instruction can be paced in such a way that as a child progresses, he or she gets closer to the goal of proficiency. Proficiency levels have gained significant attention recently because of the conversations around College and Career Readiness Standards. These Standards propose that students should "read and comprehend complex literary and informational texts independently and proficiently" (National Governors Association Center for Best Practices and the Council of Chief State School Officers 2010). The Standards clearly have teachers looking at the complexity of the texts they are using and questioning whether the exclusive use of leveled texts will lead to proficiency.

The way teachers use leveling systems can certainly change as guided reading moves forward. The bottom line is levels help teachers find texts that might be a better fit for readers; however, it is important to be mindful of other factors in finding the right text for a reader. Teachers should not let levels be the only thing that guides them in selecting texts and planning instruction. Rather, teachers should consider how they can supplement leveled texts with the use of trade books, poems, magazine articles, digital texts, or stories students have written. The levels of some of these texts may also be publicly available. If not, a quick check through the use of a student oral reading of the text will allow teachers to determine if it is within the instructional level of the students in the guided reading group. Looking for something that can be read with 90–95 percent accuracy is the goal. With more flexible use of all texts, we can lead more readers to not just make progress but actually become proficient.

## Basic #5 Guided Reading Needs to Be Structured Differently for Different Learners

Guided reading acknowledges and addresses the common developmental patterns of learners and their individual pathways. If plans do not recognize the different needs of learners, then guided reading becomes a less-effective, one-size-fits-all model. It needs to be conceptualized with different plans for different learners. For example, models of guided reading for learners in the primary grades should look different from those in the intermediate grades.

Purpose should always drive the instructional decision-making of teachers and is mainly determined by the common patterns shared by learners. These are starting points for making decisions. Teachers can begin by thinking about four common phases for readers' development: emergent, early, transitional, and fluent. Once the general phase has been determined, teachers should adapt guided reading for that phase. For example, in the emergent phase, readers are trying to determine how print works. The student has to come to understand concepts of print, phonological including phonemic awareness, and alphabetic knowledge. The emergent reader is expanding the vocabulary and world knowledge needed to bring meaning to the page. By contrast, older readers are often in the transitional phase and have the tools they need to deal with the texts they encounter. For them, the challenge is using the tools. They shift their focus to the texts as they try to become more sophisticated meaning makers. Goals are focused on understanding what is read and creating comprehensible texts when writing. Comprehension outcomes continue to expand. Students use text elements to summarize what was read. They use their ability to identify main ideas and themes to support personal response, including genuine connections. They attend to author's craft and link it to their writing. Clearly one important basic element of guided reading is that decisions about texts, teaching points, and other grouping issues need to be adapted for the common patterns of the learners in those different phases (Ford 2016, 92–96).

Each reading development phase gives a sense of the outcomes for which instruction needs to be planned. It identifies the direction in which the readers are headed. The heart of guided reading is using instruction to build the bridge between two points: where the readers are at (baselines) and where the readers need to be (outcomes). Teachers need to plan instruction intentionally and thoughtfully to help students in the small groups learn more about the reading process. While intentionality is critical, it should not preclude the teacher from being flexible. If guided reading is about common patterns, it is also about following individuals' paths. The latter requires a degree of flexibility. Teachers should be careful about operating with orthodoxy and ignoring the responsiveness that expert teaching requires. For each phase, there are critical decisions that need to be made about texts, teaching points, discussion opportunities, and fostering positive affective outcomes. Part of the decision-making requires prioritizing which teaching moments are most needed. Most guided reading sessions will last around 20 minutes, so instruction needs to be tightly focused and quickly paced.

Group membership should be considered for each session. Planning involves addressing both common patterns and individual pathways. These needs may determine initial membership in a group. As needs differ, group membership should be reconsidered. Baseline assessments provide the starting points, but ongoing formative assessments are critical to monitor progress and target instruction. Guided reading groups are flexible. When students have clearly demonstrated the need for different instruction, they should be moved to a new group. Students should be making growth if instruction is effective. If students are not making growth, then it might be important to look at the instruction they are receiving.

The good news is the instructional activities, techniques, and resources to support instruction can come from a variety of sources. Teachers need to consider whether their materials and methods send readers the kind of messages that are at the heart of effective guided reading. While isolated skill and strategy work may be needed, it is best done in the context of authentic reading and writing. While a focus on word level activities is certainly critical, students should also engage in text-level meaning making and reading that encourage positive affective outcomes. One thing that is basic to guided reading

is the teacher must be intentional but not inflexible in planning for different learners.

## Basic #6 Intentionally Plan for What the Rest of the Class Is Doing During Guided Reading

When classroom literacy programs returned to the use of small groups for guided reading, the focus was often on what to do with the students in the small group. Only limited attention was given to what to do with the rest of the class who are working away from the teacher. This issue quickly surfaced as the most frequently asked question about guided reading from educators. A decade later teachers were still asking the question (Guastello and Lenz 2005, 144). Coming up with plans for the rest of the class is basic for effective guided reading instruction.

Guided reading needs to be conceived as having two critical parts. First, guided reading is defined by what is done by the teacher with the students in the small group; but secondly and just as important, guided reading needs to clearly consider what the other students are doing while they are away from the teacher. If the latter is not thoughtfully considered and addressed, the ability to focus targeted instruction with small groups is virtually impossible. Bottom line: The instructional model of guided reading is inherently flawed and probably doomed to fail if work away from the teacher is not considered and addressed.

On average teachers have four guided reading groups they meet with for about 20 minutes three to four times a week. So students are actually away from the teacher more than they are with the teacher. On some days, a group of students may actually spend all of the time away from the teacher. The time away from the teacher must engage students in powerful work. So what do we do with the rest of the kids? Historically, the work away from the teacher often involved completing every worksheet and workbook page recommended in the basal lesson (Durkin 1978, 52–53). Then learning stations or centers became the next phase of many teachers' evolution. Guided reading programs became linked with centers and stations. (Look at the chapter starting on page 155 for suggestions on how to effectively use centers in a comprehensive literacy program.)

Beyond centers, teachers continued to look for ways to operate more effectively and efficiently. Teachers discovered the value of workshop approaches. They began to see the benefits of process-oriented classroom structures. With these workshops in place, individual students engage in productive work, and the teacher is freed up for small group work or conferences. Workshop approaches include times when students read and write either individually or with partners or small groups. Teachers started to see that they could meet with guided reading groups while everyone else was engaged in independent and peer-based reading and writing activities.

While many teachers achieved some success integrating guided reading with workshop approaches, some felt that the big blocks of time in which learners were expected to stay engaged were too long for young readers and writers. These approaches did little to prepare young students for long periods of time away from the teacher. That led to another major way of conceptualizing work away from the teacher. With their Daily 5 structure, Boushey and Moser suggested the use of routines as a way to manage learners away from the teacher. They recommended teaching young children how to stay engaged in five different routines: read to self, read to someone, work on writing, work on words, and listen to reading (2006, 11–12). As students were taught the routines and the expectations and behavioral guidelines, an intentional effort was made to help them gradually increase their stamina so they could self-regulate behaviors while involved in these routines. As stamina and engagement levels increased, teachers found the time needed to meet with small groups for guided reading.

## Basic #7 High-quality Guided Reading Needs to Be a Part of Universal Instruction Before It's Considered for Intervention

A new role for guided reading has emerged—its use as an intervention. Contributing to this change was the reauthorization of the Individuals with Disabilities Education Act (IDEA) in 2004. Within this reauthorization of federal law and subsequent state policies that followed was the opportunity for states to redefine how they determined students with Specific Learning Disabilities (SLD). Historically, IDEA supported an IQ-achievement discrepancy model, theorizing that a student's academic performance below his or her academic potential is evidence of a learning disability. State policies defined formulas for determining how much of a discrepancy would indicate a learning disability. Many experts, however, found fault with the discrepancy model because it often meant that a student had to wait to fail before receiving needed help. This model placed all the focus on student factors and rarely looked at the instruction the student was receiving. It documented a discrepancy but revealed little about why the gap existed.

While IDEA did not do away with the IQ-achievement discrepancy model, it provided states with another option. Policies permitted the use of a process that focuses on a child's response to scientifically based interventions. For the first time, schools could consider the student's response to instruction as a factor in determining if he or she had an SLD. In a relatively short time, response to instruction options became codified in Response to Intervention (RtI) frameworks. Districts quickly operationalized identification tools, rules, and processes for schools and classrooms. RtI was envisioned as a broad framework for thinking about helping all children with needs. One of the most significant shifts was the implementation of general education interventions prior to special education identification. RtI brought a promise of being both a way to reduce the number of students with learning problems while also more accurately identifying students with an SLD (Wixson and Lipson 2012, 387).

What role does guided reading play in interventions? If RtI is a regular education initiative, then it must focus initially on providing ALL students with quality, equitable opportunities to learn. All students need access to high-quality instruction within a comprehensive literacy program, including read-alouds, shared reading, independent reading, and *guided reading*. Sometimes "regular" guided reading is positioned as a small group intervention, but that needs to be rethought. Before guided reading is adapted and modified as an intervention, it should be included first as an effective instructional opportunity provided to all students. As previously discussed, a comprehensive literacy program would mean that within regular classroom instruction all students would have already received effective large group, small group (i.e., guided reading), and individualized instruction. Dorn and Soffos (2011, 7) strongly recommend that interventions should always be supported by high-quality regular classroom instruction. RtI requires that the quality of classroom instruction is always examined when discussing the needs of a child. Before looking at how a student responded to instruction, we must look at whether the student had an opportunity to learn.

So what is the role for guided reading beyond universal instruction? Can it be used as an intervention for subsequent levels? Allington (2008, 25) identified the research-based characteristics of interventions that accelerate reading growth:

- very small groups or tutoring
- majority of time spent reading
- match between reader and text level
- use of texts that are interesting to students
- coordination with core classrooms
- expert teacher delivers intervention
- expand daily reading activity
- meaning and meta-cognitive focus

Obviously, the models of guided reading presented in this chapter align with those characteristics. Fountas and Pinnell (2008, 498–501) also remind us that interventions are typically intensive, short term, supplementary, low in teacher to student ratio, and taught by an expert teacher who is in communication with the classroom teacher. Again many of those characteristics are at the heart of guided reading sessions, though the last characteristic seems to suggest that an expert teacher outside of the classroom handles the intervention. So what would have to change to position guided reading as an intervention?

Guided reading may have greater impact if the frequency of meetings is increased. Similarly, the duration of the guided reading sessions could be adjusted so students with greater needs are given more time (and instruction) with the teacher. Guided reading may also have greater impact by changing who is at the table. By decreasing the number of students taught, students are provided with more targeted instruction, greater potential for engagement, and less distraction than in regular guided reading groups. Another adjustment could be to refocus the content taught and time allocation for specific content within the lesson. This would allow for instruction that might differ from the lessons typically taught during guided reading. Guided reading sessions could also include more and/or different formative assessments to closely monitor the progress (or lack of it) with the learners than is typically seen in other guided reading sessions. Finally, one more way to adjust guided reading is to look closely at the instruction being offered. The delivery of instruction could be monitored more closely either through self-reflection, including taping the sessions, or with the help of outside supervision. Teachers should always look at their instruction to see if it is all that it needs to be to reach the students.

The reauthorization of IDEA has changed today's classrooms. It presents all of us with a huge challenge. To achieve the intent of RtI, which is to improve education for all students, we need to start by tightening up effective guided reading instruction within a comprehensive literacy program. We must be willing to take a look at guided reading when it is not working as well as it could for some learners and reflect on whether adjustments could improve the practice. Only after that occurs are we ready to add a more intensive type of guided reading instruction to reach learners with the greatest needs. In the end our willingness to move in these directions could help us resist and reduce the temptation to label and sort students.

## Conclusion

When we think about guided reading basics, we need to remember that it has a strong historical grounding and a clearly defined purpose. It has an important role to play in a comprehensive literacy program. In this chapter, we have examined insights and ideas on how to make effective decisions related to planning and implementing guided reading instruction within a comprehensive literacy program. There are intentional decisions that need to be made about the integration of guided reading with other dimensions of the literacy program, selection and use of appropriate texts, planning around common patterns with the potential for responsive teaching, structures of work away from the teacher, and intensification of guided reading as an intervention. When these decisions are made effectively, the power of guided reading will only grow stronger in a comprehensive literacy program.

## References and Resources

Allington, Richard. 2008. *What Really Matters in Response to Intervention*. Boston: Allyn & Bacon.

———. 2012. *What Really Matters for Struggling Readers: Designing Research-based Programs, 3rd ed.* Boston: Pearson.

Anderson, Richard. C., Elfrieda Hiebert, Judith Scott, and Ian Wilkinson. 1985. *Becoming a Nation of Readers*. Champaign, IL: University of Illinois. Center for the Study of Reading.

Betts, Emmett A. 1946. *Foundations of Reading Instruction, with Emphasis on Differentiated Guidance*. New York: American Book.

Boushey, Gail, and Joan Moser. 2006. *The Daily 5: Fostering Literacy Independence in the Elementary Grades*. Portland, ME: Stenhouse Publishers.

Burkins, Jan. M., and Melody Croft. 2010. *Preventing Misguided Reading: New Strategies for Guided Reading Teachers*. Newark, DE: International Reading Association.

Caldwell, Joanne. S., and Michael P. Ford. 2002. *Where Have All the Bluebirds Gone? How to Soar with Flexible Grouping*. Portsmouth, NH: Heinemann.

Clay, Marie. 1993. *An Observation Survey of Early Literacy Achievement*. Portsmouth, NH: Heinemann.

Dorn, Linda. J., and Carla Soffos. 2011. *Interventions that Work: A Comprehensive Intervention Model for Preventing Reading Failure in Grades K–3*. Boston: Pearson Higher Education.

Durkin, Dolores. "What Classroom Observations Reveal About Reading Comprehension Instruction." Center for the Study of Reading Technical Report; no. 106 (1978).

Ford, Michael. P. 2016. *Guiding Reading: What's New, and What's Next?* North Mankato, MN: Capstone.

Ford, Michael P., and M. F. Opitz. 2011. "Looking Back to Move Forward with Guided Reading." *Reading Horizons* 50: 3.

Fountas, Irene. C., and Gay Su Pinnell. 1996. *Guided Reading: Good First Teaching for All Children*. Portsmouth, NH: Heinemann.

———. 2008. *When Readers Struggle: Teaching that Works*. Portsmouth, NH: Heinemann.

———. 2012. "Guided Reading: The Romance and the Reality." *The Reading Teacher* 66: 268–284.

Glasswell, Kathy, and M. P. Ford. 2011. "Let's Start Leveling about Leveling." *Language Arts* 88: 208–216.

Guastello, E. Francine, and C. Lenz. 2005. "Student Accountability: Guided Reading Kidstations." *The Reading Teacher* 59: 144–156.

Halladay, Juliet. L. 2012. "Revisiting Key Assumptions of the Reading Level Framework." *The Reading Teacher* 66: 53–62.

Holdaway, Donald. 1979. *The Foundations of Literacy*. Sydney, Australia: Ashton Scholastic.

Kelly, Sean, and J. Turner. 2009. "Rethinking the Effects of Classroom Activity Structure on the Engagement of Low-achieving Students." *The Teachers College Record* 111: 1665–1692.

Mere, Cathy. 2005. *More than Guided Reading: Finding the Right Instructional Mix, K–3.* Portland, ME: Stenhouse Publishers.

Mooney, Margaret. 1990. *Reading To, With, and By Students.* Katonah, NY: R.C. Owens.

National Governors Association Center for Best Practices and the Council of Chief State School Officers. 2010. *Common Core State Standards for English Language Arts and Literacy in History/Social Studies, Science, and Technical Subjects.* Washington, DC: Authors.

Opitz, Michael F., and Michael P. Ford. 2001. *Reaching Readers: Flexible and Innovative Strategies for Guided Reading.* Portsmouth, NH: Heinemann.

Routman, Regie. 2000. *Conversations: Strategies for Teaching, Learning and Evaluating.* Portsmouth, NH: Heinemann.

Taylor, Barbara. M., P. D. Pearson, K. F. Clark, and S. Walpole. 1999. "Effective Schools/Accomplished Teachers." *The Reading Teacher* 53: 156–159.

Wixson, Karen. K., and M. Y. Lipson. 2012. "Relations Between the CCSS and RTI in Literacy and Language." *The Reading Teacher* 65, 387–391.

Worthy, Jo, and M. Sailors. 2001. "'That Book Isn't on My Level': Moving Beyond Text Difficulty in Personalizing Reading Choices." *New Advocate* 14: 229–239.

# Engaging Students by Differentiating Independent Reading

Michelle J. Kelley and Nicki Clausen-Grace

You walk into the classroom and can immediately tell reading is important here. Bookcases are bursting with a wide variety of genres. A cozy reading area is tucked in the corner. Text is everywhere. On closer inspection you notice a bulletin board devoted to notable authors and another highlighting recommended book titles for intermediate students. Independent reading is announced, and a small cheer goes up. Moments later, students appear to be transported to another world. Some children are devouring informational text, while others are immersed in fictional works. None are rotating from the bathroom to the bookshelf in a bid to pass time. Would you like to know the secret to creating a room full of eager readers?

## Introduction

You have been reading about the role of whole group and small group reading instruction, including the importance of teaching skills and strategies to support comprehension. Instruction in reading comprehension, fluency, vocabulary, and word work are critical to developing competent readers. But these practices alone do not necessarily create avid readers. It also takes access to compelling books, a supportive classroom culture, and time. Making room for supported independent reading during the school day is critical if we want our students to be engaged readers. It allows us to assess whether students are using the skills and strategies we are teaching them during instruction. It also gives us the perfect opportunity to provide differentiation for each student. Far from being an extra activity when time allows, independent reading is a vital component of the literacy block in order to create competent, engaged, lifelong readers.

In 2007 Trudel noted that a "sustained reading epidemic" (308) plagued our classrooms, indicating independent reading had all but disappeared from elementary classrooms, even though research supported its use. Unfortunately, for myriad reasons, this plague still exits a decade later. In fact, only "one third of children aged 6–17 (33 percent) say their class has a designated time during the school day to read a book of their choice independently, but only 17 percent do this every day or almost every school day" (Scholastic's Kids and Family Reading Report 2015, 2). In this chapter we will explore the rationale, issues, and best practices for implementing independent reading. We will also introduce a model that supports a differentiated approach, allowing you to assess, guide, intervene, and support your students as they engage in choice reading.

## Independent Reading Defined

Uninterrupted Sustained Silent Reading (USSR), Sustained Silent Reading (SSR), Drop Everything and Read (DEAR), or Daily Independent Reading Time (DIRT) are just a few of the acronyms used for in-school independent reading programs. Although they go by different names, they each involve setting aside time for students to read books of their choosing. Other common aspects might include the teacher reading along with students, students maintaining a reading log, and students completing a follow-up activity when they finish a book. Hunt (1984, 192) suggests that SSR is "the pinnacle of achievement with regard to teaching skillful reading." Educators often cite the following reasons for in-school independent reading: to build students' vocabulary, to provide practice time for reading skills taught during direct instruction, to enhance students' reading achievement, to build students' background knowledge, and to increase students' desire to read. But is it really worth taking time out of the already jam-packed literacy block to have students read independently? What does the research say are the effects of independent reading on students?

## Why Independent Reading?

The number of students ages 6–17 who report reading a book for fun has declined steadily over time, yet what has not diminished is the need to have students read often and read more. Research has demonstrated that students who read a lot have better vocabularies, read more fluently, write better, have greater grammatical command, and know more about social studies and science content (Krashen 2011). Additionally, there is a powerful link between the time students spend reading and their reading achievement (Cunningham and Stanovich 1997; Guthrie, Wigfield, Metsala, and Cox 1999; Schaffner, Schiefele, and Ulferts 2013). The more students read, the better readers they become. And according to Gambrell (2015), proficient reading has been linked to a more productive academic, civic, and social life.

## Engaged Readers and Motivation

But being a competent reader does not equate to being an engaged reader. Engaged readers choose to read because they are motivated to do so, they enjoy it, and they are interested in it (Guthrie et al. 1996; Guthrie and Wigfield 2000), often losing themselves in a text (Rosenblatt 1978). Engaged readers are metacognitive, applying a variety of strategies to comprehend and gain conceptual knowledge (Guthrie et al. 1996; Guthrie and Wigfield 2000; Kelley and Clausen-Grace 2007). Engaged readers share books with their peers and are more likely to read independently as the result of these collaborations (Morrow, 1996). Jang, Conradi, McKenna, and Jones (2015, 240) refer to reading motivation "as what moves students to pick up a book (or a magazine or a device) and what moves students to persist in reading that text, even when it might be challenging or boring." Guthrie and Wigfield (2000, 405) suggest that "engaged readers can overcome obstacles to achievement to become agents of their own reading growth" by fulfilling reading goals they have personally set. Because they believe they will have success, they are more than likely to engage in reading (Schunk and Zimmerman 1997).

## Obstacles to Independent Reading

Time is often cited as the number one roadblock to employing independent reading in the classroom. Teachers are typically expected to use a variety of formats (whole group, small group, learning stations, partner work, and independent work) to teach all aspects of literacy. As you have read in the other chapters, teachers use these structures to deliver instruction in various skills, such as vocabulary, fluency, comprehension, word work, writing, and conventions. With all of that crammed into a 90–120 minute block, it's easy to see why some teachers have trouble finding time for anything that isn't mandated. When the benefits of independent reading are fully understood, it makes sense to allocate instructional time to this practice. And once you begin strategically employing it with students, it will soon become an indispensable part of the school day.

With respect to providing time for independent reading, Kelly Gallagher cites another very real, related obstacle. He believes that "High-interest reading is being squeezed out in favor of more test preparation practice" (2009, 4). He describes this lack of reading for pleasure as "Readicide" (2009, 2). When teachers value independent reading enough to use it regularly, readers will be and are more motivated.

In addition to a lack of time allocated to independent reading, students can be negatively influenced if they think teachers don't value the practice. If students are asked to read while the teacher is working on grading or other tasks, they may view reading as busywork instead of a meaningful learning experience. While avid readers will engage in reading any chance they get, many others will use the time less productively. Effective teachers monitor and respond to children as they read and write, rather than assigning a worksheet or sitting at a desk correcting papers (DeVries 2004). Thus, the teacher must be similarly involved in the independent reading process.

Another issue relates to struggling readers. Sadly, struggling readers, those who need the most extra time reading, actually spend the least amount of time engaged in reading for pleasure (Allington 2006; DeVries 2004). They are often pulled from independent reading for an intervention group or to complete unfinished work from earlier in the day. We want all students in our classroom to have the opportunity to read independently and to see themselves as capable, confident readers.

Engagement is certainly the most critical factor to determine the effectiveness of any independent reading program. If students are not engaged, then independent reading is not critical (Bryan, Fawson, and Reutzel 2003). Fake reading, when students look like they are reading but are really just passing their eyes over the print without attending to meaning, is perhaps the biggest obstacle to overcome during independent reading (Kelley and Clausen-Grace 2007; Tovani 2002). This behavior can be seen in both struggling readers and high-achieving readers, such as when they select inappropriate texts to read. They do not know how to choose books based on their interests and abilities, or they may not have access to compelling texts they can read. And though book selection is often the culprit, there are also other issues.

Another contributing factor to fake reading involves difficulty settling into reading. The reasons can range from physical to cognitive to motivational issues. Stamina can sometimes be the cause of this problem; students can't focus for more than a few moments. Regardless of the cause, the result is these students rarely actually read. They may fidget, talk, gaze around the room, go from the bookcase to their seats and back, switch books, or never finish reading a single book (Kelley and Clausen-Grace 2006). Many of these students do not know how to engage in and enjoy a text, and some don't even realize that they are supposed to. So what are some of the types of reading behaviors you might see in your classroom, and how can you help engage students during independent reading? This next section will provide tips in these areas.

## Types of Reading Behaviors

We have developed a continuum of reading behaviors based on the readers we have worked with over the past 24 years (Kelley and Clausen-Grace 2008). They range in behavior type from the most disengaged to the most engaged. (See Figure 1 on p. 144.) By acknowledging and anticipating different types of reading behaviors, you are better prepared to validate students' strengths and in turn differentiate instruction for them during independent reading. The goal is to move them along the continuum toward more engaged reading.

FIGURE 1 CONTINUUM OF READING BEHAVIORS

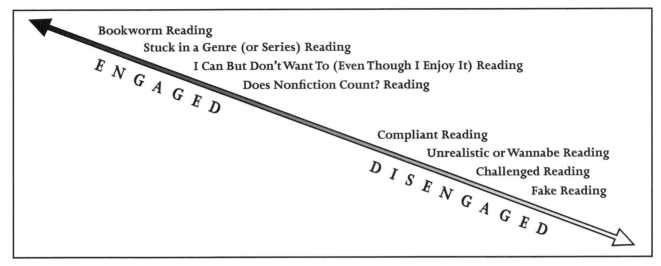

Adapted from Kelley and Clausen-Grace 2008, published with the International Reading Association

## Disengaged Reading Behaviors

### Fake Reading

Students who display fake reading behaviors rarely ever read. They might appear to read by staring at the text and flipping the pages at the appropriate time, or they might be avoiders who do the everything-but-reading shuffle between the bookcase, desk, bathroom, and pencil sharpener. These students will say you do not have any books for them to read, even though they are faced with hundreds of options in your classroom library. Students who fake read need a strong purpose, structure, ongoing support, close monitoring, and accountability for their reading. Book selection is key for these readers. They need texts that they want to read. You can best support them through check-ins during reading and more frequent one-on-one reading conferences. These readers need your help and the help of classmates to nurture a love of reading. Consistently communicate that your goal is to help them find texts they love and don't want to put down.

### Challenged Reading

Students displaying challenged reading behaviors may have physical challenges (visual tracking, anxiety disorder, Attention Deficit Hyperactivity Disorder), cognitive limitations (learning disabilities, poor memory, language deficits), or social obstacles (dysfunctional home life, extreme poverty, learning English as a second language)—any of which make independent reading difficult or low on their priority list. They can only independently comprehend texts well below their grade level. Since they struggle with the act of reading, they must be carefully monitored. Reading a story for pleasure is often not enough to sustain interest.

Some of these readers respond extremely well to structure, and some need an added purpose and extra support as they read. One great way to provide both is by teaching the sticky note strategy. Give your reader a stack of sticky notes and instructions to pause at the end of a section of text to reflect. Determine the length of text that is appropriate for the student to read before pausing. At the end of the section, have the student write a sentence, summarizing what has been read. He or she might add another sentence to predict, visualize, question, or connect with something on the page. If summarizing is difficult, tell the student to reread before going on. This keeps the student from getting too far without comprehending the text. Make sure to check in and read the student's reflections as this provides validation for the student and is valuable insight for you. Also monitor to ensure the student isn't spending way more time writing than reading. Of course, just like those exhibiting fake reading behaviors, students with challenged reading behaviors need more frequent check-ins and help with book selection.

### Unrealistic or Wannabe Reading

Readers displaying unrealistic or wannabe reading behaviors choose books that are far beyond their current ability. Thus, they are infamous book switchers, discarding one book for another inappropriate choice. Often they are able to read the words, but making meaning is so difficult that they easily get tired and are unable to sustain their efforts. Another common characteristic of this reading behavior is for students to provide you with continual updates on their reading, such as "I'm on chapter four now." They view reading as finishing the book, rather than truly enjoying a book. Lessons on book selection followed by frequent, targeted conferences can help them find the right book and stick with it. Sometimes these students can be tenacious in their lack of desire to find an appropriate book. Give them a few moments of your time at the bookshelf each week, suggesting texts you think they will like. Connecting with a reading mentor in this way is very powerful for many readers, but especially students exhibiting unrealistic or wannabe reading traits.

### Compliant Reading

Readers showing compliant reading behaviors read because it is required. Since they do not read for pleasure, they do not usually pick something they would be interested in reading. They may read the easiest or closest text around. There is no intentionality in their book selection; therefore, they have difficulty engaging. The good news is most of these readers can read. They benefit from careful book selection and monitoring, as well as a culture that supports an enthusiasm for reading. Partner these students with your avid readers to build the desire to read and tempt them with engaging book discussions. Make sure you and your students take time for book talks, both to model enthusiasm and to introduce a wide variety of titles. Also place these students front and center when you read aloud or talk enthusiastically about what you are reading.

## Engaged Reading Behaviors

### Does Nonfiction Count? Reading

Students who have a preference for nonfiction may not view themselves as readers because they have difficulty focusing on narrative story lines. They might initially appear to show fake or disengaged reading behaviors if nonfiction is not valued in the classroom. Allowing them to read what they want to read and having a plethora of informational text in your classroom library will contribute to their view of themselves as readers. You can also affirm their choices by having them do quick book talks about the text they are reading. When you are working in whole group or guided reading groups on challenging nonfiction texts, tell the students that these children are expert nonfiction readers, and ask your experts to share their strategy use with others.

### I Can But Don't Want To (Even Though I Enjoy It) Reading

Some students lack the passion for reading even though they can choose a book that interests them and enjoy reading it. They might only read the required amount of time, therefore taking a long time to finish reading a book. When given the choice to read or do something else, something else always wins. You will most likely identify this behavior when you take the status of the class, which is when the title of the book and page number being read is recorded each time students read independently. This avoidance behavior can be changed with support during reading conferences. Encourage students to add reading minutes at home. Helping these students with book selection and having students share and discuss texts they are reading can also move them along the engaged reading continuum.

### Stuck in a Genre (or Series) Reading

Many readers know what they like to read. They'll devour a reading series, like Junie B. Jones, and are reluctant to try anything else. Readers who are stuck in a genre don't see any reason to move beyond their comfort zone. Although sticking with one genre is a hallmark of some adult readers, we do not want our elementary students to limit their reading potential. You can help change this behavior during conferencing by suggesting texts based on their interests but in different genres. Having other students share what they are reading will also entice these children to broaden their reading horizons and become wide readers.

### Bookworm Reading

Students who are bookworms may be addicted to books and opt to read rather than pay attention in class or work on homework. They read beyond what is expected. They read a variety of genres but do tend to have a preference. Having to log what they read or reflect on their reading may seem cumbersome to them because they would rather just keep reading. Providing a purpose in addition to pleasure will help move these readers to the next level. These readers serve as excellent reading role models who really help build enthusiasm for reading in your class. Therefore, capitalize on their excitement and voracity.

After determining reading behaviors, create a classroom culture that positively enforces independent reading.

## Best Practices in Independent Reading

When implementing independent reading, it is helpful to be aware of some common characteristics effective independent reading programs share (Pilgreen 2000). The most obvious is having an extensive classroom library, in terms of genre, level, and text types. Krashen (2011) found that the number of titles available to students was a significant predictor of reading comprehension improvement in SSR programs. Simply put, text matters. Access to appealing books is critical to successful independent reading. The texts we invest in need to be compelling enough for students to want to read. Therefore knowing what your students are interested in will help you match them to books. When students are

allowed to read texts they are interested in, they make time to read. Ninety-one percent of children ages 6–17 say, "my favorite books are the ones that I have picked out myself" (Scholastic 2015, 56). Therefore, offering students choice is also an important characteristic. Teachers can manage this choice by placing parameters on book selection while offering relevant texts students would want to read.

In addition to having a quality classroom library, a comfortable environment that promotes engagement is essential. The classroom should invite reading with nooks and crannies where students can get cozy with a good book. If practical, scatter rugs, reading lamps, and beanbag chairs to encourage students to relax and enjoy independent reading.

Marinak, Molloy, Gambrell, and Mazzoni (2015) propose that promoting the value of reading necessitates more than just words but also requires action and intentionality, so offering time to read and being consistent with this time is integral to independent reading success. Providing encouragement/feedback by guiding book selection, commenting on reading progress, celebrating success, and facilitating self-assessment and goal-setting can help students understand the purpose of independent reading and the connection to your reading instruction.

We also suggest independent reading be explicitly connected to the reading block and your teaching. A typical literacy block includes time for whole group lessons, small group lessons, station work, and independent work. The sample schedule in Figure 2 on the next page shows one possible suggestion for grades 2 and up. It includes 30 minutes for a whole group lesson, a 30-minute small group/literacy stations rotation, and 30 minutes for choice reading, including literature circles and R[5] (Read, Relax, Reflect, Respond, and Rap)—the latter of which is our independent reading block and will be discussed later. The variety of reading block time allocations and configurations vary greatly from school to school, and this is just one suggestion for how to fit it all in. While it may be tempting to relegate independent reading to an independent activity while you work with small groups, this might be a mistake in some classrooms. The students who need the most support, and therefore need independent reading the most, would be left to fend for themselves.

R[5], or any independent reading structure, is ideally 25–30 minutes for primary students and 30–35 minutes for intermediate students and occurs at least three times per week. Incorporating social interaction through discussion with independent reading encourages engaged reading (Bryan, Fawson, and Reutzel 2003). In order to participate in discussions about what they have read, students must actively engage with each other (Almasi 1996). Discussion not only increases reading comprehension and motivation (Gambrell, Mazzoni, and Almasi 2000), it also contributes to their self-efficacy in reading (Hall 2012).

## A Model for Differentiating Independent Reading

### R[5] (Read, Relax, Reflect, Respond, and Rap)

Once we decided that independent reading was an indispensable part of our literacy block, we tweaked it to eliminate some of the obstacles we referred to earlier in this chapter. In addition to thwarting the common issues related to independent reading, R[5] was developed based on students' needs, best practices research, and our collective teaching experiences. Our structured independent reading block includes aspects of SSR, Reader's Workshop, and Self-Selected Reading, along with an added twist. (See Table 1 on p. 148.)

R[5] has a predictable structure and differentiates learning for students in two distinct ways, through process and content (Theroux 2004). Differentiation occurs within the structure of R[5], as well as the conferences and conversations that occur during R[5]. R[5] was designed to maximize student engagement and promote strategic reading for all readers (Kelley and Clausen-Grace 2006). There are three distinct phases in R[5]: Read and Relax, Reflect and Respond, and Rap. The time allotted for R[5] is 30 minutes, but the time in each phase varies as students develop reading stamina.

FIGURE 2 SAMPLE INTERMEDIATE LITERACY BLOCK SCHEDULE

|  | Monday | Tuesday | Wednesday | Thursday | Friday |
|---|---|---|---|---|---|
| 9:45–10:15 am Whole Group Lesson |  |  |  |  |  |
| 10:15–10:45 am Small Groups |  |  |  |  |  |
| 10:15–10:45 am Literacy Stations | word study | fluency | computer | comprehension | make up |
| 10:45–11:15 am Choice Reading | R[5] | literature circles | R[5] | literature circles | R[5] |
| Specials (Music, PE, Art, Spanish, STEM) |  |  |  |  |  |
| 12:00–12:20 pm Read Aloud |  |  |  |  |  |

## Table 1 A Comparison of Common Independent Reading Structures

| R⁵ | Reading Workshop | Sustained Silent Reading | Self-Selected Reading |
|---|---|---|---|
| **Read and Relax:**<br><br>Students read a book of their choice in a comfortable spot in the classroom.<br><br>Students actively read and employ reading strategies that have been taught during whole group instruction and those most necessary to comprehend the text being read.<br><br>The teacher completes a Status of the Class and confers with one student about his or her reading goal(s). | **Mini-lesson:**<br><br>The teacher conducts a brief lesson. This lesson typically sets a purpose for that day's reading.<br><br>**Independent Reading:**<br><br>Students read a book of their choice. The teacher does a Status of the Class, then reads while students are reading. The teacher may confer with students one-on-one or in a small group. | **Read:**<br><br>Students read a book of their choice while the teacher reads. | **Teacher Read-aloud:**<br><br>The teacher launches a lesson with a read-aloud from a wide range of literature. |
| **Reflect and Respond:**<br><br>Students reflect on what they have read and respond to prompts in a log. The teacher will use the students' responses to scaffold the discussion they will have in Rap and to promote strategic thinking.<br><br>The teacher circulates and observes while students complete the log. | **Record/Respond:**<br><br>Students record book titles read and may or may not complete a response for their reading. | **Record:**<br><br>Students record book titles read in a log. | **Read:**<br><br>Students read a book at their reading level, typically from a set of books identified in their reading range.<br><br>The teacher may confer with several students individually or in small groups. |
| **Rap:**<br><br>Part 1 (in pairs): The teacher listens in as students share what they read that day with a partner. Students actively listen to each other, so they are able to share in Part 2.<br><br>Part 2 (whole-class): The teacher facilitates oral pair-sharing and asks questions to help students identify the strategy(ies) discussed in each student's share. | **Sharing:**<br><br>The teacher facilitates a whole-class or pair-sharing activity.<br><br>The teacher may also recap the mini-lesson content, or students may share journal entries. | **Sharing:**<br><br>Students may or may not share what they have read with classmates. | **Sharing (Optional):**<br><br>Students share what they have read with peers. |

## Read and Relax

During Read and Relax, students read self-selected books (often with guidance) in a comfortable spot in the classroom. For some students this might be under a desk, on a beanbag chair, or at their desks. While students settle in, the teacher notes what they are reading and the page number, or a "Status of the Class." This is done each time. It allows the teacher to quickly monitor book selection (appropriate text level and interest) and progress with reading (Are they reading at an appropriate rate and/or switching books?). The teacher can provide some feedback or guidance while taking the status. For example, she may comment on a student who is reading a book at an unrealistic rate or suggest a mini-conference with a student who is reading a book far above his or her reading level. In addition, the teacher may identify a student for a more in-depth conference about a reading goal. The conference form (see Figure 3 on p. 150, Kelley and Clausen-Grace 2008) can help to guide these discussions, keep a record, and ensure important topics are hit when conferring. In addition, we have included a transcript of a conference between Nicki Clausen-Grace and a student (Figure 4 on p. 151) to show the type of conversation that occurs between the teacher and a student while conferring.

FIGURE 3 R⁵ CONFERENCE FORM

# R⁵ Conference Form

Student: _____  Date: _____

Is this an intervention conference?    Yes ____    No ____

If yes, check appropriately:

____ Changing books    ____ Stuck in a genre/series    ____ Choosing books too difficult/
                                                             too easy

1. "Tell me a little about what you are reading."
   Title _____

   Behaviors observed:
   ____ includes characters        ____ includes problem/solution and/or events
   ____ includes setting           ____ can identify the genre

2. "Can you give me an example of a strategy you have used today while reading
   (or recently)?"

   ____ connecting       ____ predicting        ____ questioning
   ____ visualizing      ____ summarizing        ____ other _____

   Example was:
   ____ nonspecific    ____ demonstrates use of strategy    ____ unable to give example

3. "Let's take a look at your reading folder."

   ____ folder is neatly maintained    ____ student accurately completes Response Log

4. "How can I help you become a better reader?

5. "What would be a good goal for your next conference?"

Adapted from Kelley and Clausen-Grace 2008, published with the International Reading Association

FIGURE 4 CONFERENCE TRANSCRIPT TO ILLUSTRATE R⁵

Nicki: *Tell me a little about the book you are reading today.*

Student: "So far Hobbes did a cannonball in the bathtub, and he made all the water splash out and splashed himself out of the bathtub. It was funny."

Nicki: *I am wondering if you were actually watching it, would it really be happening that way?*

Student: "No, it would be more like in his [Calvin's] imagination because maybe he did a cannonball and he slung shot Hobbes right into the bathtub."

Nicki: *Let's look at your questioning plan. You are working on questioning to help you connect to the text. You said here that you will read more nonfiction and books about Jamaica. Have you done that?*

Student: "No, but I did find some books I could question to connect to, and I've done that with Calvin and Hobbes."

Nicki: *Did you do this today?*

Student: "Not so far."

Nicki: [Trying to find out if he was using any strategy at all.] *Well, have you had any connections in this book?*

Student: "Yes, like when he plays with his food at lunchtime and he really grosses out the people around him . . . I sometimes do that at home."

Nicki: *How can I help you become a better reader?*

Student: "You could make me read more."

Nicki: *Do you mean assign reading to you?*

Student: "Yeah, because I don't really read at home."

At the beginning of the year, students might Read and Relax for only five minutes but as they gain reading stamina, more time is devoted to Read and Relax. The goal is to reach 10–15 minutes of reading in this phase for primary students and 15–20 minutes for intermediate students.

## Reflect and Respond

After Read and Relax, students Reflect and Respond. They think about the cognitive reading strategies they used while reading and complete a brief log about what they read that day, along with noting their strategy use. Reflect and Respond lasts three to five minutes. This remains consistent throughout the year.

## Rap

Rap is divided into two parts. In Part 1 students meet with a partner and share what they read that day. The goal is for them to have a mini-conversation about their reading. The teacher strategically pairs the partners. This might be based on social-emotional needs, developmental needs, interests, or reading goals. The partners are typically not "best friends" or "worst enemies." Each partner shares what he or she read that day, along with what he or she was thinking while reading (this could be a prediction, a question, a connection, and/or something he or she visualized), and the other partner listens carefully, asking clarifying questions if needed. The listening partner needs to be prepared to share what his or her partner explained. This partner share occurs during a whole group share out, which is Part 2. Rap Part 1 takes about five minutes. This time also remains consistent throughout the year. During Rap Part 2, the teacher facilitates a whole-class share and calls on pairs to share each other's thoughts about what they read that day. The teacher then asks the remainder of the class to identify the reading strategy or strategies being shared. At the beginning of the year, most of the R⁵ time is spent in Rap Part 2, sometimes up to 15 minutes. This allows for everyone to share and holds students accountable for their reading and sharing. As engagement improves and time spent in the Read and Relax phase increases, the time spent on Rap Part 2 decreases to around five minutes.

## Benefits of R$^5$

The biggest difference between R$^5$ and most other independent reading models is the teacher plays an active role in all phases of the process. Second, there is an explicit connection between the reading strategies taught in whole and small group to R$^5$. And third, there is subtle, daily accountability via Rap. R$^5$ has far exceeded our original goals. It provides structured, supportive independent reading practice, necessitates engagement, enhances metacognitive awareness, supports wide reading, promotes social interaction, and develops active listening (Kelley and Clausen-Grace 2007). In addition, Rap exposes students to a variety of books and often entices students to try to new genres, authors, and titles. Most importantly, R$^5$ is the ultimate differentiated, culminating activity for all of your reading instruction.

## Conclusion

Sometimes in the rush to cover standards, prepare for assessments, incorporate project-based learning, teach text-based writing, facilitate STEM, take class pictures, attend assemblies, and so on, we can overlook one of the most impactful instructional strategies around—structured independent reading. Teaching requires educators to make decisions about which practices to emphasize and which to spend less time on. No one can argue the value of direct instruction in reading strategies, but to get the full impact of these efforts, purposeful independent reading is vital. It allows students to practice what they have learned in a supportive environment. It holds them accountable for applying what they know and, more importantly, it helps create an ongoing desire to read for pleasure and information. This desire will continue to help readers grow long after they leave your classroom.

## References and Resources

Allington, Richard L. 2006. *What Really Matters for Struggling Readers: Designing Research-based Programs*. Boston: Pearson.

Almasi, Janice F. 1996. "A New View of Discussion." *In Lively Discussions! Fostering Engaged Reading*, edited by Linda B. Gambrell and Janice F. Almasi, 2–24. Newark, DE: International Reading Association.

Booth, David. 2002. *Even Hockey Players Read: Boys, Literacy, and Learning*. Markham, ON: Pembroke.

Bryan, G., P. C. Fawson, and D. R Reutzel. 2003. "Sustained Silent Reading: Exploring the Value of Literature Discussion with Three Non-engaged Readers." *Reading Research and Instruction* 43: 47–73.

Cunningham, Anne E., and K. E. Stanovich. 1997. "Early Reading Acquisition and Its Relation to Reading Experience and Ability 10 Years Later." *Developmental Psychology*, 33: 934–945.

DeVries, Beverly A. 2004. *Literacy Assessment and Intervention for the Elementary Classroom*. Scottsdale, AZ: Holcomb Hathaway.

Gallagher, Kelly. 2009. *Readicide*. Portland, ME: Stenhouse Publishers.

Gambrell, Linda B. 2015. "Getting Students Hooked on the Reading Habit." *The Reading Teacher* 69 (3): 259–263.

Gambrell, Linda B., Susan A. Mazzoni, and Janice F. Almasi. 2000. "Promoting Collaboration, Social Interaction, and Engagement with Text." In *Engaging Young Readers: Promoting Achievement and Motivation*, edited by Linda Baker, Marian J. Dreher, and John T. Guthrie, 119–139. New York: Guilford Press.

Guthrie, John T., P. VanMeter, A. D. McCann, A. Wigfield, L. Bennett, C. C. Poundstone, and A. M. Mitchell. 1996. "Growth of Literacy Engagement. Changes in Motivations and Strategies During Concept-oriented Reading Instruction." *Reading Research Quarterly* 31 (3): 306–332.

Guthrie, John T., and A. Wigfield. 2000. "Engagement and Motivation in Reading." In *Handbook of Reading Research*, edited by Michael L. Kamil, Peter B. Mosenthal, David Pearson, and Rebecca Barr, 403–422. Mahwah, NJ: Erlbaum.

Guthrie, John T., A. Wigfield, J. Metsala, and K. Cox. 1999. "Motivation and Cognitive Predictors of Text Comprehension and Reading Amount." *Scientific Studies of Reading* 3 (3): 231–256.

Hall, Leigh A. 2012. "Moving Out of Silence: Helping Struggling Readers Find Their Voices in Text-Based Discussions." *Reading & Writing Quarterly* 28 (4): 307–332.

Hunt, L. C., Jr. 1984. "Six Steps to the Individualized Reading Program (IRP)." In *Readings on Reading Instruction*, edited by Albert J. Harris and Edward R. Sipay, 190–195. New York: Longman.

Jang, Bong G., K. Conradi, M. C. McKenna., and J. S. Jones. 2015. "Motivation: Approaching an Elusive Concept Through the Factors that Shape It." *The Reading Teacher* 69 (2): 239–247.

Kelley, Michelle and N. Clausen-Grace. 2006. "R⁵: The SSR Makeover that Transformed Readers." *Reading Teacher* 60: 148–159.

———. 2007. *Comprehension Shouldn't be Silent: From Strategy Instruction to Student Independence.* Newark, DE: International Reading Association.

———. 2008. *R⁵ in Your Classroom: A Guide to Differentiating Independent Reading and Developing Avid Readers.* Newark, DE: International Reading Association.

Krashen, Stephen. 2011. *Free Voluntary Reading.* Santa Barbara, CA: Libraries Unlimited.

Marinak, Barbara A., J. B. Molloy, L. B. Gambrell, S. A. Mazzoni. 2015. "Me and My Reading Profile: A Tool for Assessing Early Reading Motivation." *The Reading Teacher* 69 (1): 51–62.

Morrow, Linda M. 1996. *Motivating Reading and Writing in Diverse Classrooms: Social and Physical Contexts in a Literature-Based Program* (NCTE Research Rep. No. 28). Urbana, IL: National Council of Teachers of English.

Pilgreen, Janice. 2000. *The SSR Handbook: How to Organize and Manage a Sustained Silent Reading Program.* Portsmouth, NH: Heinemann.

Rosenblatt, Louise M. 1978. *The Reader, the Text, the Poem: The Transactional Theory of the Literary Work.* Carbondale, IL: Southern Illinois University Press.

Schaffner, Ellen, U. Schiefele, and H. Ulferts. 2013. "Reading Amount as a Mediator of the Effects of Intrinsic and Extrinsic Reading Motivation on Comprehension," *Reading Research Quarterly* 48 (4): 369–385.

Scholastic. 2015. "Kids and Family Reading Report." New York, NY: http://www.scholastic.com/readingreport/index.htm.

Schunk, Dale. H., and Barry J. Zimmerman. 1997. "Developing Self-efficacious Readers and Writers: The Role of Social and Self-regulatory Processes." In *Engagement: Motivating Readers Through Integrated Instruction*, edited by John T. Guthrie and Alan Wigfield, 4–50. Newark, DE: International Reading Association.

Smith, Michael W., and Jeff D. Wilhelm. 2002. *Reading Don't Fix No Chevys: Literacy in the Lives of Young Men.* Portsmouth, NH: Heinemann.

Theroux, Priscilla. 2004. "Enhance Learning." Accessed January 11, 2008. members.shaw.ca/priscillatheroux/differentiating.html.

Tovani, Cris. 2002. *I Read, But I Don't Get It: Comprehension Strategies for Adolescent Readers.* Portland, ME: Stenhouse.

Trudel, Heidi. 2007. "Making Data-driven Decisions: Silent Reading." *The Reading Teacher* 61: 308–315.

Wiesendanger, Katherine D., and L. Bader. 1989. "SSR: Its Effects on Students' Reading Habits After They Complete the Program." *Reading Horizons* 29: 162–166.

# Differentiating Through Literacy Centers

## Connie Dierking

## Introduction

When my daughter was 4 years old, I decided it was time to begin formal swimming lessons. My family lives in Florida, so being able to swim fluently is really a need rather than a want. I signed up Madeline for classes at the local swim school, and off we went. On arrival, Maddie joined her group of "minnows" and hung to the side of the pool for dear life. For the first couple of lessons she screamed whenever the instructor ventured off the side of the pool with Maddie in her arms. But with proper modeling and practice, Maddie progressed to kicking her feet, blowing bubbles, and even laughing when her teachers would bob her up and down in and out of the water. She was definitely making progress toward becoming a swimmer in a few short weeks.

When the time came to begin a new session, I was disappointed to learn there were no openings in the 30-minute group sessions. I was told, however, Maddie could enroll for a few 10-minute private swimming lessons. I was apprehensive that any progress could be made in just 10 minutes of instruction. But . . . my goal was to make sure that my daughter could swim by the end of the summer. So we enrolled. I sat in the bleachers and watched Maddie work hard for 10 minutes. Her instructor didn't spend any time on kicking or blowing bubbles as he had in the group session. He realized quickly that Maddie had already mastered those skills. He spent time teaching her to put her face in the water and float on her tummy, then her back. He taught her what **she** needed, not what was best for the whole group. Her differentiated instruction in a mere 10 minutes managed to accomplish as much or even more than her 30-minute whole group instruction. After three weeks of whole group instruction and three 10-minute differentiated sessions, Madeline became a swimmer. I often think about this swimming school experience when I reflect on the powerful differentiated instruction that happens daily inside an elementary classroom. Swimming lessons, literacy instruction; the similarities are there!

The spectrum of needs in any elementary classroom is deep and wide. It is only through differentiation that a teacher can meet the needs of all students in his or her classroom. Differentiation requires knowledge of materials, teaching methods, and organization. This differentiation provides practice to the curriculum for all students. While there are many opportunities to differentiate instruction, a common and effective way to provide this type of practice is through literacy centers or stations. A literacy center or station is an area within the classroom where students work independently or in small groups to practice reading, writing, speaking, and listening. This area may be a physical space in the classroom or a space that changes according to availability. These spaces can be called literacy centers, literacy stations, or literacy workstations. Whatever the name, the intent is the same: providing students opportunities to practice skills and strategies—that have already been taught—both independently and collaboratively.

# Setting Up Your Literacy Centers

When designing a literacy center, there are questions that can guide your planning. If the goal is to provide materials and time for literacy practice, then it helps to plan with the end in mind. You will want to consider the following:

- Have I taught the skill or strategy?

- Is it tied to a standard I am responsible for teaching?

- Is there an accountability or feedback piece to ensure correct practice of the skill?

- Is this activity building stamina?

- Is the activity engaging and motivating?

- Does this activity provide differentiated practice?

- As a result of this activity will the student become a better reader, writer, speaker, or listener?

Every classroom has unique challenges around physical space. While many classrooms have nooks and crannies that outline specific center boundaries, in others you may need to put a center in a tub or basket to be carried back to a desk or table for practice. When collecting materials for your centers, you will want to provide everything a student would need to complete the center, including student-supported directions and the expected outcome for the center. You will want the activities to be open-ended. There should be multiple entry points, paths to solutions, and possible outcomes.

While the activity within the center may be the same, the materials or the final product may differ. Some students may show what they know through art or drama while others prefer written tasks. Affirming that the skill or strategy has been taught to all students will lead you to envision the outcome of the practice in the center. For example, in the writing center, some students may choose to write an opinion essay to share why recess should be extended by 10 minutes. Another student may create a poster to expose his thinking while another may write a letter to the principal. While each student is practicing the structure of opinion writing, the format is differentiated, allowing students to be confident and comfortable in their practice.

Differentiation allows for students to highlight their strengths while extending practice in areas where they need it. For example, students can practice reading strategies in a literacy center through multiple text types. Picture books, chapter books, magazines, comic books, electronic texts, and texts related to a popular television show or movie are all appropriate for practice. However, each of these text types will provide engagement for different students. Remembering to differentiate materials within the literacy center is an important first step in getting centers up and running.

When introducing literacy centers or stations to your class, introduce one center at a time. Review the materials and how to use them as well as what to do with the completed center activity or project. Some ways to house literacy center work include individual student folders, crates with hanging folders marked with student names, or a common basket for all center work. Provide clear expectations for work at the center, and review them often when introducing the purpose for the work within the center. Expectations can be differentiated. For example, one group of students may need to illustrate five vocabulary words while another group may need to illustrate and use the words in meaningful sentences. It is important to be very explicit with posted reminders inside the center. For example, "At the writing center you will . . . ." When adding a new center to the mix, expectations for an old center, or brand new materials, remember to take the time to review this new information with the class.

Provide practice with lots of positive reinforcement when discussing the literacy center routines. Doing so will provide time for you to teach small group differentiated instruction without interruption. It will also allow students to solve problems without you while reinforcing literacy skills and strategies in meaningful ways. Create a clear road map for yourself with student-friendly goals and appropriate materials for student success. See the example of a road map on the next page.

## Writing Center Road Map

| Purpose<br><br>What does it look like? | Materials<br><br>What does it include? | Student Actions<br><br>What will the students do there? |
|---|---|---|
| an area that promotes practice in the writing process. | · many different kinds of paper, including different colors, shapes, thickness, lined, and unlined<br><br>· stapler<br><br>· tape<br><br>· colored pencils and markers<br><br>· colored paint chips (from the paint section of a discount store)<br><br>· photographs<br><br>· pictures from magazines<br><br>· stickers of people, places, or things | · create their own book<br><br>· make a list<br><br>· write a sticker story<br><br>· compose sentences to go with photographs or magazine pictures<br><br>· compose an innovation from a picture book |

It is helpful to provide mentor examples for students, so they can see exactly what a completed project or activity would look like. For example, post an example of a student-created book, so students at the center can refer to it as they compose their own stories. As students complete one of the activities, post it so other students can admire and then imitate quality work.

Differentiation lies in the choice of materials, practice, and the product. You may have students who work best with only two material choices. For these students, you will need to minimize their choices. It might sound like, *Today, I want you to choose paper from the red bin and a picture from the green bin. See how many sentences you can write to describe the scene. When you are finished with one picture, then choose another picture from the green bin.* Students can compose their own sentences and pictures but you are scaffolding their material choice. This will provide support for choosing an activity so practice time isn't wasted with decisions about magazines, photographs, etc.

## Transitions

For literacy centers or stations to be most effective, students should be able to independently move from center to center with little direction from the teacher. A management board will help with this. Some teachers use a bulletin board with pocket envelopes and Popsicle sticks with student names to assist their students. The name of the center is posted on the pocket envelope with the Popsicle stick names of the students assigned to that center placed inside. Some teachers use paper plates and clothespins.

Other teachers use a large circle with each pie piece of the circle naming a center. Student names are posted on sticky notes inside the slice naming their center assignment for the day.

Often, a simple four square is used with center names highlighted in each square and student names listed underneath. Older students may sign up for centers as part of their morning routine or refer to an assignment board for the day. Literacy centers, or work stations, at the intermediate level may be differentiated by need. For example, students may be working on a research paper or project that requires additional reading on a particular topic. During center time, students may sign up for the reading center or the computer center in order to do work toward completion of a project.

Finally, teachers may label themselves as a center. Small group differentiated instruction becomes part of the student rotation. Teachers may pull students from each center assignment when it is their turn for small group differentiated instruction.

A consideration for differentiation is always the makeup of the group of students collaborating at the literacy center. Heterogeneous grouping allows for students with different strengths and abilities to support each other. Students of differing literacy levels can work nicely together. Teaching students ways to assist a classmate when faced with a learning struggle is an important life skill. This skill can be practiced and reinforced when students are working together outside of the scaffold of the teacher. Children who are second language learners will benefit from working with English speaking students inside of centers. The oral language exposure will be as important as the work inside the center itself. See the chapter on ELLs (starting on page 179) for more information on ELL considerations. Literacy center groups can be fluid, allowing for differentiated learning with various work partners. For example, students who find success in artistic expression can work with a partner who prefers responding in writing. This partnership will do well creating a book together in the writing center.

Students can be alerted that it is time to rotate between centers by the sound of a bell, a song, or a teacher announcement. It is important to limit transition time. It shouldn't take more than 3–4 minutes to move between centers. Students should practice how to clean up centers and get moving to the next activity quickly so as not to take from instruction time.

As you are setting up literacy centers, remember that you want to see what students are doing at all times. While little nooks and crannies are fun places to huddle around an activity, you want your students to be aware that you are monitoring their success in the center at all times. In addition, take the time to share the work done at centers. It only takes a few minutes to highlight exemplary work with the group. This public positive reinforcement reminds students that you are reviewing their center work and you expect quality. It also gives you the opportunity to honor all approximations toward mastering standards practiced inside centers.

# Primary Literacy Centers

Literacy centers or stations in the primary grades should provide practice in early literacy skills. Emergent and early readers require differentiated practice in phonological awareness, phonics, print awareness, oral language, and writing. While many centers provide multifaceted practice in several areas, the focus should always be on what is pertinent to the age and development of the reader and writer. Typically, a center in a primary classroom would include the following and allow for differentiated practice:

## Word Study Center

Focus: working with letters, making words, writing and reading high-frequency words, word sorts, name puzzles

## Writing Center

Focus: drawing stories, writing labels, writing stories of your life, making different kinds of books (list, ABC, wordless, all about, how to, fairy tales, innovations), making cards, writing letters, making brochures or posters

## Retelling Center

Focus: sequencing familiar nursery rhymes or fairy tales; acting out stories; recounting events; putting the written version of a story in order; using retelling props; using a graphic organizer to show beginning, middle, or end

## Computer Center

Focus: using technology to differentiate practice in literacy

## Listening Center

Focus: listening comprehension, choosing a favorite page to illustrate

## Reading Center

Focus: independent or partner reading, rereading a guided reading book, reading a book at your independent reading level, reading across a series, rereading a teacher read-aloud

# Primary Literacy Center Activities

## Writing Center

### Make an ABC Book

1. Look through the ABC books.

2. Choose a topic, such as desert animals or types of machines.

3. Make a list of words or pictures that go with your nonfiction topic.

4. Put your words in ABC order to make a book.

Materials: alphabet books, topic lists, blank books, pencils, crayons

### Make a Research Notebook

1. Choose a topic to research.

2. Read the books in the correct topic basket.

3. Take a research notebook from the basket, and jot down your notes.

4. Remember to study the text features.

Materials: basket of different nonfiction topics, research notebooks, pencils

### Create a Labeled Diagram

1. Look through the books in the basket.

2. Find a diagram to study.

3. Choose a topic.

4. Decide on a diagram to support your topic.

5. Draw your diagram.

6. Label your diagram.

Materials: basket of different nonfiction books, plain white paper, colored pencils

### Make an Alphabet Chart

1. Choose several alphabet books from the basket to study.

2. Choose a template with the number of boxes that match the number of letters you want for your own alphabet chart.

3. Draw a picture to go with each letter of the alphabet you chose.

4. Write the word to go with the picture.

Materials: ABC templates, ABC books, colored pencils, black marker

### Make a Flip-book

1. Choose a topic to study.

2. Read the books in the basket.

3. Choose four questions that go with your topic.

4. Take a flip-book from the basket.

5. Write a question about your topic on the top of each flap.

6. Write the answer underneath the flap.

Materials: flip-books, basket of nonfiction books, colored pencils, pencils

**Write a Riddle**

1. Choose a topic.

2. List the facts you know about this topic on paper.

3. Number your facts in the order of importance. Number one should be the most important fact.

4. Rewrite your facts in the order you just numbered.

5. Read your riddle to a friend to see if they can guess the answer.

Materials: basket of riddle books, paper, colored pencils, pencils

## Big Book Center

**Make a Label**

1. Read the big book using a pointer.

2. Write labels to go with the pictures in the book.

3. Place your labels in your book.

4. Reread your book using the pictures and words.

Materials: big books, large sticky notes, pencils, pointers

## Reading Center

**Text Feature Hunt**

1. Read through your big book to find text features.

2. Use the class text feature chart to help you.

3. Tally the number of text features that you found.

Materials: nonfiction big book, text feature chart, paper, pencils

## Listening Center

1. Choose a book to listen to.

2. Listen to the book.

3. Draw a picture that matches something you heard.

Materials: audio book, paper, colored pencils

## Computer

1. Log in with your student number.

2. Make sure you are in the right spot.

3. Make sure your headphones are on.

Materials: computer station

## Word Study

1. Go over your word cards.

2. Have your partner show the cards to you, one at a time.

3. Flash your partner's cards to him or her.

4. Play concentration or Memory with your partner by putting your cards together.

Materials: word cards

Literacy centers or stations provide a much-needed venue for differentiated practice independent of the teacher. Practice within the center can be differentiated by assigning the appropriate activity to each student through color-coding or by assigning students to a particular center. Then students receive the practice that is just right for them.

The chart on the next page outlines core instruction and how practice inside of literacy centers can be differentiated.

| Core Instruction | Differentiated Instruction/Literacy Centers |
|---|---|

I can retell stories by using the pictures and words.

**Mini-lesson**

### Connection

*Last night at dinner I asked my daughter to tell me everything she did at school. She told me she went to P.E., and they ran races. There was pizza for lunch. Then her teacher read them a story, she drew a picture in the writing center, and she got on the bus and came home. Wow! She gave me a lot of information. So I told her that I was going to meet her at school for lunch the next day. I said, "So you have lunch after P.E., right?" And my daughter said, "No, we have P.E. the last period of the day. It wouldn't make sense to come for lunch after P.E." I told her I was a little confused because when she told me the story of her day, she said she went to P.E. and then she ate pizza. "Oh," she said, "I didn't know that I was supposed to say it in order!" So this made me start thinking about retelling a story that you would read in a book. It is really important that you retell the story in the order that the events happen or the story won't make sense. So today I want to teach you how to retell a story in the order that the events happened by using the pictures and words.*

### Teach

*The title of this book is Yoko by Rosemary Wells. Yoko is about a kitten who acts like a person. While I am reading today I want you to watch how I use the pictures and words to help me remember how each page goes.*

Read a few pages. Study the illustrations, and model how to look for key words to remember how each page goes.

Then model how to go back to the beginning and retell the pages you have read so far. Highlight how the pictures and words help you remember the story.

### Active Engagement

*Now you give it a try. I am going to read the next three pages. You listen carefully to what is happening with Yoko on each page. I will hold the book up high so you can see the pictures as well.*

After reading the next three pages, have students retell what has happened on those pages.

Now go back and retell the pages that you modeled and the pages the students practiced retelling.

### Link

*So remember readers, anytime you want to remember how a story goes, look at the pictures and the words to help you remember the story. Then when you go back to retell the story, you can use both the pictures and words to help you.*

I can practice retelling stories using the pictures and words.

### Retelling Center 1

**Pre-emergent Readers**

- Follow along as you listen to the story online.
- When you are finished, return to the first page of the book.
- Tell what happened on the first page quietly to yourself.
- Turn the page, and say what happened next.
- Turn the page, and say what happened next.
- Turn the page, and say what happened next.
- Go back and retell the whole story using the pictures and words.
- Listen to the story again to make sure that you remembered everything that happened!

### Retelling Center 2

**Emergent Reader**

- Reread the story, *Yoko*, using the pictures and words.
- Think about the most important parts, and sketch those parts.
- Add labels to the pictures.
- Use your pictures to retell the story to a partner also in your center.
- Touch your sketches to tell how the story goes.

### Retelling Center 3

**Early Reader**

- Listen to the story, *Yoko*, on the computer.
- Use the picture cards to put the events in the order that they happened in the story.
- Check the book to make sure you have the pictures in the right order.
- Retell the story to a partner in your center.

### Retelling Center 4

**Transitional Reader**

- Read the book, *Yoko*, independently.
- Fill in the retelling graphic organizer using pictures and words.
- Practice retelling the story by using your graphic organizer, rereading your words, and pointing to the pictures.
- Read your graphic organizer to a partner in your center.

# Intermediate Literacy Center Activities

Literacy centers at the intermediate level are different from centers at the primary level. Because students are older, they are able to sustain themselves independently for longer stretches of time. Thus activities must be rigorous and hold a high degree of accountability. If students are going to spend time engaged in differentiated practice, they must have something to show for it in the end.

While the center names for intermediate centers may be the same, the practice at them should look different. It is always important to remember that no matter the level, centers should be aligned with the curriculum, based on ongoing assessment, ensure independence, and have an accountability system built in. If centers are matched to the needs of each student, everyone will stay engaged in the practice throughout the duration of independent work time. Intermediate students will benefit from practice in vocabulary, fluency, retelling, grammar, writing, reading, and computer. Typically, a center in an intermediate classroom would include the following and allow for differentiated practice:

## Vocabulary Center

Focus: working with academic vocabulary, vocabulary four square (Frayer model), drawing and defining idioms, creating an individual thesaurus, making lists of word degrees ("mad," "angry," "furious"), matching words and definitions

## Fluency Center

Focus: reading and rereading familiar text or passages, working with a partner, timing rate and using a rubric to analyze expression, reader's theatre

## Retelling Center

Focus: sequencing using a graphic organizer. An effective comprehension strategy for retelling is to use Somebody-Wanted-But-So. Students record the character (somebody), the problem (wanted), the events (but), followed by the outcome (so).

## Grammar Center

Focus: identifying and using parts of speech, making sentences, adding prefixes and suffixes, editing your own writing

## Writing Center

Focus: writing stories of your life, making different kinds of books (sequels, wordless, all about, how to, fairy tales, realistic fiction, etc.), making cards, writing letters for social justice, making brochures, posters, book reports, or reviews

## Reading Center

Focus: independent or partner reading, rereading a guided reading book, reading a book at your independent reading level, reading across a series, rereading a teacher read-aloud, asking and answering questions about text

## Computer Center

Focus: using technology to differentiate literacy skill practice, creating a report using PowerPoint or Prezi, researching, typing practice, publication of a piece of writing

# Specific Examples of Activities Inside Intermediate Literacy Centers

## Writing Center

### Make a Wordless Book

1. Look through the basket of wordless books.

2. Study the themes or lessons learned.

3. Make a list of themes or lessons learned found in the books.

4. Choose a theme or lesson and storyboard your book.

5. Illustrate your book using markers, pencils, colored pencils, or crayons.

Materials: wordless books, theme lists, blank books, pencils, crayons, markers, colored pencils

### Make a Research Notebook

1. Choose a topic to research.

2. Read the books in the topic basket of your choice.

3. Take a research notebook from the basket, and jot down any facts and details that are important to the topic.

4. Remember to study the text features. Include information found in the illustrations, captions, diagrams, etc.

5. Organize your information using your own text features.

Materials: basket of different nonfiction topics, research notebooks, pencils

### Create a Brochure

1. Look through the books and brochures in the basket. Note how the information is shared.

2. Choose a place to research. Make a list of everything you know about that place.

3. Design a brochure to convince someone to visit your place.

4. Create the brochure.

5. Plan to present your brochure to the class.

Materials: basket of books and brochures about travel, plain white paper, colored pencils

### Make a Flip-book

1. Choose a topic to study.

2. Read the books in the basket.

3. Choose four main ideas that would go with your topic. For example: giraffes, main idea: Habitat, Habits, Predators, Unusual Body Parts

4. Create a flip-book by folding a piece of paper provided in half. On one side of the paper, cut four flaps

5. Write one main idea on the top of each flap.

6. Record the facts and details about each main idea underneath the corresponding flap. Add a diagram or chart if you choose.

Materials: white paper, scissors, colored pencils, pencils

### Write a Riddle

1. Choose a topic.

2. List the facts you know about this topic.

3. Number your facts in the order of importance. Number one should be the most important fact.

4. Rewrite your facts in the order you just numbered.

5. Read your riddle to a friend to see if he or she can guess the answer.

Materials: basket of riddle books, notebook paper, colored pencils

## Final Thoughts

We know the best way to ensure success at any process, procedure, or practice is to model, model, model. It is also the seamless orchestration of the differentiation that will make literacy centers or stations a success in your classroom. Remember to spend the time needed to model expectations not only of the materials and outcomes but of behavior at the centers as well. The early childhood director in my district reminds us often to, "Slow down to go fast." This is excellent advice for getting literacy centers up and running. Be reflective—if a center is not working, there is a reason. Don't overwhelm yourself with materials. Keep your centers simple and open-ended. Less is more. Finally, look around your classroom and take pride in the well-oiled machine that you have created. This small area in your classroom is where students work alone or in small groups to practice in a differentiated way. It doesn't necessarily come easily, but it is well worth the time spent up front!

## References and Resources

Campbell Dierking, Connie. 2014. *Linking K–2 Literacy and the Common Core: Mini-lessons That Work*. North Mankato, MN: Maupin House by Capstone Professional.

Cobb, Charlene, and Camille Blachowicz. *No More "Look Up the List" Vocabulary Instruction*. Not This But That. 2014. Portsmouth, New Hampshire: Heinemann.

Diller, Debbie. 2016. *Growing Independent Learners, From Literacy Standards to Stations, K–3*. Portland, ME: Stenhouse.

Kelley, Michelle, and Nicki Clausen-Grace. 2016. *Teaching Text Features to Support Comprehension*. North Makato, MN: Maupin House by Capstone Professional.

Richardson, Jan. 2009. *The Next Step in Guided Reading: Focused Assessments and Targeted Lessons Helping Every Student Become a Better Reader*. New York, NY: Scholastic.

Taberski, Sharon. 2011. *Comprehension from the Ground Up: Simplified, Sensible Instruction for the K–3 Reading Workshop*. Portsmouth, New Hampshire: Heinemann.

Wells, Rosemary. 1998. *Yoko*. NY, New York: Disney Hyperion Books.

# Sharing and Assessment During the Language Arts Block

Adele T. Macula

. . . . . . . . . . . . . . . . . . . . . . . . . . . . . . . . . . . . . . . . . . . . . . . . . . . . . . . . . . . . .

> A teacher who establishes rapport with the taught, becomes one with them, learns more from them than he teaches them.
> —Mahatma Gandhi

## Introduction

By design, classrooms are the first-tier level of true "learning communities" in which comprehensive instruction is facilitated and/or delivered by the teacher and authentic student learning occurs. When a teacher and students meld together as a classroom community, and as learning unfolds, there is an unending stream of classroom conversation, communication, and interaction that reflects an exchange of information and ideas. This sharing is enhanced by a trust-based setting. From the first day that the class comes together, and especially over time during the course of a school year, this sharing environment develops and deepens. As teaching and learning envelop each day's classroom activities and events, both the students and the teacher impart information; disclose important thoughts; ask valuable questions; wonder about possibilities; pose and discuss potential solutions to problems, situations, and challenges; and pursue avenues of further research and learning to support their thoughts and ideas. The entire class becomes invested as a class, not just as individuals within the class.

For students and teachers in kindergarten through grade five classrooms, much passion for teaching and learning abounds. Lively, thoughtful conversations and dynamic discussions are fostered by students' interests and sparked by their exploratory minds. Their questions about an event or the subject being studied never seem to end and are usually generated from other students' thinking. Harrison (2006, 67) believes that "learning is shaped by the experiences that we engage in and also that the power to fashion ideas and beliefs is both greater and more flexible through oral communication than written." Young students surely rely on talk as their foremost method of communication with peers and others. Their vocabulary grows exponentially in the early years as their experiential learning expands, grows, and deepens. The teacher's knowledge and expertise, coupled with the thoughtfully developed, standards-based curriculum units and the planned lessons and instructional activities, strategically lead students into a scaffolding and deepening connection to the content while causing them to think critically about what they are learning. A student's new learning and analytical thinking often trigger connections to real-life situations about which they are eager to share. This cycle of new learning and communal sharing embodies rich assessment opportunities—formatively and summatively.

The continual interchange during the learning experience provides much data to the teacher about what the students know and are able to do, how they think about what is being taught and learned, what questions the students still have, and what they do not understand and/or can't do. Throughout this process, both the teacher and the students are able to adjust their thinking, formulate new questions, explore alternative possibilities, and rethink prior solutions. Additionally, modifications to teacher plans are expected to occur seamlessly based on the needs of the students. Ford-Connors, Robertson, and Paratore (2016, 51) state, "Teachers who learn to attend and respond to the talk of the classroom typically do so seamlessly, making in-the-moment decisions to shape and refine their instruction and strengthen the learning experience for students. The dynamic and interactive nature of these instructional exchanges allows teachers and students to forge collaborative partnerships in the learning process as they work together to construct a trustworthy understanding of what students know and can do."

When students are engaged in language arts instruction and activities during the literacy block, there are ample opportunities for whole class sharing that enables the teacher to gain assessment information related to student progress and learning in literacy. Sharing occurs individually by students, in one-to-one situations, in pairs, in small groups, and as the larger class. The teacher gleans details, information, and anecdotal data that become evidence to support the confirmation of student learning, individually and collectively as a class. Allington (2016, 1) reports that there was "lots of talk across the school day" related to curriculum topics in exemplary teachers' classrooms and that the talk was "more often of a conversational nature than an interrogational nature." Allington further states, "teachers and students discussed ideas, concepts, hypotheses, strategies, and responses with others. The questions teachers posed were more 'open' questions, where multiple responses would be appropriate." Johnston (2004, 4) elaborated on classroom talk by saying, "Teachers play a critical role in arranging the discursive histories from which these children

speak. Talk is the central tool of their trade. With it they mediate children's activity and experience, and help them make sense of learning, literacy, life, and themselves."

This chapter on sharing and assessment looks at these two integral aspects of literacy instruction that cross all components of the language arts block, yet are sometimes considered so basic and seamless that preparing for these critical elements are casual and unplanned. Often, one or both domains might be cut short or left out totally due to a lack of time. Similarly, implementation and reflection in these areas often lead to possible unintended outcomes and a blurry sense of what was accomplished, what skills were mastered, and what students actually learned. This chapter on sharing and assessment examines the concepts, centers on related core principles, emphasizes the class as a whole, and zeros in on effective practices.

"Sharing" and "assessment" are both global themes so, in the next few pages, these big ideas, illuminated through both the teacher and student perspectives, will be channeled to reinforce essential fundamentals. This chapter aims to offer classroom practitioners: (1) tips for purposeful planning, (2) techniques for focused, targeted implementation to increase student motivation and engagement, and (3) strategies for ongoing formative assessment of student progress to maximize learning, improve mastery of skills, and increase student achievement.

## When Does Sharing Typically Occur during Comprehensive Literacy Instruction?

There are varying models for comprehensive literacy instruction and programs in K–5 classrooms. Most programs address state and national Standards and focus on English language arts competencies for all students—fluency, vocabulary development, reading comprehension, and writing. Many literacy programs follow a balanced literacy approach in a literacy block format and include these components: read-aloud, shared reading, guided reading, independent reading, word study, and writing. As teachers prepare and plan for instruction in each of the component areas, sharing activities are woven into each area appropriately with extensions and connections across all of the component parts.

## What Does Sharing Look Like in the Literacy Classroom?

During the language arts block, sharing is such an important priority because it creates a classroom culture that builds relationships between the teacher and the student(s) and also among student(s), while validating rich conversations about books, videos, and other media. Sharing occurs in many different ways during literacy instruction.

- Read-alouds set the stage for demonstrating to students that reading can be a pleasurable learning experience. Read-alouds also develop students' ability to use comprehension strategies to think about a text. When the teacher reads to students expressively and fluently, students learn to enjoy stories, books, and novels in a new way; anticipate reading on their own; and come to understand that reading can be fun. The teacher verbally interacts with the students in many ways during read-alouds. As the teacher introduces a text to be read, possibly through showcasing authentic visual objects or by previewing brief selections, students talk about the text in a substantive conversation. They answer questions, analyze events in the story, make predictions about what will happen next, clarify misconceptions, and make connections. Sharing occurs often and widely during this process.

- During shared reading students are provided many rich opportunities to discover the joys of reading. In this setting students are actively involved in the multiple readings of the chosen book. A sense of community is developed and communication opportunities are abundant for student sharing that extend beyond repeating lines and responses to direct questions. As part of the shared reading session, the teacher enthusiastically supports all students to feel encouraged and confident in making predictions, sharing comments, and relating the book to their personal experiences.

- Guided reading is a time during the literacy block when the teacher works directly with a small group of students and can meet the needs of all the students, so they become more proficient readers. Using this strategy, students read a text that is precisely at their reading ability level, and instruction is directly streamlined to individual needs. The teacher is able to give individual attention to each of the group members and can guide, support, and reinforce skills. The sharing that occurs during guided reading provides the teacher with examples, patterns, and candid illustrations of each student's progress. As the reading materials reach more challenging levels, the teacher can assess how well students apply the strategies learned and observe and document their paths to becoming more successful readers. The teacher can also adjust instruction to better scaffold students' improvement and advancement.

- As a reflective writing activity, students make an entry in their reading logs. There are wide-ranging opportunities for students to share thoughts through writing. Sometimes students may write in response to a question the teacher has asked, sometimes they may write a summary, and sometimes they may reflect on their use of strategies while reading.

- Word study encourages students to explore words and strengthen their vocabulary by learning new words and constructing language. They also learn by manipulating words into meaningful sentences, paragraphs, and stories. During word study, there might be whole class discussion to explore students' understanding of a particular vocabulary word. For example, a term used in the curriculum for the day's journal writing prompt may need to be studied or investigated. The teacher knows the concept of/definition of the vocabulary word is necessary for students to understand the prompt's central focus. Therefore, the teacher spends time having students share their understanding of the meaning of the word and looking up varying definitions, while providing strategies for developing consensus (reading the word in context to ascertain meaning), prior to having them do the task.

- Independent reading time provides students with a voice in the reading process. By selecting the book(s) they wish to read, they have control over what they are interested in and want to learn. Sharing their thoughts about book choice with the teacher provides insight. After reading a fascinating, enlightening, or interesting book, the students will want to tell someone about it. They will want to share what a "really good book it was" and want to tell about the characters, story details, and events; what they learned; etc. Conversations can occur with learning partners, in small groups, or with the entire class about different texts the students read and enjoyed.

- As part of writing workshop, when students develop and refine pieces of writing on topics they've chosen themselves, they can also work with one or more classmates to share, revise, and edit their rough drafts. Their drafts are also then shared with the teacher during a final editing conference.

- The "author's chair" is a literacy strategy that is often integrated into a reading and writing workshop and in which sharing is the essential goal. Students take turns reading their final products aloud to an audience (classmates). Author's chair is an opportunity for writers to receive positive feedback from their classmates. Their classmates enjoy listening to them read aloud because the students have learned how to read with expression, thereby holding their classmates' interest.

- Becoming a savvy and skilled presenter takes practice and involves extemporaneous interaction with audience members. Students develop and perfect their presentation skills by sharing their authentic works in the form of published pieces. They can also share the results of research related to class projects in the form of reports that are informational or explanatory in nature. These presentations are typically made formally and from the front of the class. As a presentation unfolds, the student presenter is expected to provide depth and vividness by sharing core information, clarifying explanations, adding details, answering questions, and including impromptu commentary. This effective sharing activity is designed to also support the development of active speaking and listening skills, including a focus on questioning.

"Talking with others about ideas and work is fundamental to learning. . . . But not all talk sustains learning. For classroom talk to promote learning it must be accountable: to the learning community, to accurate and appropriate knowledge, and to rigorous thinking" (Michaels, O'Connor, and Hall, with Resnick 2013, 1). This is the premise for the research and development of the Accountable Talk program. In their research on accountable talk, Wolf, Crosson, and Resnick examined the relationship between the quality of classroom talk and academic rigor in reading comprehension lessons. The results of their study "provided supportive evidence that a classroom discourse including listening to others, questioning other's knowledge, and exploring one's own thoughts is positively correlated with the academic rigor of reading comprehension." They concluded, "the quality of classroom talk should be considered as a lens with which to look at the classroom culture" (Wolf, Crosson, and Resnick 2005, 50).

Sharing as a whole class is important and produces improved student interaction and achievement. Sharing as a group supports meaningful student-led discussions in which students actively engage with texts, interact verbally and nonverbally with one or more other students, and take ownership of the time and the text. Furthermore, questions become the keystones to new and deeper learning. Powerful targeted questions stimulate complex answers, inspire higher-level vocabulary usage, and instigate the use and synthesis of evidence. Text-dependent questions challenge students to seek out facts and inferences from a text to substantiate their response with proof and data.

Whole class sharing widely kindles innovative thinking, risk-taking, and authentic problem-solving. As this culture of sharing is practiced, students learn to hold themselves more accountable. They also learn to provide understanding through paraphrasing another student's response and/or develop insight into another student's thoughts more completely.

## What Is Formative Assessment, and How Does It Inform Instruction and Learning?

Data used to inform instruction and student progress should be linked with day-to-day interactions between teachers and students. Collecting evidence about student learning is an ongoing and systematic process widely known as formative assessment. The accumulation of evidence assists the teacher in assessing a student's or students' current level of learning, identifying specific learning needs, and providing differentiation, adaptations, and/or modifications to help improve learning to reach the identified learning goals or outcomes. Heritage (2007, 141) classifies three types of formative assessments as means of gathering evidence on student learning. "On-the-fly assessment occurs spontaneously during a lesson . . . . In planned-for-interaction, teachers decide beforehand how they will elicit students' thinking during the course of instruction . . . . Curriculum-embedded assessments . . . solicit feedback at key points in a learning sequence and . . . are part of ongoing classroom activities."

Formative assessment also provides the teacher with a process to assess one's own teaching and decision-making. Self-reflective questions can be asked after creating and delivering an instructional unit or lesson. Questions posed by a fifth-grade teacher (Stephens 2013, 120–121) include: "Is there a better way to ask that question? Can I teach that skill another way? Should I pull a small group to revisit that concept? What did I say that confused students so badly? Well, that worked well, so can I incorporate that same structure into other units? Did I assess a

student on a genre she or he was unfamiliar with? Why was that student unsuccessful with that text?"

## How Does Sharing Inform Assessment?

Throughout the formative assessment process, students should be engaged and participate actively with the teacher. As part of the daily literacy instructional period, ongoing interactions occur, and sharing (oral and written) is the fundamental mode of communication among teacher and students. Ford-Connors, Robertson, and Paratore (2016, 50) tell us that "When considering the range of classroom-based assessment tools available to teachers, one of richest sources is also one of the most accessible: teacher and student talk. These dialogic exchanges often provide the first, and perhaps most spontaneous and telling glimpses into students' developing understandings (Auckerman 2007)."

Students in kindergarten through grade five are capable of being involved as real partners in their learning. And students of all ages can contribute thoughtful commentary on likes, dislikes, areas of interest, successes, challenges, and possible solutions. During informal conversations and formal conferences, students will reflect on and share insights about their personal learning, how their learning is progressing, what they are having trouble with, and what steps might help them to do better. Feedback from the teacher and other classmates, with numerous opportunities to "try out" and use the feedback, provide students with information about how they are doing in the effort to reach a goal.

Often, assessment data gathered from informal and formal sharing sessions by students in one-on-one and small group instruction informs the teacher's plan for whole class instruction. Linking assessment in the literacy classroom with student growth and achievement meshes together perfectly. Marzano (2006, 7) indicates, "major reviews of the research on the effects of classroom assessment indicate that it might be one of the most powerful tools in a teacher's arsenal." Ongoing informal and formal classroom assessment is the connective tissue that holds teaching and learning together, especially during literacy instruction. It can shape learning and instruction and assist teachers in gauging student mastery of grade-level language arts and literacy skills required by national and state Standards and summative assessments. If students are included in the assessment process/cycle, they will be better able to improve their personal performances as they have insight into the expectations and the tasks.

Assessment of sharing experiences and activities is an important priority that should always be a prime feature of every literacy unit, daily lesson, mini-lesson, workshop, and activity. In actuality, assessment and the goals for what will be assessed should be planned for even before a unit, lesson, mini-lesson, workshop, or an activity is prepared. Assessment benchmarks should be correlated with national and state Standards that have been unpacked, represent mastery of knowledge and/or skills, and are a component of the district's approved curriculum.

Formative assessment is assessment for learning and provides information needed to adjust teaching and learning while they are happening in real time. Formative assessment conversations in which feedback, supported by evidence, is provided bolsters the student's understanding of the expected learning outcomes by clarifying the task(s) and the level of desired performance. The teacher is also able to provide specific steps that can be taken to accelerate progress.

## Sharing and Assessment in Literacy Classrooms: Two Perspectives— the Teacher and the Student

### The Teacher's Role

#### Focus on Students: Who Are the Learners?

More than ever, all teachers in twenty-first century classrooms must be prepared to meet the wide-ranging spectrum of educational, social, and emotional needs of students from widely divergent cultures possessing diverse perspectives, experiences,

strengths, and challenges. Every student brings rich and varied language and cultural experiences, and these attributes and experiences must be recognized and valued. Equally importantly, each student's academic characteristics must be understood and addressed through a spectrum of learning options and designs that maximize their potential and represent the highest quality instruction.

The role of the teacher in the literacy classroom promotes the success of each child through multiple pathways—motivation, student interest, scaffolding of skill development, differentiation to accommodate strengths and challenges, support for struggling students, and providing enrichment and acceleration of content and materials designed to challenge all students. In the literacy classroom, each student must intrinsically feel valued, engaged, supported, and academically challenged. Transforming students into prolific readers and writers is a complex, challenging mission. Teachers must actively plan and prepare effective lessons and dynamically demonstrate successful strategies that skilled readers and writers embody.

The beginning of the school year is generally centered on defining common expectations, developing student behaviors, and setting up procedures and routines. Students become acclimated to this instructional model while "testing the waters" and developing trust between each other as classmates in a learning community. As the school year progresses, the process moves quickly into more authentic experiences, which are held more and more frequently so the model becomes more comprehensive. A plan of established classroom practices(s) is set forth on a daily basis. It is the vision in a sharing-based classroom that student participation is nonnegotiable, meaning every student must participate.

Teachers in literacy classrooms are likely to implement proven and effective literacy instructional strategies applicable for the whole class. They are expected to carry out the instructional changes they believe are likely to improve student performance in reading and writing and raise student achievement. Changes they choose to implement may include, but are not limited to, one or more of the following:

- allocating more time for topics with which students are struggling;

- reordering the curriculum to shore up essential skills with which students are struggling;

- designating particular students to receive additional help with particular skills (i.e., grouping or regrouping students);

- attempting new ways of teaching difficult or complex concepts, especially based on best practices identified by teaching colleagues;

- better aligning performance expectations among classrooms or between grade levels; and/or

- better aligning curricular emphasis among grade levels.

## Focus on Content: What Do We Teach?

For English language arts teachers who provide literacy instruction to students in kindergarten through grade five, the focus on curriculum and content is critical. In research-based literacy models, most purchased literacy programs, and in many district-designed customized programs of study, literacy skill development is aligned with the goals of national and state Standards and the recently implemented ELA summative assessments. According to the English Language Arts Common Core State Standards (National Governors Association Center for Best Practices and the Council of Chief State School Officers 2010, 8), there are key features in each of the component areas of the Standards.

- Reading: text complexity and the growth of comprehension

- Writing: text types, responding to reading, and research

- Speaking and Listening: flexible communication and collaboration

- Language: conventions, effective use, and vocabulary

Research-based best practices inform us that curriculum, instruction, assessment, and professional learning are the foundational elements upon which an effective program of instruction is built. Teachers should be focused on the core content of the subject, teaching an integrated curriculum, differentiating instruction to meet individual student needs, and providing active learning opportunities for students to internalize learning. Additionally, teachers need to focus on the following aspects of curriculum implementation:

- proactive planning and preparation

- rigorous, purposeful objectives that are measurable

- sequential skill development

- supporting, challenging, enriching, and accelerating content

- scaffolding content supports for students

- protocols of sharing skills

- demonstrations of knowledge

- applications of understandings and learning

The curriculum is the cornerstone of teaching and learning. Time and effort need to be invested into constructing a robust and rigorous curriculum that is flexible. It must be adaptable to accommodate ever-changing mandates while maintaining integrity to content, standards, and research-based best practices.

## Focus on Assessment: How Are Students Performing?

Formative assessment helps to ensure students achieve targeted standards-based learning goals within a set time frame. Formative assessment:

- serves as practice for students; these assessments should not be graded (only assessed).

- provides information and evidence to the teacher to adjust teaching and learning in "real time."

- helps teachers differentiate instruction and thus improve student achievement.

- promotes checking for understanding along the way.

- guides teacher decision-making about planning and conducting future instruction.
- embeds proven effective instructional strategies for the whole class into the scheduled assessment opportunities.

For assessment to work and make a difference in the literacy classroom, the teacher must focus on each student's individual needs while teaching the required grade-level curriculum. Assessments such as classroom experiences and planned activities, performance tasks, and work products provide evidence of student progress toward mastery. In a sharing-focused classroom these elements can be assessed regularly as the teacher is engaged with the whole class.

The teacher can consider all of these as formative assessment artifacts that can be embedded into a whole class sharing experience. Many of the suggestions are based on sharing experiences that are student-focused.

- Observations—While students are engaged in an activity, the teacher walks around the room. The teacher may be observing for ability with a specific skill upon which the lesson is focused or student interactions in pairs or in small groups. The teacher will record what he or she sees as informal notes in order to drive future instruction.

- Questioning—Asking high-quality questions provides students with opportunities for deep thinking. Throughout the interplay of questioning, teachers gain substantive insight into the breadth of student knowledge and depth of student understanding. Questioning also engages students in conversation, dialogue, and discussion; strengthens students' confidence; and increases student learning. It is important that questions be well designed, elicit higher-order thinking skills, and lead students to more questions of their own. Using text-based questioning as a strategy in a close reading of a text is used in literacy to increase reading comprehension through text analysis.

- Discussion—Classroom discussions play an important role in the sharing classroom. Discussion is an exchange of ideas usually focused on reaching a decision, solving a problem, or exploring a particular topic with varying viewpoints. Teachers plan discussions for student interactions on content topics, texts being read, open-ended questions, and so on. The goal is for students to build knowledge, develop critical and creative thinking skills, and enhance listening and speaking skills. Discussions allow students to learn new information from others, deepen their understanding of a topic, and provide new perspectives about the issue. It is also an opportunity for teachers to observe depth of understanding.

- Journals—Using journal writing and integrating journals across the curriculum have many documented benefits. Higher-order student thinking and critical writing skills are embedded in the process of keeping journals. There are many types of journaling that can be done. In language arts students can use a writer's notebook where they keep all their writing. This includes drafts and finished samples. The teacher reviews selected writing artifacts periodically throughout the year and conferences with students to discuss strengths and weaknesses related to the work samples.

- Assignments and Projects—Assignments and projects are performance-based assessments directly related to the goals of the curriculum unit and/or the planned lesson. Assignments and projects engage students in structured activities in which they are able to practice, integrate, or extend new learning. They grow out of the content, speak to students' interests, and encourage students to do research, show evidence, and provide documentation. They can be completed individually or in small groups. The teacher can create a rubric to assess student performance and learning. Some sample assignments that engage students in sharing what they have read might include:

- creating a visual representation of an important character or event in the story;

- producing a word wall with unfamiliar words from the novel they are reading;

- writing a letter to the author of the assigned book, asking questions about a particular character;

- examining newspaper articles, television reports, and websites about a particular topic and asking if they agree or disagree with the way the stories were told;

- creating a collaborative Twitter poster in which students summarize the main idea of a short written piece on a sentence strip using 140 characters and pin their strips to the poster to resemble a Twitter feed.

- Peer and Self-assessments—Peer and self-assessments help to foster the concept of the classroom as a learning community. Students who set personal instructional goals and then self-assess become more engaged in their own learning. Students are far more aware of their personal strengths and weaknesses and share that information when conferencing with the teacher. Peer assessments enable students to view each other as resources for checking for understanding and quality work against predetermined criteria. The teacher can analyze the self-assessments and the peer assessments to identify strengths and weaknesses.

- Practice Presentations—Teachers schedule "practice sessions" for students to present to the entire class or as part of a small group. During these sessions students practice their presentation skills, following a prescribed presentation model and an established rubric, and receive peer feedback. These sessions are held in advance of the final presentations, so students get to authentically practice their skills. This process enables students to enhance their speaking and listening skills, work on vocabulary and grammar, and demonstrate their knowledge of the content. Through the peer feedback, students receive constructive information they can use to enhance their skills. By simply viewing the practice and final presentations, the teacher can appraise the improvement in student performance and the level of student understanding of the content, concept, and topic. The teacher also gains significant insight to plan future lessons accordingly.

## The Student's Role

The student has an equally valuable position in the whole class sharing model. The role of the student is that of a learner, collaborator, and team member. There is a responsibility on the part of every student to become actively involved in his or her own learning and care about how he or she interacts within the classroom setting. Students must also become invested in learning how to learn. Therefore, their advances in achievement are built on their own increased capabilities and solid, core learnings. In addition, future learning becomes easier and current understandings continue to grow and deepen exponentially. For example, students should contribute to classroom discussions by answering questions posed by the teacher and questions posed by their classmates. Students should also ask questions or express their own ideas about a subject to their teacher and their peers.

## Engagement in Learning

According to *The Glossary of Education Reform* (2014), "Student engagement refers to the degree of attention, curiosity, interest, optimism, and passion that students show when they are learning or being taught, which extends to the level of motivation they have to learn and progress in their education . . . the concept of 'student engagement' is predicated on the belief that learning improves when students are inquisitive, interested, or inspired." In a sharing-based classroom, these attributes are important qualities that permeate the culture of the class and add to the level of teacher enthusiasm that, in turn, promotes more and more quality sharing experiences.

The student, personally and as a member of the class community, is expected to actively engage in learning. Moreover, the student should wholly immerse himself or herself in total participation to demonstrate knowledge and apply understanding of the content in new and novel situations. The goal is to capture student interest and couple it with a vibrant level of enthusiasm and engagement shared by the entire class.

## Participation as a Speaker and Listener

Conversations and discussions that are rich and enlightening experiences for students are important aspects of a sharing classroom. A classroom climate and culture steeped in mutual caring and respect is the hallmark of a safe and trusting environment in which students feel secure in sharing, providing feedback, and communicating thoughtfully. These are the skills that are needed to be college and career ready, and there are practices to put in place to reinforce these skills.

"To build a foundation for college and career readiness, students must have ample opportunities to take part in a variety of rich, structured conversations—as part of a whole class, in small groups, and with a partner. Being productive members of these conversations requires that students contribute accurate, relevant information; respond to and develop what others have said; make comparisons and contrasts; and analyze and synthesize a multitude of ideas in various domains" (National Governors Association Center for Best Practices and the Council of Chief State School Officers 2010, 22). Furthermore, Macula (2016, 123) articulates, "Students must be able to pay attention to the flow and content of conversations and actively take part in discussions, building off other students' ideas and thoughts. High-quality, structured classroom discussions focus all students on considering relevant information, assessing facts, making comparisons with other sources, developing their speaking points using evidence, and cementing their point of view on the topic." As we prepare students for their future lives and to communicate

in the world of work, students need to exhibit both active speaking and attentive listening skills. These skills are developed daily in literacy experiences in language arts classrooms.

## Examine One's Own Data and Set Personal Learning Goals

Students should be provided with explicit instruction on using achievement data regularly to monitor their own performance and establish their own goals for learning. They can keep a record or a log of their academic progress and grades. The data analysis can motivate elementary students by mapping out accomplishments that are possible and achievable, revealing actual achievement gains, and providing students with a sense of control over their own outcomes. Teachers can then use these goals to better understand factors that may motivate student performance and adjust their instructional practices accordingly. Similarly, students should be encouraged to maintain a "work folder" or a "portfolio" containing artifacts demonstrating their progress over time, as well as completed projects, work samples, and exemplars that have been graded and include written feedback.

A sample weekly "Student Learning Goals and Grade Log" is offered for use in the language arts classroom. The log is student-centered and provides an opportunity for students to initiate their performance goals and express how they will work on their goals during the weekly time frame. This log also provides an interactive way for the teacher to provide comments about student progress.

## Student Learning Goals and Grade Log

Student Name:

For the Week of:

### In Language Arts Class

| My strengths are: | 1. | 2. | 3. |
| I need to work on: | 1. | 2. | 3. |

### My Weekly Learning Goals

My first goal is to:

To achieve this goal, I plan to . . .

My second goal is to:

To achieve this goal, I plan to . . .

My third goal is to:

To achieve this goal, I plan to . . .

### My Progress this Week

| | Yes | No | Comments | Teacher Signature |
| --- | --- | --- | --- | --- |
| My progress on Goal 1 is satisfactory: | | | | |
| My progress on Goal 2 is satisfactory: | | | | |
| My progress on Goal 3 is satisfactory: | | | | |
| My assignments are up to date: | | | | |
| My behavior is appropriate: | | | | |
| My participation is acceptable: | | | | |

## Use Feedback to Improve Performance

Effective feedback for students contains information that a student can use. In the language arts classroom, students have many opportunities to receive feedback about aspects of their performance or understanding from their teachers and peers. Feedback should be provided clearly, so students understand the recommendations and suggestions. Feedback should also be given in a timely manner so students remember the task and skills being assessed. Assessment data should be returned to students within a week of collecting an assignment, and sooner when possible. Feedback should provide concrete information and tangible suggestions for improvement. Explanations, examples, and suggestions for additional practice are more concrete and easier for students to act on than a score or letter grade alone, and the remarks and commentary may increase students' confidence and motivate better performance.

The students are responsible to translate the feedback into action. They need to be able to articulate the knowledge or skills they are aiming to develop or improve. Additionally, the students need to know: Where am I now? How close am I to meeting the expected goal? How do I get there? What do I need to do next? What steps should I follow? Creating and using rubrics are an effective means to assist students in assessing their personal performance and showcasing the tasks to be completed. They also indicate the acquisition of knowledge and skills needed to scaffold the students' current performance to a potential level of mastery and/or completion.

## Engage in Rigorous Assignments

Students should be engaged with assignments that match the rigor of grade-level or above assignments. The work students complete should be more substantive, more challenging, and require more self-regulation. Particularly in the literacy setting, and following the balanced literacy approach, it is critical that students have many opportunities for reading and writing engagement with grade-level materials,

in addition to the "just-right" levels, so students can systematically progress in their development and reach higher proficiency levels.

## Develop Autonomy and Independence

The gradual release of responsibility model of instruction (Duke and Pearson 2002, 211) "requires that the teacher shift from assuming all the responsibility for performing a task . . . to a situation in which the students assume all of the responsibility." One of the four interrelated components of a gradual release of responsibility model (Fisher and Frey, 2008) is "independent work." According to Fisher (2008, 1), independent learning provides students "practice with applying information in new ways. In doing so, students synthesize information, transform ideas, and solidify their understanding."

The English Language Arts Common Core State Standards (National Governors Association Center for Best Practices and the Council of Chief State School Officers 2010, 7) portray students who have met the Standards as demonstrating independence. Students can "comprehend and evaluate complex texts across a range of types and disciplines, and they can construct effective arguments and convey intricate or multifaceted information. Likewise, students are able to independently discern a speaker's key points, request clarification, and ask relevant questions. They build on others' ideas, articulate their own ideas, and confirm they have been understood. Without prompting, they demonstrate command of standard English and acquire and use a wide-ranging vocabulary. More broadly, they become self-directed learners, effectively seeking out and using resources to assist them, including teachers, peers, and print and digital reference materials."

In order to thrive in our global society that is entrepreneurial, technology-forward, and innovative, students need to develop skills and dispositions that will enable them to be successful as independent performers, as well as collaborators and global community contributors. They will be creating their own world of work. It is critical that students possess literacy skills that enable them to communicate effectively, solve complex problems creatively, think quantitatively and qualitatively, and produce quality products, documents, and reports that analyze data efficiently. Students will be expected to apply their knowledge in new and novel situations and must be able to do so seamlessly, thoughtfully, and thoroughly.

## Summary

The chapters in this book examine specific components of effective literacy instruction. This chapter is intended to provide a context for understanding how to create and implement sharing opportunities for students. It also explains how sharing supports learning goals and strengthens formative assessment to inform students' progress as effective readers and writers. Throughout this chapter, sharing and assessment were developed as critical components of effective literacy instruction and integral to all component parts of the literacy block.

Working with a whole class provides students with a shared experience every day in a literacy environment. This experience is as rich and diverse as every one of the students in the class. Every student has much to offer and contributes in a unique and real way, bringing a cultural background; home, school, and worldly experiences; and ideas, dreams, and perspectives forward during every sharing opportunity.

Although the teacher is the foremost model, each student has daily opportunities to model knowledge, skills, and behaviors that exemplify excellent and appropriate sharing techniques and practices. Students develop effective communication, collaboration, complex thinking, discovery, and creativity skills in an extraordinary, but natural and routine way. Students learn a great deal from each other and about each other through sharing. These skills are internalized over a long period of time—the school year. The culture of the classroom, given this instructional model for sharing, develops

a more sophisticated level of communication and interaction, thereby providing students with intense and powerful opportunities to maximize their fullest potential.

Assessment, in all forms, provides teachers with evidence-based data to determine adjustments in instructional practices, based on students' distinctive needs. Effective teachers use a variety of assessments to learn from and with their students, as students are active contributors and have a responsibility for being committed participants. As discussed in the chapter, formative assessment is not an event, but an ongoing process. Teachers are the designers and observers throughout the process and need to flexibly make instructional decisions with the goal of impacting instruction and student learning.

Sharing and assessing seem like simple constructs, but together, when implemented in the literacy classroom, they are powerful in their possibilities. Both collectively shape an instructional blueprint for student success and improved performance. This potent experience positions students toward increased achievement and better performance on formative and summative English language arts assessments.

Leveraging the power of sharing and assessment to strengthen and enhance students' literacy skills in reading, writing, speaking, and listening must become a top priority. If we are to prepare students to become college and career ready and to live in society as twenty-first century global citizens, then we need to strategically utilize these two constructs as the transformational change-agents to inspire, develop, and escalate students as literate human beings possessing premier literacy knowledge and skills.

## References and Resources

Abbott, S. (Ed.). 2014. "Hidden Curriculum." *The Glossary of Education Reform*, August 26. http://edglossary.org/hidden-curriculum.

Allington, Richard. 2016. "The Six Ts of Effective Elementary Literacy Instruction." Reading Rockets. http://www.readingrockets.org/article/six-ts-effective-elementary-literacy-instruction.

Auckerman, Maren S. 2007. "When Reading It Wrong Is Getting It Right: Shared Evaluation Pedagogy Among Struggling Fifth Grade Readers." *Research in the Teaching of English*, 42 (1), 56–103. https://sites.ehe.osu.edu/bedmiston/files/2013/03/AukermanRTE2007.pdf.

Donnelly, Amy and Amy Oswalt. 2013. "Chapter 2—Portrait 8: Amy Oswalt, Fifth-Grade Teacher: Finding Children's Strengths: Assessment as a Thinking Process." In *Reading Assessment: Artful Teachers, Successful Students*, edited by Diane Stephens, 119–134. Urbana, IL: NCTE. http://www.ncte.org/library/NCTEFiles/Resources/Books/Sample/30773Portrait8.pdf.

Duke, N. K. and P. D. Pearson. 2002. "Effective Practices for Developing Reading Comprehension." In *What Research Has to Say About Reading Instruction*, edited by A. E. Farstup and S. J. Samuels, 205–242. Newark, DE: International Reading Association.

Fisher, Douglas. 2008. "Effective Use of the Gradual Release of Responsibility Model." Author Monograph, December. https://www.mheonline.com/_treasures/pdf/douglas_fisher.pdf.

Fisher, Douglas, and Nancy Frey. 2008. *Better Learning Through Structured Teaching: A Framework for the Gradual Release of Responsibility*. Alexandria, VA: ASCD.

Ford-Connors, Evelyn, Dana A. Robertson, and Jeanne R. Paratore. 2016. "Classroom Talk as (In)Formative Assessment." *Voices from the Middle* 23 (3): 50–57. http://www.ncte.org/library/NCTEFiles/Resources/Journals/VM/0233-mar2016/VM0233Classroom.pdf.

Harrison, Christine. 2006. "Banishing the Quiet Classroom." *Education Review*, 19 (2): 67–77. https://www.researchgate.net/publication/275340695_Banish_the_Quiet_Classroom.

Heritage, Margaret. 2007. "Formative Assessment: What Do Teachers Need to Know and Do?" *Phi Delta Kappan*, 89 (2): 140–145. http://www.pdkmembers.org/members_online/publications/Archive/pdf/k0710her.pdf.

Johnston, Peter H. 2004. *Choice Words: How Our Language Affects Children's Learning*. Portland, ME: Stenhouse.

Macula, Adele T. 2016. *From the Classroom to the Test: How to Improve Student Achievement on the Summative ELA Assessments*. North Mankato, MN: Maupin House by Capstone Professional.

Marzano, Robert J. 2006. *Classroom Assessment and Grading That Work*. Alexandria, VA: ASCD.

Michaels, Sarah, Mary Catherine O'Connor, and Megan Williams Hall, with Lauren B. Resnick. 2013. Accountable Talk® Sourcebook: For Classroom Conversation That Works. Pittsburgh, PA: Institute for Learning—University of Pittsburgh. http://ifl.pitt.edu/index.php/educator_resources/accountable_talk.

National Council of Teachers of English. 2013. "Formative Assessment That Truly Informs Instruction." Urbana, IL: NCTE. http://www.ncte.org/library/NCTEFiles/Resources/Positions/formative-assessment_single.pdf.

National Governors Association Center for Best Practices and Council of Chief State School Officers. Common Core State Standards for English Language Arts and Literacy in History/Social Studies, Science, and Technical Subjects. 2010. Washington, DC: Authors. http://www.corestandards.org/wp-content/uploads/ELA_Standards1.pdf.

Public Schools of North Carolina Department of Public Instruction: Elementary Division. "Best Practices: A Resource for Teachers." North Carolina: Authors. http://www.ncpublicschools.org/docs/curriculum/bpractices2.pdf.

Wolf, Mikyung Kim, Amy C. Crosson, and Lauren B. Resnick. 2005. "Classroom Talk for Rigorous Reading Comprehension Instruction." *Reading Psychology*, 26: 27–53. DOI: 10.1080/02702710490897518 https://msimplementation.wikispaces.com/file/view/wolfclassroom.pdf.

# English Language Learner Support in a Comprehensive Literacy Program

Becky McTague and Kristin Lems

## Introduction

As we have seen in previous chapters of this book, a good comprehensive literacy program offers a wide range of activities and projects, which, taken in combination, comprise a memorable experience for young learners. When teachers design and implement a comprehensive literacy program, they offer appealing projects across the school year, so students are nurtured, challenged, and supported. Students enjoy taking part in activities such as journaling, paired reading, project-based learning, self-paced fluency practices, read-alouds, author studies, and a wealth of other techniques, all of which instill in young learners a lifelong love of literacy. English language learners (ELLs) also derive great benefit from such an approach.

However, there are important ways in which ELLs in an elementary language arts classroom need specific kinds of language support, and these need to be intentionally embedded in the teaching plan. This chapter lays out some of the ways teachers can meet the special talents and needs of ELLs.

## Learning a New Language

The way in which a literacy program is designed and delivered can positively impact the educational outcomes of ELLs. There are some elements that need to be in place, however, because learners of a second language may require different considerations than those acquiring a native language. Here is a brief review of some of the important features of second language acquisition (SLA).

## Social Language vs. Academic Language

One of the important findings in the field of second language acquisition has been the realization that children obtain skills in a new language in two different ways. Social language, which has been called the language of "BICS" or "Basic Interpersonal Communicative Skills" (Cummins 1981), can be acquired through social contact with others, and it takes 1–3 years for a child to attain (Thomas and Collier 2002). Once ELLs master BICS language, which is mostly oral, they speak as quickly and comfortably as native speakers of English, and for this reason, teachers may assume they have the same knowledge of the language as native English speakers. Academic language, called "CALP" or "Cognitive Academic Language Proficiency," on the other hand, is not acquired naturally, but must be learned in school. Becoming proficient in CALP often takes 7–8 years to achieve, and it takes a great deal of sustained effort on the part of the learner and the instructors (Thomas and Collier 2002). While all children are charged to learn the content areas of the curriculum in school, ELLs also have to learn and perform in the language in which the content areas are being taught. This is no small task, and this grand undertaking deserves our utmost respect and commitment to them.

## Language Develops Differently

ELLs' language and literacy develops differently from that of native English speakers. A child's language growth depends on many factors, including the age at which he or she is introduced to English, prior schooling, first language literacy, the family's educational level, closeness of the first language to English, and the instructional program. Some of these differences are completely individual to each child. Others, such as the following three factors, apply to many learners and are based on an understanding of second language acquisition.

- The *silent period*: In general, listening comprehension precedes speaking, and reading comprehension precedes writing. This explains why some ELLs experience a preproduction period, or *silent period*. During the silent period, learners are actively absorbing and mentally organizing their new language, but they are not at the point of being ready to produce speech. When students are in this phase, teachers may think they have a cognitive impairment, but it is a common stage of language acquisition. There are several ways to keep students involved in the classroom when they are in the silent period. They can perform a nonverbal activity, such as pointing out something in a picture or sorting objects. They can also act out procedures to indicate comprehension using a technique called Total Physical Response (Asher 1969). When children move out of the silent period, teachers are often startled by how much the child is able to say (Lems, Miller, and Soro 2010, 56). The silent period may last up to most of an academic year.

- *Listening level:* ELLs will have less listening stamina than native English speakers because processing oral language in a new language takes a tremendous amount of mental energy. For this reason, they will also be less likely to remember what they have heard. Francisco Jimenez, author of the book *The Circuit*, recollects his school days learning English:

> By the end of the day, I was very tired of hearing Miss Scalapino talk because the sounds made no sense to me. I thought that perhaps by paying close attention I would begin to understand, but I did not. I only got a headache, and that night, when I went to bed, I heard her voice in my head.
> — *The Circuit* by Francisco Jimenez (1997, 17–18)

ELLs may appear inattentive during teacher-centered instruction because they are simply tired from the mental exercise. It is important to avoid lengthy teacher-centered instruction, including long oral directions. Also, clear directions for all procedures should be posted in the room, so ELLs can check for anything they missed when it was spoken.

- *Spelling and writing:* The nature of an ELL's spelling and writing will be greatly influenced by his or her first language writing system and first language literacy. In general, first language literacy is a big aid to second language acquisition (Cummins 1981). That being said, ELLs may write English words using letters from their first language. For example, a Spanish-speaking ELL might spell the English word "city" as "siri" because that is the way the Spanish letters would sound when saying the English word "city." Spelling mistakes made by ELLs are different from spelling mistakes made by native English speakers, and this should not be considered a learning disability but a developmental stage. In writing, ELLs may need more explicit instruction in the skills of writing, and peer editing may not be appropriate (Lems, Miller, and Soro 2010).

## The Affective Filter

This phrase was coined by Krashen (1982) to describe the emotional stress that language learners may face when they cannot understand or communicate in a new language. When the "filter" is high, ELLs cannot produce, understand, or remember new language because they are in a state of high anxiety. Of course, we all feel stress when we are trying to learn new things, but stress is even more paralyzing in language learning because language is a primary way we communicate with others, and it forms a central part of our identity.

These classroom practices tend to raise the affective filter:
- calling on a student to answer in front of the whole class
- mispronouncing a student's name
- requiring a student to read aloud
- pointing out or correcting errors when the student is trying to express him or herself
- high-stakes timed tests
- basing assessments on "cold readings" of a text

Fortunately, there are many ways to create and maintain a classroom with a low affective filter.

Classroom practices that lower the affective filter:
- using formative assessments and allowing more time
- putting students in pairs or small groups and reporting to only 1–2 others
- focusing on students' expression of ideas and feelings, both orally and in writing
- avoiding assignments that require learners to react to a single exposure to a text, by giving opportunities to read or hear a text more than once
- using a system of corrections using "recasts" (teacher rephrases the student's sentence correctly, in a natural context, without mentioning that it is a correction) resulting in student "uptake" (students modify their output to match the teacher's corrected sentence) (Doughty and Williams 1998)
- finding out how children wish to be called, pronouncing their preferred names correctly, and not calling attention to your own attempts

## Providing ELL Support in Whole Groups and Small Groups

Now let's look at ways that teachers can apply effective practices in a language arts classroom. Because ELLs need a low affective filter as well as extensive opportunities to practice English, small groups are often the best arrangement. We will touch upon these areas:

- Building Background Knowledge
- Collaborative Learning
- Multiple Representations of Content
- Formative Assessments
- Affirming Cultures

### Building Background Knowledge Through Interactive Read-aloud

Building background knowledge is just as important for native speakers of English as it is for ELLs. Background knowledge is the fertile soil upon which the child's learning grows. It can be built in both whole group and small group arrangements. One powerful technique that builds background knowledge is the interactive read-aloud. We chose the book *Katie Woo Tries Something New* (Manushkin 2015) as an exemplar, not only because it's a fun and popular book, but because kids who enjoy a book that is part of a series are more likely to read more books in the series, thus increasing their reading volume. Note that this book includes several stories within it. Teachers can conduct an interactive read-aloud using the following steps:

1. Hold up the book, slowly read the title and examine the cover art, and ask students what they think the book will be about. Questions for beginning level ELLs, spoken slowly, might include, "What is the name of the girl in the picture?" "What is she doing in the picture?" Or "How many words are in the title?" For children with greater proficiency, consider questions such as, "Who learned something new this week?" Providing generous wait time gives ELLs the time needed to gather their thoughts and words. After a child provides a response, repeat it slowly and correctly, so the learner hears it again.

2. Do a "picture walk" through the first story, slowly turning the pages, commenting on the pictures, and pausing to think aloud. This procedure helps to teach new vocabulary and text features. The vocabulary for the first story includes common activities in the early grades, such as "cartwheel" and "somersault," and activities about learning something new. Since *Katie Woo* is divided into stories, previewing the story titles to predict coming events helps children learn about text features. Other books in this series have a great deal of information about school and community activities, which are important background knowledge for ELLs. When children hear these books read aloud, they will have this background knowledge in mind by the time they read later by themselves. Time spent building background knowledge before reading a book is time well spent, and it should not be rushed.

3. After the picture walk, ask students to predict what they think is going to happen in the story.

4. Read the story aloud expressively.

5. Connect the story to children's own experiences. For children in the silent period, ask them to point to activities performed by Katie. For beginning level learners questions might include, "What is Katie learning to do?" or "Was it hard for Katie to learn something new?" For more proficient learners, ask them to relate stories about a child who tried a new sports activity or someone who joined a club or team. Narrate your own stories before inviting students to tell theirs. Engaging in dialog about the students' stories is time well spent because it builds oral language skills.

The interactive read-aloud of a book can take place over several days because there are so many aspects of balanced literacy that can be performed and rehearsed with ELLs. It can even lead to having students write or dictate stories (Lems and Abousalem 2014). For ELLs, the combination of a teacher's clear explanations along with patient coaxing and encouragement lets students know their own voices are valued. Over time, they will begin to find the means to tell about their lives and the lives of their families and to feel part of the classroom community.

## Collaborative Learning

Collaborative learning is done in small groups. The groupings can be structured either by cooperative learning (Johnson, Johnson, and Holubec 1993) or collaborative learning (Panitz 1999). Both foster more student participation than in a whole group. In cooperative learning the teacher assigns tasks to members of a small group, and each student is responsible for a piece of the work. ELLs in the silent period might be given a nonverbal assignment, such as creating a drawing. However, cooperative learning is still teacher-directed, and some students find it stressful due to the element of competition, which can occur when teachers verbally or nonverbally favor one group's project. Collaborative learning, on the other hand, is student-directed. Students talk and work on a project together, creating their own processes and sharing their work. In cooperative learning, completing the product is the most important part, whereas in collaborative learning, the process is just as important as the product.

In order to have effective collaborative learning, carefully consider the current English proficiency levels of the ELLs and the purpose of the small group activity. Although there is "chemistry" to small groups that cannot always be boiled down to a checklist, there are some factors that make small groups more likely to succeed:

Considerations to facilitate small groups with ELLs:
- Take care that one or more of the group members has a sufficient proficiency level in English to perform the activities, modify the activities, or find first language resources to assist.
- Model procedures before breaking into small groups, so ELLs can see what you are expecting.
- Assign three students to a group if language proficiency levels in the class make that possible; if not, try four students.
- When completing a whole class activity within small groups, use an adaptation of the "think/pair/share" technique. Students share thoughts in response to something they listen to or read within the small group before they share it again with the whole class. Think/pair/shares give ELLs a "dry run" and more time to practice saying the words, which lowers the affective filter.
- Use purposeful grouping according to the project. If reading together, group students by similar reading levels (homogeneous grouping). If there is an oral activity or a creative project, mixed reading levels (heterogeneous grouping) may do better.
- Use a variety of criteria to group students, including teacher assigned and student chosen groups. Decide in advance which one you want, and state your choice clearly to students.
- Use groupings not just for academic purposes, but for other classroom routines as well, such as tidying up the class at the end of the day or preparing and passing out a snack.

Besides making deliberate decisions about grouping, teachers need to act as facilitators of the group process. Here are some suggestions:

---

Suggestions for facilitating the small group process:

1. Create problem-based tasks. For example, ask students to solve a logic problem together and explain their reasoning.
2. Use "essential questions" with tasks. For example, ask more "how" questions than "what" questions.
3. Create "think questions" for use at centers. For example, post "What is happening in this story?" at a listening center.
4. Provide high-quality, open-ended questions for discussions.
5. Establish a clear start date, end date, and assigned time for the project each week.
6. Make expectations clear, and keep them posted and visible.

---

Such projects help ELLs acquire social language (BICS) and academic language (CALP) at the same time, which is just about the perfect balance. Key to framing collaborative learning is thinking about the purpose for the groups and making the purpose clear to the students. Is it connected to regular classroom routines, like center work? Is it connected to part of a larger unit? How long will the students be working in this group, and what is the expectation at the end? These projects need to be connected to a unified concept, both in their purpose and their techniques (Frey and Fisher 2013).

## Multiple Representations of Content

Content can be represented and accessed in many different forms, including written and spoken words, images, body language, graphic organizers, videos, songs, manipulatives, and many others. Some of these representations can be easily implemented in the classroom, such as three we have chosen to highlight on the pages that follow: language walls, hand signals, and realia. These techniques support text and provide increased paths of access to learners still becoming proficient in English. Some learners might know how an object looks but not know how it is represented in written form. Other learners might know the meaning of a word in spoken form but not know how it works as part of a sentence. Multiple representations of content increase an ELL's possible points of entry into the material.

**Language walls** (Policastro and McTague 2015) are similar to word walls, but language walls support language and vocabulary development. Word walls are a systematic and organized collection of words posted on a wall or displayed in a classroom. This visual presentation of the words can be a reference for students for sight words, spelling words, or other collections of words. Many times word walls become merely decorative and are not used to their full potential. Language walls, in contrast, represent words, in poster form, that have been part of instruction, discussions, readings, or other sources. They pull out and emphasize the language from these activities and routines, so students can learn the specific language, vocabulary, and concepts associated with the content area. Language walls are also similar to anchor charts, which have specific groups of words, new vocabulary, and concepts that a teacher and learners create, then are posted in the classroom. Language walls encourage students to review language phrases, new and interesting vocabulary words, and categories of words.

We have chosen the historical fiction second grade text *Brave Girl: Clara and the Shirtwaist Makers' Strike of 1909* (Markel 2013) to model the use of language walls.

Some language walls might be explicitly related to an instructional unit while other language walls might be specific to a book as illustrated here. Language walls are not limited to words but can incorporate pictures and other visual cues. Since the

Procedure for using language walls:

1. Read the story interactively while sitting next to a poster board.
2. Invite students to choose new and interesting words as they appear in the book, and write them on the poster. *Brave Girl* might include words and phrases, such as "strike," "tenement house," "filthy," "condemned," and "poor as dirt."
3. After reading, talk about the words and phrases you have pulled out of the story, paraphrasing parts of the story to use the words.
4. Post the language wall, and keep it posted for follow-up activities, including writing activities.
5. Add to the language wall at any time.
6. Use drawings or doodles, especially to represent actions.

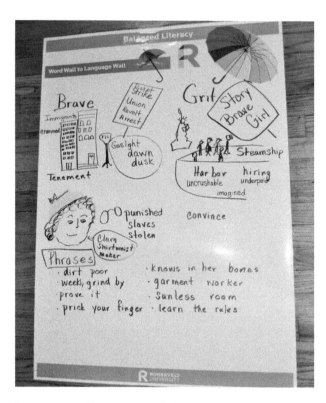

language walls are created during instruction, the words emerge from a meaningful context and involve classroom discourse. The language walls make the vocabulary visible and easily accessible.

**Hand signals**, like other body language, are language- and culture-specific and need to be explicitly taught, just like the sounds, appearance, and meaning of the words of a language. There are common hand signals used in the classroom, and teachers need to take an inventory of their own hand signals and teach them at the beginning of the year. For example, Grzegorsz G., a social studies teacher in the Chicago Public Schools, teaches the hand gesture of rotating his hand around to indicate "more" or "keep going" when a student is speaking. Now that he has taught it, he finds he can even give the "continue talking" signal from across the room, and students understand that he is encouraging more language production.

Sometimes, a hand signal can be used specifically to guide a cognitive function. Calkins (2015) suggests developing a set of hand signals for cognitive cues that guide students toward greater metacognitive awareness. For example, the right hand can be used to signal comparisons, the left hand can be used to signal contrasts, and we can point to our heads to signal "critical thinking." Gestures like these can serve as a useful "shortcut" to cognitive processes.

**Realia** and symbolic objects support reading strategies. Realia are "real-life" props, artifacts, and authentic materials that are set up in the classroom to support learning. They might include simple objects such as plastic fruit, dolls, or tools; historical objects such as old catalogs or princess telephones; or more complex installations that stay in the classroom for some time. Realia can be used for building background knowledge, as a scaffold to introduce a new unit or topic, or even for a metaphorical purpose, such as a toy airplane to represent travel.

An example of realia might come from a simple accessory owned by most children in the class: hats. A great trio of books by Jon Klassen, *I Want My Hat Back* (2011), *This Is Not My Hat* (2012), and *We Found a Hat* (2016) can be used with learners in the early elementary grades. Along with exploring the stories and images in the books, the teacher can bring in a variety of hats, and these can be admired, described, compared, and tried on, building oral language in a classroom that creates a sense of delight—and maintains a low affective filter.

An example of more complex realia is establishing a small ant farm in a corner of the classroom and performing observations and experiments related to it. Watching the changes and activities in the ant farm can provide the basis for a hands-on science unit that develops such skills as making observations in a journal, creating class charts and tables, and talking about ecosystems.

In these ways, teachers can provide multiple representations of content in order to make learning much more accessible for ELLs (Waxman and Tellez 2002), and a lot more fun.

## Formative assessment

Formative assessment is a process of providing feedback to move a student's learning forward during instruction (Wiliam 2011). It includes collecting data about the student's learning during instruction and giving the student positive cognitive and behavioral feedback in order to move his or her learning ahead in real time. The ultimate goal is to have the teacher's verbal and written feedback become part of the "inner talk" students use to improve their own learning. This type of assessment is important for all students but even more crucial for ELLs as they negotiate two languages. Peers give each other informal formative feedback in collaborative learning situations, but for ELLs still learning English, teachers should provide most of the formative feedback.

Teachers collect formative student data through observations, conferencing, running records, and many other strategies. However, two pitfalls need to be avoided: delayed feedback and general compliments (Policastro, McTague, and Mazeski 2016). Delayed feedback is not meaningful to students because many will have difficulties connecting the feedback to the event. Also vague compliments such as "Good job!" make a student feel good and have an important role, but they do not move the student's learning forward because they are not specific. When a teacher is very specific with positive formative feedback, and it is given immediately, student uptake is more likely to occur. For example, when second grader Aracely, an ELL student, read a sentence aloud and made a reading error, the teacher observed that at the time of the error. After Aracely was made aware of the error, her eyes darted to the picture on the page, and she corrected the word. The teacher then said, *I like the way you noticed the word "beat" didn't sound right, and by looking at the picture and thinking about the story, you successfully read the sentence. Keep looking at the pictures and thinking about the story when you read, Aracely, like you did just now.* Because the feedback is given immediately after the student's successful reading and it contains specific formative feedback, the child knows to use this strategy for reading.

## Self-Assessment of Metacognition

The goal of formative feedback is to create metacognitive learners who are able to assess their learning and work out solutions for themselves. Students who hear, see, and experience formative assessment from their teachers and peers are more likely to create a metacognitive system for themselves. It is important for the students to have an environment to develop their metacognitive system.

Recently, Becky McTague was in a primary classroom she was observing for the first time. A little girl came up to Becky and said, "In this class we learn to think about our thinking while we are reading and writing." Becky replied, "OK." The little girl pressed on by asking, "Do you know how to think about your thinking while you read and write?" At first Becky thought she was a uniquely precocious little girl; however, after talking with many of the students, who were bilingual and monolingual, Becky realized that all of the students could discuss their metacognitive thinking and wanted all visitors to think about their thinking. By using formative feedback, the teacher had clearly created an environment that enabled her students to be aware of and use metacognitive strategies.

## Affirming Cultures

The final consideration for ELLs is to affirm languages and cultures represented in the class, and multiculturalism in general. How can we tap children's "funds of knowledge" (Moll, Amanti, Neff, and Gonzalez 1992)? So often children know more than teachers think they know and more than they themselves realize they know. For example, a third grade reading specialist went through a picture vocabulary assessment with a young bilingual student and was surprised when the student was able to produce the word "caliper," the final and hardest word on the assessment. Asked how he knew such a technical word, he shrugged and said, "My dad changed those on our car."

One way to tap into students' background knowledge is to get to know families and caregivers. Also consider having family members visit with the class. Which family members can come in to demonstrate a special craft, such as needlework or woodcarving, or an art, such as playing a musical instrument or performing a traditional dance?

We can also celebrate holidays around the world while studying geography and ecology. For example, there are many New Year's days observed around the world, using different national, religious, and ecological calendars. When we look at the classroom as a living festival of world cultures, we find rich resources all around us. In so doing, we create happy classrooms that nurture, challenge, and support English language learners.

In this chapter, we have presented some of the features of second language acquisition that help teachers understand the language and literacy development of English language learners in their classrooms. These include such factors as the silent period, the difference between BICS and CALP language, and the importance of keeping a low affective filter. To address these features, we have chosen several areas that have strong research support as effective methods in teaching ELLs: building background knowledge, collaborative learning, multiple representations of content, formative assessments, and affirming cultures. The chosen examples we have provided within each of these areas can be considered a "starter kit" that can be used to explore many other valid ways to successfully work with these wonderful students.

## References and Resources

Asher, James. 1969. "The Total Physical Response Approach to Second Language Learning." *The Modern Language Journal* 53 (1): 3–17.

Calkins, Lucy. 2015. *Units of Study: Reading.* Portsmouth, NH: Heinemann.

Cummins, James. 1981. "The Role of Primary Language Development in Promoting Educational Success for Language Minority Students." In *Schooling and Language Minority Education: A Theoretical Framework,* edited by the California State Department of Education, 3–49. Sacramento, CA: State Department of Education.

Doughty, C. J., and Jessica Williams, eds. 1998. *Focus on Form in Classroom Second Language Acquisition.* Cambridge, UK: Cambridge University Press.

Frey, Nancy, and Douglas Fisher. 2013. *Rigorous Reading: 5 Access Points for Comprehending Complex Text.* Thousand Oaks, CA: Corwin.

Jimenez, Francisco. 1997. *The Circuit: Stories from the Life of a Migrant Child.* Albuquerque, NM: University of New Mexico Press.

Johnson, David D., Roger T. Johnson, and Edythe Johnson Holubec. 1993. *Circles of Learning: Cooperation in the Classroom.* Minneapolis, MN: Interaction Book Company.

Klassen, Jon. 2011. *I Want My Hat Back.* Somerville, MA: Candlewick Press.

———. 2012. *This Is Not My Hat.* Somerville, MA: Candlewick Press.

———. 2016. *We Found a Hat.* Somerville, MA: Candlewick Press.

Krashen, Stephen. 1982. *Principles and Practices of Second Language Acquisition.* New York City, NY: Prentice-Hall.

Lems, Kristin, and Samar Abousalem. 2014. "Interactive Read-aloud: A Powerful Technique for Young ELLs." In *The Common Core State Standards in English Language Arts for English Language Learners: Grades K–5*, edited by Pamela Sypcher, 5–16. Arlington, VA: TESOL Publications.

Lems, Kristin, Leah D. Miller, and Tenena M. Soro. 2010. *Teaching Reading to English Language Learners: Insights from Linguistics*. New York: Guilford.

Manushkin, Fran. 2015. *Katie Woo Tries Something New*. Katie Woo. North Mankato, MN: Picture Window Books.

Markel, Michelle. 2013. *Brave Girl: Clara and the Shirtwaist Makers' Strike of 1909*. New York, New York: Blazer-Bray, a division of Harper Collins.

Moll, Luis, Cathy Amanti, Deborah Neff, and Norma Gonzalez. 1992. "Funds of Knowledge for Teaching: Using a Qualitative Approach to Connect Home and Classrooms." *Theory into Practice* 31 (2): 132–141.

Panitz, Ted, 1999. Collaborative Versus Cooperative Learning—A Comparison of the Two Concepts. ERIC document ED 448 443: http://files.eric.ed.gov/fulltext/ED448443.pdf.

Policastro, Margaret M., and Becky McTague, 2015. *The New Balanced Literacy School: Implementing Common Core*. North Mankato, MN: Capstone Professional.

Policastro, Margaret M., Becky McTague, and Diane Mazeski. 2016. *Formative Assessment in the New Balanced Literacy Classroom*. North Mankato, MN: Capstone Professional.

Stanford University. 2013. "Key Principles for ELL Instruction" *Understanding Language: Language, Literacy, and Learning in the Content Areas*. (January): http://ell.stanford.edu/content/six-key-principles-ell-instruction.

Thomas, Wayne P., and Virginia P. Collier. 2002. *A National Study of School Effectiveness for Language Minority Students' Long-term Academic Achievement*. Santa Cruz, CA: Center for Research on Education, Diversity and Excellence, University of California-Santa Cruz.

Waxman, Hersh C., and Kip Tellez. 2002. *Research Synthesis on Effective Teaching Practices for English Language Learners*. Philadelphia, PA: Temple University, Mid-Atlantic Regional Educational Laboratory, Laboratory for Student Success. ERIC Document Retrieval No. ED474821: http://files.eric.ed.gov/fulltext/ED474821.pdf.

Wiliam, Dylan. 2011. *Embedded Formative Assessment*. Bloomington, IN: Solution Tree Press.

# Intervention: Differentiated Instruction within the Classroom

Nancy L. Witherell and Mary C. McMackin

## Differentiated Instruction Takes Center Stage

**M**any states and school districts underscore the need for differentiated instruction. Throughout the country, teachers are expected to be able to design and implement tiered instruction. We've selected a few examples to illustrate this point: In Massachusetts, which is our home state, teacher candidates must demonstrate they can use data from assessments to "identify and/or implement appropriate differentiated interventions and enhancements for students" (Massachusetts Department of Elementary and Secondary Education 2016, 23). And in Michigan students engage in district-administered diagnostic assessments to "assess at a deeper level to provide data that can be used to plan, modify, and differentiate instruction and interventions" (Michigan Department of Education 2016).

Connecticut also pledged to support districts as they implement differentiated instruction, as detailed in the Connecticut State Board of Education's *Ensuring Equity and Excellence for All Connecticut Students: Five-Year Comprehensive Plan* (2016–2021) (Connecticut State Board of Education nd).

In the state of Washington, the 2013 *Comprehensive Literacy Plan* is organized around three essential facts, one being that "[Literacy] is improved through responsive and differentiated teaching" (State of Washington Office of Superintendent of Public Instruction 2013).

Dr. John D. Barge for the Georgia Department of Education (2014) identified differentiated instruction as one of 10 performance standards as part of Georgia's Teacher Effectiveness Measure, a teacher evaluation system that seeks to ensure consistency in teacher effectiveness across the state.

We even noticed a recent job posting for a New York City primary grade reading coach that had as preferred skills "Knowledge and ability to apply effective literacy practices in . . . differentiated instructional strategies" (New York City Department of Education 2016).

From coast to coast, classroom teachers, literacy specialists, and school and district administrators are aware of the need to determine where students are in their academic development. And educators use that information to design rigorous instruction so each student grows to his or her full potential.

When teachers differentiate instruction, they are tailoring academic needs to each and every student in the classroom. If progress monitoring shows a student is falling behind, intervention is put into place. Intervention techniques set up goals and initiate a set of steps to help the child reach the specified goal, so the learning gap does not increase. Intervention begins with the teacher as the teacher would be the first to notice any discrepancies in the learning process. In the Response to Intervention (RtI) Model, the first level of help for students who appear to be struggling would be a teacher differentiating lessons in some way to meet the needs of all students. Offered in this article is how the role of tiered instruction can aid in initial intervention and help classroom teachers meet the needs of all students.

## Differentiation in the 21st Century

Going back too many years, as young teachers, we prided ourselves in meeting the needs of all students through "individualized instruction." Nancy was in a team-teaching situation, and she and another teacher implemented what was then considered stellar instruction. Together they divided and taught six different leveled reading groups using the mandated basal reading program. Math was divided into a high and low class, but spelling was handled by each teacher and Nancy had four spelling groups. The Super Spellers spelled the required spelling list correctly on the pretest, they were given more words, and they still had to write the required spelling list words on the post-test. Now we know better and would contract the students out of spelling for the week or forget the list entirely and incorporate spelling into writer's workshop. Although all practices were not bad, and hopefully none were harmful, we have come a long way in our knowledge of differentiation in the classroom.

Much of the differentiation in today's classroom is guided by Carol Ann Tomlinson's work with differentiation using tiered instruction (not to be confused with the three tiers or levels used in Response to Intervention). Tomlinson's tiered instruction is based on meeting the same objective or outcome for all students, but differentiating for students through process, content, or product (Tomlinson 2001, 51). For instance, when teaching leveled guided reading groups the differentiation is done by content, as students are reading books that are at their instructional level. So in second grade, one group could be reading several first grade level books, while another group could be reading a fourth grade level book. It's important to ensure that all students are reading a significant amount of text each day, so they can practice literacy skills and strategies as well as gain content knowledge. In addition, the teacher would take intensive steps to increase the reading vocabulary of the first grade level reading group. This could be accomplished in a variety of ways through whole class activities, such as using read-alouds with higher level vocabulary, using flexible grouping techniques with text sets in which the teacher preteaches vocabulary, or independently by using software that scaffolds unknown words. Through this differentiation we are meeting the main goal of Tomlinson's work, which is giving children an opportunity to grow as much as possible from their starting point (Tomlinson and Imbeau 2010, 1).

Tomlinson and Imbeau (2010) define content as the knowledge, understanding, and skill we want students to learn. Using leveled reading books is differentiating by content. Process is defined as the way in which students come to understand or make sense of the content. Sometimes children can gain more understanding of a concept or skill with changes to the instructional approach. For instance, using visuals while explaining vocabulary greatly aids English language learners and others. Product is the demonstration of that knowledge (Tomlinson and Imbeau 2010). For instance, when teaching past tense, a teacher can have some students circling words in a copied text, while students who need more challenging work are told to find two past tense words in the text and write sentences using the two words.

In essence, content is the material used, process involves the instruction, and product is how we have students apply the knowledge in their work. When differentiating through product, the outcome remains the same, and the product is "cloned" to an easier or more complex level. For example, if the outcome is "students will be able to identify a character's goal," all students will meet this outcome. The students who need intervention might be required to state the main character's goal. The on-grade level students might be required to state the main character's goal and motive. The students who need a challenge might be required to state the main character's goal and motive as well as comment on how other characters within the text could influence the main character's goal. As you read back on these three levels, you will notice the tasks become progressively more complex.

## Growth vs. Fixed Mindset

When differentiating instruction, the teacher first models the targeted skill or strategy, and then students engage in guided practice. The practice provides students with an opportunity to "have a go" with the task, and it provides teachers time to assess how well each student is doing. The benefit of this formative assessment is the teacher can match students with the most appropriately tiered follow-up activity for the lesson.

An underlying principle of our work is based on what Carol Dweck (2006) refers to as a "growth mindset." Students and teachers who believe in a growth mindset recognize that intelligence isn't something that remains unchanged from birth to death. Rather, everyone has the ability to learn and grow and extend his or her intelligence through hard work and confidence. They believe everyone can realize new goals, especially when faced with challenging tasks. Dweck (2006) also presents a "fixed mindset" way of thinking. Those who believe in a fixed mindset accept they are either capable of success or not. They tend to avoid challenges because they believe that needing to work hard at something is an indicator of limited intelligence. In an interesting conversation with students, Dweck (2006, 24) asked when they felt smart. She wanted to know if it was when they were "flawless" or when they

were truly learning something. What she found was that students with a fixed mindset thought they were smart when they got everything right, when they worked quickly, or when they could do things other students couldn't do. Conversely, those who held a growth mindset believed they were smart when they were working on something new or difficult and were able to figure it out.

We've all worked with students who don't want to attempt anything unless they are certain they will be successful. These students may be gifted, on level, or need intervention of some sort. What they have in common is they don't want to take any risks that might bring into question how "smart" they are. They come to their learning events with a preconceived, fixed mindset that doesn't allow them to take risks for fear they might fail.

Most relevant to our work is Dweck's recognition that everyone who interacts with students (e.g., teachers, parents, coaches) plays a critical role in providing both the encouragement and also the specific instruction students need in order to develop and maintain a growth mindset. Dweck (2016, 41) clearly states,

> . . . In the name of growth mindset, some adults blithely assure children that they can do anything if only they work hard enough. But if a child lacks the necessary skills, strategies, support or mentoring, such reassurance is hollow and even misguided. On the flip side, some parents and educators have taken to lavishly praising effort, even when a child has not in fact worked hard or effectively.
>
> This tactic, too, sends a discouraging message: 'You are not capable of anything better.' To convey a true growth mind-set, adults must help kids understand what they need to do to develop their abilities and to guide them in that process.

Dweck's work (2015) has shown that learners with a growth mindset achieve more than those who adhere to a fixed mindset. This appears to be particularly true for struggling students. Effective differentiated instruction, coupled with the fostering of a growth mindset, may prove to be a highly successful intervention combination.

## The Role of Differentiation in Intervention: What Does It Look Like?

Intervention, by educational definition, means that we are working differently to help a child who is behind in an aspect of learning. In reading instruction, it may be a lack of phonics, inability to comprehend, fluency issues, and so forth. When working with children we need to start from where they are (Tomlinson and Imbeau 2010). This is extremely important in intervention when the child gets further behind and needs modified instruction. For intervention the focus is on modifying the content, process, or product, but remaining with the same intended outcome. So what might this look like?

During a second grade classroom lesson, one of the authors was pairing nonfiction with fiction. Using Chris Van Allburg's *Two Bad Ants* (1988) as a read-aloud, she paired the book with four different levels of informational texts about ants. The differentiation was done through content as students read books at their instructional level. Although the books were different for each group, each book contained information on ant colonies, queen ants, soldier ants, and/or worker ants, along with an ant anatomy diagram. With guidance and look backs into the books, each child was able to complete the same product. Students had to define the queen ant, soldier ant, or worker ant and then label the parts of the ant body. The follow-up discussion was completed with the whole class because all students were able to contribute to a discussion about the common factors. They were able to share equally. In this lesson, the group of students needing the most support worked with the aid of a teacher, but all students met the expected outcomes: to define the different types of ants that could be found in a colony and label the parts of an ant.

In another lesson with fourth graders, the outcome was to do a character analysis. Students were expected to analyze Anna's character in *Sarah, Plain and Tall* (MacLachian 1985). During the lesson the teacher used Caleb's character to model how a character's actions can help a reader understand and identify a character's traits. For the model the teacher used a grade-level graphic organizer. Students were then given a graphic organizer that the teacher matched to their level of instruction. Two levels of graphic organizers were provided, one on grade level and one that was less complex (Witherell and McMackin 2005, 40–41). In this lesson the differentiation for targeted students was done by product: the character analysis. At the end of the lesson, a discussion was held on Anna's character traits and how actions could help a reader understand a character. All were able to participate in that discussion.

## Model Lessons

As Watts-Taffe, et al. (2012, 306) report, "[Effective differentiated instruction] is found in the decisions teachers make based on their understanding of the reading process, in-depth knowledge of their students, consideration of an array of effective instructional practices supported by research, and ability to select models, materials, and methods to suit particular students as they engage in particular literacy acts." In this next section, we provide two differentiated instruction lessons. You'll see that we incorporate Pearson and Gallagher's (1983) gradual release of responsibility model as we move from teacher modeling to guided practice to individual practice. The latter includes three tiers of differentiated materials. The following model lessons, though somewhat abbreviated, show how differentiation can be done at three levels, with the less complex model as intervention. We purposefully chose concepts that are difficult for most third and fourth grade students to understand.

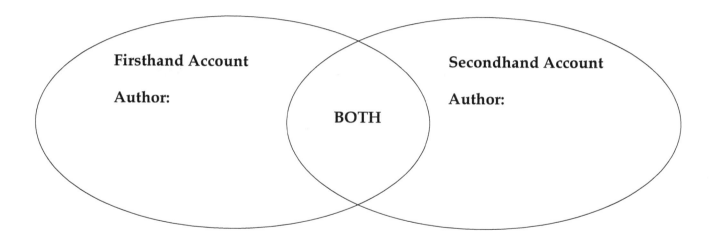

## Model Differentiated Lesson #1: Firsthand and Secondhand Accounts

At the conclusion of this lesson, fourth graders should be able to distinguish between firsthand and secondhand accounts and be able to explain why information may appear or not appear in different accounts. Firsthand accounts are told by eyewitnesses who experience an event or who have direct, personal knowledge of a subject that is being discussed. The words "I" and "we" are often used in firsthand reports. Conversely, secondhand accounts are told by people who heard about, read about, or researched an event. Words such as "they," "he," and "she" appear in secondhand narratives. When we read informational texts, we determine if it is a firsthand account or a secondhand account. Having this information allows us to evaluate the accuracy and authenticity of the information. It also enables us to assess whether or not the writer has lived through the event, has had hands-on experiences with the subject matter, or has interpreted an event.

CCSS.ELA-Literacy.RI.4.6: Compare and contrast a firsthand and secondhand account of the same event or topic; describe the differences in focus and the information provided.

## Teacher Modeling

Begin the lesson by explaining the difference between firsthand and secondhand accounts, and then have the following scenarios available for students to read (perhaps on a whiteboard, documentation camera, or tablet). Also have available the Venn diagram above.

### Text A (a text message):

*Have you heard the good news? TC just got his new puppy. He's about 12 weeks old and weighs about 4 pounds. TC is going to name him Cotton because he's so soft and white.*

### Text B (a diary entry):

*Today was so amazing. I picked up my new puppy from the shelter. He was born 12 weeks ago tomorrow. My mom wanted me to call him Caleb because that's her favorite name, but as soon as I saw him, I thought he should be called Cotton. When I held him, I knew Cotton was the perfect name. He's still tiny—only 4 pounds—but he likes to eat, so he'll grow fast. I can't wait to teach him some tricks.*

Read aloud texts A and B, letting students know you'll be determining which one is a firsthand account and which one is a secondhand account. Next, complete the Venn diagram (above) as you think through a comparison of the two accounts. Let students know that B is an example of a firsthand account because we know that TC wrote the diary entry about his new puppy and that A is the secondhand account because someone who knows TC wrote about TC's experience.

Next, reread the two texts looking first for any information that both accounts share, and jot down the notes in the center of the Venn diagram (e.g., the puppy is 12 weeks old, is 4 pounds, is called Cotton because he's white and soft). Explain why you think the information is in both accounts (e.g., They are key, essential facts).

Next, jot any information that only appears in the firsthand account (left side of diagram) or only in the secondhand account (right side of the diagram). For example, the firsthand account lets us know that TC's mom wanted him to call the puppy Caleb. This information is missing from the secondhand account.

Talk about why this information may appear in Text B and not the other (e.g., perhaps TC didn't tell his friends that his mother already had a name in mind for the puppy). Before concluding this part of the lesson, display the following two sentences and explain why each text may have been written: *I think the author of the firsthand account wrote the text so* _____. *I think the author of the secondhand account wrote the text to* _____.

(Possible responses: I think the author of the firsthand account wrote the text so he would always remember what it was like the day he got his new puppy. I think the author of the secondhand account wrote the text to let others know about TC's exciting news.)

Share another example and explain your reasoning. You might read aloud excerpts from *Through My Eyes* (Bridges 1999) and *The Story of Ruby Bridges* (Coles 1995) or texts of your choosing.

Once students understand the difference between firsthand and secondhand accounts, they can compare and contrast the information in them and can begin to articulate why an author may include or leave out information. Provide some guided practice so students can try out the skills. While they work, you should informally assess their ability to "compare and contrast a firsthand and secondhand account of the same event or topic; describe the differences in focus and the information provided" (CCSS.ELA-Literacy.RI.4.6). You'll use the information from your informal assessment to match your students with the most appropriate follow-up activity.

## Guided Practice

Provide a set of firsthand and secondhand accounts about the same event or subject. One text should be a firsthand account (e.g., autobiography, interview, original letter); the other text should be a secondhand account (e.g., such as those reported in *Time for Kids*, a biography, a local newspaper article, pages from a textbook). For this guided practice, you might want to have students work in pairs. Ask them to read the two accounts and fill in the information on a Venn diagram. When complete, have students report out their answers. If students need more guided practice, have two or three other scenarios available.

## Student Application: Tiered Activities for Differentiation

For this follow-up activity, use excerpts from texts that are at students' independent reading levels.

**Initial:** *For Students Needing Intervention*

Have students identify which account is the firsthand account and which one is the secondhand account. Students should be able to justify their decision when you ask them to do so. Using a Venn diagram, have them write down the author of each text, what the two texts have in common, and why both authors included the same information.

**Transitional:** *For On-grade-level Students*

Have students complete the same task as students at the Initial level. Then have students use the Venn diagram to include information appearing in only one of the accounts and say why this information may have appeared where it did.

**Accomplished:** *For Students Who Need a Challenge*

In addition to completing what the students at the Transitional level will do, have students at this level complete these sentences on the back of their paper:

*I think the author of the firsthand account wrote the text so* _____.

*I think the author of the secondhand account wrote the piece to*

_____.

## Differentiated Lesson #2: Understanding Metaphorical Language

The outcome of this lesson is to have third grade students understand that authors use metaphors as a literary device to show a hidden or implied comparison. A metaphor states one thing is another, and it is not a literal comparison. The two things being compared have something in common.

CCSS.ELA-Literacy.RL.3.4: Determine the meaning of words and phrases as they are used in a text, distinguishing literal from nonliteral language.

### Teacher Modeling

Begin the lesson by explaining that authors use metaphors as a literary device to make their writing more interesting, colorful, and unique. In addition, metaphors describe and make an unusual comparison. For example, "My mom's car was the town's favorite bus." Discuss this comparison. How are Mom's car and a bus alike? (both have wheels, both carry people) Ask students to explain what can be inferred about Mom's car? (Mom must take a lot of people in her car and get them to where they want to go.) Explain to students that a metaphor says one thing is another, and the two items being compared have something in common. If possible, read a piece of literature in which the author has used metaphors in a description. You might use the chapter titled "Hairs" in *The House on Mango Street* (Cisneros 1984, 6). In this short chapter, the author says the mother's hair is rosettes, candy circles, and the warm smell of bread. After reading these examples (or those in a book of your choice), explain the comparisons as a think-aloud: *Each of these metaphors imply something beautiful about the main character's mother's hair and the mother.* Then, put the following three metaphors and four questions up on whiteboard or projector:

**Metaphors**

• My dad, a night owl, stayed up until three in the morning!

• My sister, her royal highness, thinks she's my boss.

• My mom says my room is a disaster.

**Questions**

1. What two things are being compared?

2. What seems to be common between the two?

3. What does this imply or suggest?

4. What other comparison might we have made if we wrote this metaphor?

Read each metaphor and answer each question for the students. Unpack your thinking as you answer the questions about each metaphor. Explain why you are giving these answers and how authors make us think a bit differently when they use metaphors. By the third metaphor, students might want to begin to help. And if they are ready, let them. Here are the answers for each metaphor:

(1) comparing dad with a night owl (2) both up late (3) implies dad is up late a lot (4) hamster (another nocturnal animal)

(1) comparing sister with a royal highness, (2) special, uppity (3) She thinks she has a right to boss me around. (4) her ladyship

(1) comparing my room to a disaster (2) both are a mess (3) A disaster is horrible, so the room must look horrible. (4) junkyard or pigpen

### Guided Practice

Using the following metaphors, have students answer the four questions written above. Read each metaphor and then each question, and have students write each answer.

• Meet my son, the Babe Ruth of his baseball team.

• My brother, the couch potato, likes it when I get his snacks for him.

• The lawn, a green carpet, was perfect for a game of golf.

The answers should be something like:

(1) son and Babe Ruth (2) good baseball players (3) The father is really proud of his son and thinks the son is a really good baseball player. (4) Mickey Mantle

(1) brother and a couch potato (2) they don't move (3) The brother sits around too much watching television. (4) lazybones

(1) lawn and a green carpet (2) very level (3) Good to play golf on because it is so even, straight, and level (4) a tightly made-up bed

## Student Application: Tiered Activities for Differentiation

When students are ready to apply this skill independently, begin this portion. For student application, use the following metaphors, and have students complete the activity suggested for the level in which you think they would be successful.

- The ice cream, now a small red lake, was all over the counter.
- Our teacher, a fairy princess, gave us an extra recess.
- My older brother, a walking encyclopedia, knows everything.
- The royal carriage, my dad's car, has arrived to pick up my sister.
- My sister, the brain, got all As on her report card.

**Initial:** *For Students Needing Intervention*

Have students answer the first two questions: What is being compared, and what do the two have in common?

**Transitional:** *For On-grade-level Students*

Have students answer the first three questions: What is being compared, what do the two have in common, and what does this imply?

**Accomplished:** *For Students Who Need a Challenge*

Have students answer all four questions: What is being compared, what do the two have in common, what does this imply, and what else might it be compared to?

# Differentiation and Response to Intervention (RtI)

If we differentiated our instruction effectively, there would be less need for intervention. The federal program, Response to Intervention (RtI), was created to encourage teachers to differentiate more in their classrooms to enable students to be more successful in the classroom setting. RtI began with the reauthorization of IDEA in 2004. RtI requires the use of scientifically researched-based instruction. Commonly in the RtI model there are three tiers (not to be confused with Tomlinson's tiered instruction) of instructional levels. The goal of this intervention program is to identify those students in need of special education programs and to ensure children do not get further behind in their learning as they go through the grades. In the three-tiered RtI model, student progress is continually and carefully monitored to ensure all students, especially those needing intervention, are receiving the help they need. The three tiers of RtI are usually defined as:

Tier 3: The students with the greatest needs are placed in Tier 3 in the RtI model. This is usually the level with the least number of students as effective differentiation is expected to ensure fewer students need aid from specialists. This level offers intensive intervention and targeted instruction to specially meet the needs of individual students. One-on-one instruction is often employed.

Tier 2: Students requiring Tier 2 support receive service by both the classroom teacher and the specialist. Intervention is based on student needs and supplements the classroom curriculum and instruction. Intervention is usually done in small groups by the teacher, specialist, or coach. If a student does not show adequate progress, he or she receives Tier 3 level of support. Tomlinson's tiered differentiation would be used by the classroom teacher at this level.

Tier 1: In the RtI model, this is the large majority of students (approximately 80 percent). Instruction is provided by the classroom teacher. All students get high-quality scientifically researched-based instruction. Tomlinson's tiered differentiation could also be used by the classroom teacher at this level. Students who do not make adequate progress would be moved to Tier 2.

As indicated by our descriptions of the tiers, RtI Tiers 1 and 2 are most likely to employ Tomlinson's tiered instruction and would be used in the classroom for differentiation. Although aspects could be used at Tier 3, the instruction at this level is more individualized for intensified intervention.

We believe it's essential for all students and teachers to maintain "growth mindsets" (Dweck 2006). Every student deserves to know that he or she is capable of reaching his or her full potential. Teachers who know their students and apply effective research-based instruction can ensure every student succeeds.

## References and Resources

Barge, Dr. John. D. 2014. "Teacher Assessment on Performance Standard 4: Differentiated Instruction TKES Quick Guide." Georgia Department of Education Teacher Keys Effectiveness System, July 1. https://www.gadoe.org/School-Improvement/Teacher-and-Leader-Effectiveness/Documents/FY15%20TKES%20and%20LKES%20Documents/QG%20TAPS%204%20Differentiated%20Instruction%202014-15.pdf.

Bridges, R. 1999. *Through My Eyes.* New York: Scholastic.

Cisneros, Sandra. 1984. *The House on Mango Street.* New York: Vintage Books, Random House.

Coles, R. 1995. *The Story of Ruby Bridges.* New York: Scholastic.

Connecticut State Board of Education. n.d. "Ensuring Equity and Excellence for All Connecticut Students: Five-Year Comprehensive Plan (2016–2021)" http://www.sde.ct.gov/sde/lib/sde/pdf/board/five_year_comprehensive_plan_for_education.pdf.

Dweck, C. S. 2006. *Mindset: The New Psychology of Success.* New York: Ballantine Books.

———. 2015. "Growth." *British Journal of Educational Psychology* 85: 242–245.

———. 2016. "The Remarkable Reach of Growth Mind-sets." *Scientific American Mind* 27 (1): 36–41.

MacLachlan, P. 1985. *Sarah, Plain and Tall.* New York: HarperCollins.

Massachusetts Department of Elementary and Secondary Education. 2016. "Guidelines for the Candidate Assessment of Performance." June. http://www.doe.mass.edu/edprep/cap/guidelines.pdf.

Michigan Department of Education. 2016. "District-Administered Diagnostic Assessments." http://www.michigan.gov/mde/0,4615,7-140-28753-363936--,00.html.

National Governors Association Center for Best Practices & Council of Chief State School Officers. 2010. *Common Core State Standards for English Language Arts and Literacy in History/Social Studies, Science, and Technical Subjects.* Washington, DC: Authors.

New York City Department of Education. 2016. Division of Human Resources, Teacher Assigned Vacancy. http://schools.nyc.gov.

Pearson, P. D. and M. C. Gallagher. 1983. "The Instruction of Reading Comprehension." *Contemporary Educational Psychology* 8: 317–344.

State of Washington Office of Superintendent of Public Instruction. 2013. "English Language Arts Comprehensive Literacy Plan: Instruction and Intervention." August 27. http://www.k12.wa.us/ELA/CLP/InstructionIntervention/default.aspx.

Tomlinson, C. 2001. *How to Differentiate Instruction in Mixed-ability Classrooms, 2nd Edition.* Alexandria, VA: ASCD.

Tomlinson, C. and M. Imbeau. 2010. *Leading and Managing a Differentiated Classroom.* Alexandria, VA: ASCD.

Van Allsburg, C. 1988. *Two Bad Ants.* New York: Houghton Mifflin Harcourt.

Watts-Taffe, S., B. P. Laster, L. Broach, B. Marinak, C. M. Connor, and D. Walker-Dalhouse. 2012. "Differentiated Instruction: Making Informed Teacher Decisions." *The Reading Teacher* 66 (4): 303–314.

Witherell, N. & McMackin, M. 2005. *Teaching Reading Through Differentiated Instruction with Leveled Graphic Organizers.* New York: Scholastic.

# About the Contributors

· · · · · · · · · · · · · · · · · · · · · · · · · · · · · · · · · · · · · · · · · · · · · · · · · · · · · · · · · · · ·

**Dr. Nancy Boyles** is professor emerita at Southern Connecticut State University, where she was Professor of Reading and Graduate Reading Program Coordinator. Previously, she spent 25 years as a classroom teacher at various elementary grade levels. She was named Teacher of the Year in her district and was a semi-finalist for Connecticut Teacher of the Year. She received her doctorate in reading and language from Boston University and has received numerous awards for her contribution to the field of literacy. She currently consults with districts and other organizations and agencies, providing workshops, modeling best practices in classrooms, and assisting with curriculum development. Dr. Boyles is the author of several books, including *Teaching Written Response to Text, Constructing Meaning through Kid-Friendly Comprehension Strategy Instruction, Hands-On Literacy Coaching, That's a GREAT Answer!, Rethinking Small-group Instruction in the Intermediate Grades, Launching RTI Comprehension Instruction with Shared Reading, Closer Reading in Grades 3–6,* and *Lessons & Units for Close Reading.*

**Kathy Brown** enjoys teaching our youngest learners in the wonderful world of kindergarten. Her passion for early literacy instruction was ignited in 1987 when she did her student teaching in Australia. Her action research entitled Ladders to Literacy was published in 1998 after she earned her master's degree from Aurora University. She is a Nationally Board Certified Teacher in Early and Middle Childhood Literacy: Reading-Language Arts, a nominee for the Golden Apple Foundation for Excellence in Teaching Award from WGN and Disney's American Teacher Award, and a presenter at the local, university, state, national, and international levels. She has presented at the NAEYC conference, the I Teach conference, the annual IASCD Pre-K–Kdg conference, and the International Literacy Association conference. She is also the co-author of *Kindergarten and the Common Core: It's as Easy as ABC!*

**Nicki Clausen-Grace** is a fourth-grade teacher with more than 25 years of experience. She also serves as a consultant for educators and parents and is the co-author of *Teaching Text Features to Support Comprehension* and *Reading the Whole Page: Teaching and Assessing Text Features to Meet K–5 Common Core Standards.*

**Dr. Charlene Cobb** is Assistant Superintendent of Teaching and Learning in East Maine School District 63, in Des Plaines, Illinois. She has worked in the area of literacy for more than 20 years as a teacher, reading specialist, professor, and consultant. Dr. Cobb has worked nationally with schools and districts to support literacy programs and is particularly interested in the literacy development of linguistically diverse learners and struggling readers. She has contributed several articles to the International Literacy Association journal, *The Reading Teacher,* and has co-authored two books on the topics of literacy and vocabulary.

**Connie Dierking** holds a bachelor's degree in elementary education and a master's degree in special education, both from Kansas State University. During the past 32 years, Connie Dierking has experienced the joys of teaching kindergarten, second grade, third grade, and exceptional education students. She has experience as a reading/writing demonstration teacher, reading coach, and writing staff developer. She also provided guidance for literacy teachers throughout the southwest region of Florida as a Reading Coordinator. She currently writes literacy curriculum and is an instructional staff developer for Pinellas County Schools in Florida. She is the author of several books written for literacy teachers to assist with the teaching of writing and reading in the primary grades, including *Linking K–2 Literacy and the Common Core: Mini-Lessons that Work*, and co-author of *Growing Up Writing: Mini-Lessons for Emergent and Beginning Writers*. She conducts professional development in the areas of reading, writing, speaking and listening throughout the country.

**Dr. Michael P. Ford** is a former first grade and Title I Reading teacher. He is professor emeritus at the University of Wisconsin Oshkosh where he worked with pre-service and in-service teachers for 29 years as a professor and department chair in the Department of Literacy and Language. Dr. Ford has consulted with teachers throughout the world. He is the author or editor of books focused on elementary literacy classroom programs and practices. Dr. Ford has been looking at guided reading practices since his first book *Reaching Readers* was published in 2002 and has more recently authored *Guided Reading: What's New, and What's Next?* He is the co-author of *Accessible Assessment, Do-able Differentiation, Where Have All the Bluebirds Gone?, Books and Beyond*, and *Classroom Catalysts*. He is the co-editor of the *Engaging Minds in the Classrooms* series and co-author of the anchor text *Engaging Minds in the Classroom: The Surprising Power of Joy*.

**Dr. Shari Frost** has served as an elementary classroom teacher, a reading specialist, a professional developer, and an instructor at the university level. Currently, she consults with literacy coaches, intervention specialists, classroom teachers, and children in classrooms to support the improvement of literacy instruction in the Chicago Public Schools. Dr. Frost is an active member in professional organizations, including the National Council of Teachers of English and the International Literacy Association and their state level affiliates, and she presents frequently at conferences sponsored by these organizations. She is the author of *Rethinking Intervention: Supporting Struggling Readers in the Regular Classroom* and *Two Books Are Better Than One!: Reading and Writing (and Talking and Drawing) Across Texts in K–2*, a co-author of *Effective Literacy Coaching: Building Expertise and a Culture of Literacy* with Roberta Buhle and Camille Blachowicz, and a principal writer for the PARCC formative tools for grades K–2.

**Dr. Michelle J. Kelley** is an Associate Professor in Reading at the University of Central Florida, teaching pre-service educators and graduate students. She also provides professional development to teachers and administrators. Dr. Kelley previously taught in Maine and Florida and served as a professional developer for FLaRE (Florida Literacy and Reading Excellence Center). She is the co-author of *Teaching Text Features to Support Comprehension* and *Reading the Whole Page: Teaching and Assessing Text Features to Meet K–5 Common Core Standards*.

**Dr. Kristin Lems**, Professor of ESL/Bilingual Education at National Louis University in Chicago, has had two Fulbrights to Algeria and Mongolia to work with EFL teachers. As an English Language Specialist for the U.S. State Department, she worked with EFL teachers in Chile and in 2016 presented a global webinar to 2,000 teachers on using music to teach English as a second language. Dr. Lems co-authored the widely used teacher-focused textbook, *Teaching Reading to English Language Learners: Insights from Linguistics*, and has published in *Reading in a Foreign Language, Writing Systems Research, The Reading Teacher*, and *English Teaching Forum* on pedagogical literacy topics. She presents annually at International TESOL in a popular post-conference institute about using music to teach ESL. Her doctorate is in reading and language, and her dissertation on ESL oral reading fluency won a finalist award from the International Reading Association.

**Dr. Adele T. Macula** spent her professional career serving in New Jersey's second largest school district as an elementary teacher, District Supervisor for Programs that Maximize Potential, Special Assistant for the Department of Curriculum and Instruction, and Associate Superintendent-Curriculum and Instruction for grades K–12. Additionally, Dr. Macula was an Adjunct Professor at Fairleigh Dickinson University and Seton Hall University. Presently, she is the Director of Curriculum and Instruction for NJ EXCEL (Expedited Certification for Educational Leadership) and also serves as a faculty member. Dr. Macula has authored *From the Classroom to the Test: How to Improve Student Achievement on the Summative ELA Assessments*, is a consultant, and has presented numerous workshops on CCSS, PARCC, formative assessment, teacher evaluation and effective feedback, and promoting data-informed instruction. She has received several awards, including the Brian C. Doherty Community Service Award, the Dr. Ernest L. Boyer 2009 Outstanding Educator Award, the "Service Above Self" Community Service Award, the Women's History Month "Award for Contributions to Multicultural Education," and New Jersey City University's "Inaugural Distinguished Education Alumni Award." She continues to present at local, state, national, and international conferences.

**Sarah Martino** is a kindergarten teacher, author, conference presenter and kindergarten intervention teacher. She is the co-author of *Kindergarten and the Common Core: It's as Easy as ABC!* She has also written teacher's guides for educational materials. Sarah Martino received her master's degree in literacy in 2004. She focused her action research on writing in kindergarten. She was also a nominee for the Golden Apple Foundation for Excellence in Teaching Award from WGN. In addition to her site-based job, Sarah Martino presents at the university, local, state, national, and international levels. She has presented at the NAEYC conference, the I Teach conference, the annual IASCD Pre-K–Kdg conference, and the International Literacy Association conference.

**Dr. Mary C. McMackin** is professor emerita from the Language and Literacy Division of the Graduate School of Education at Lesley University, where she taught graduate literacy courses for 20 years. Until recently, she served as the Lesley University coordinator of the Lesley/Urban Teacher Center partnership, a clinically based teacher preparation master's degree program offered in Baltimore, MD, and Washington, DC. She was also the faculty mentor for the literacy courses in the Lesley/UTC partnership. Dr. McMackin has co-authored many literacy books for K–8 teachers, including *Differentiating for Success: How to Build Literacy Instruction for All Students*, and has published several articles in journals such as *The Reading Teacher*, *Phi Delta Kappan*, and *Childhood Education*. Dr. McMackin serves on the board of the Massachusetts Reading Association and has spoken at conferences across the United States.

**Dr. Becky McTague** is an associate professor of language and literacy at Roosevelt University in Chicago, Illinois. She has more than 30 years of experience, ranging from elementary schools to the university level. She holds a bachelor's degree in elementary education from Southern Illinois University, a master's degree in reading from Northeastern Illinois University, and an EdD from National-Louis University. Her teaching experiences include trainer for Reading Recovery; primary teacher in Illinois, Oklahoma, and England; and reading specialist/coach for several public school districts. She has written several articles and chapters that have been published in professional journals as well as co-authored *The New Balanced Literacy School: Implementing Common Core* and *Formative Assessment in the New Balanced Literacy Classroom*. Dr. McTague has also directed many local grants as well as worked on federal grants focused on school improvement.

**Barbara Nelson** is an Arizona-based educator, conference speaker, and consultant. During her 46-year career, she has taught at every grade level. She conducts workshops on reading and writing strategies throughout the United States on topics such as CCSS. She is also the co-author of *Guided Highlighted Reading: A Close-Reading Strategy for Navigating Complex Text*.

**Dr. Margaret Mary Policastro** is a professor of language and literacy at Roosevelt University in Chicago, Illinois, where she directs the language and literacy program and is the founding director of the Summer Reading Clinic for children. Dr. Policastro has more than 30 years of experience teaching both undergraduate and graduate students in language and literacy at Roosevelt University. She has worked more than 10 years on grant funded literacy projects in Chicago Public Schools and is currently the principal investigator of the Improving Teacher Quality (ITQ) grant from the Illinois Board of Higher Education (IBHE), funded by No Child Left Behind (NCLB). She also co-authored *The New Balanced Literacy School: Implementing Common Core* and *Formative Assessment in the New Balanced Literacy Classroom* and authored *Living Literacy at Home: A Parent's Guide*. Dr. Policastro attended Indiana University where she received her bachelor's degree in art and elementary education and her master's degree in reading. After teaching art and reading in Indiana, she earned her PhD from Northwestern University in reading and language.

**Dr. Timothy V. Rasinski** is a professor of literacy education at Kent State University and director of its award-winning reading clinic. He has written more than 200 articles and has authored, co-authored, or edited more than 50 books or curriculum programs on reading education. He is the author of the best-selling books on reading fluency, *The Fluent Reader* and *The Fluent Reader in Action*. He also co-authored *Tiered Fluency Instruction: Supporting Diverse Learners in Grades 2–5*. His scholarly interests include reading fluency and word study, reading in the elementary and middle grades, and readers who struggle. Dr. Rasinski has served a three-year term on the Board of Directors of the International Reading Association and was co-editor of *The Reading Teacher* and the *Journal of Literacy Research*. Dr. Rasinski is a past-president of the College Reading Association, and he won the A. B. Herr and Laureate Awards from the College Reading Association for his scholarly contributions to literacy education. In 2010 he was elected to the International Reading Hall of Fame.

**Dr. Sharon Vaughn**, Manuel J. Justiz Endowed Chair in Education, is the Executive Director of The Meadows Center for Preventing Educational Risk, an organized research unit at The University of Texas at Austin. She is the recipient of numerous awards, including the CEC research award, the AERA SIG distinguished researcher award, The University of Texas Distinguished Faculty Award and Outstanding Researcher Award, and the Jeannette E. Fleischner Award for Outstanding Contributions in the Field of LD from CEC. She is the author of more than 35 books and 250 research articles. Several of these research articles have won awards, including the A. J. Harris IRA award for best article published and the School Psychology award for best article. She is currently Principal Investigator on several Institute for Education Sciences, National Institute for Child Health and Human Development, and U.S. Department of Education research grants. She works as a senior adviser to the National Center on Intensive Interventions and has more than six articles that have met the What Works Clearing House Criteria for their intervention reports.

**Dr. Elaine M. Weber** has spent her career as a teacher, adjunct professor, and language arts consultant for the Michigan Department of Education, Department of Defense Schools in London, England, and in her current position with the Macomb Intermediate School District working with teachers and administrators in 21 school districts. She has also co-authored *Guided Highlighted Reading: A Close-Reading Strategy for Navigating Complex Text* and *Reading to the Core: Learning to Read Closely, Critically, and Generatively to Meet Performance Tasks*.

**Dr. Nancy L. Witherell** is a professor in the Department of Elementary and Early Childhood Education at Bridgewater State University, Bridgewater, Massachusetts, where she teaches literacy courses and is coordinator of student teachers for the department. Dr. Witherell is past president of her local reading council, the Massachusetts Association of College and University Reading Educators, and the Massachusetts Reading Association (MRA). In addition, she has been MRA's State co-coordinator for the International Literacy Association (formerly IRA). She has presented at numerous regional and national conferences. Besides the publication of numerous articles in such journals as *The New England Reading Association Journal* and *The Reading Teacher*, Dr. Witherell has co-authored several books, including *Differentiating for Success: How to Build Literacy Instruction for All Students*, and authored two books.

**Hillary Wolfe** began her career as a journalist and advertising copywriter before earning multiple- and single-subject teaching credentials. As a published author, she brought a writer's perspective to reading instruction, which served her well as a reading and writing resource specialist (elementary) and literacy teacher (high school). Her students' high pass rates on state tests earned her the position of Intervention Coordinator for an urban high school, where she built a program that helped more than 1,000 students raise their scores in reading, writing, and math. Her work was documented in *School Library Journal* (2008). She has published articles on education as a columnist and correspondent for local and national newspapers and magazines as well as authored *Writing Strategies for the Common Core: Integrating Reading Comprehension into the Writing Process* (3–5 and 6–8). Hillary Wolfe rejoined the publishing world as an editor and curriculum writer, working on more than 40 professional books and curriculum resources and earning Distinguished Achievement awards from the AEP. As an Academic Officer, she provided ELA coaching and professional development and coordinated CCSS program implementations in districts around the country and internationally (in American Samoa). She also presented at national conferences on how to incorporate literacy skills into content-area instruction. She earned her master's degree in educational leadership from California State Polytechnic University, Pomona, and currently works as a district coordinator for curriculum, instruction, and assessment.

**Dr. Chase Young** is an associate professor in the Department of Language, Literacy, and Special Populations at Sam Houston State University. Dr. Young received his PhD in Reading Education from the University of North Texas, where he was named the 2011 Outstanding Doctoral Student in Reading Education. Previously, he was the Silverman Endowed Chair in Literacy at Texas A&M University in Corpus Christi. Prior to entering higher education, he taught in the primary grades and served as an elementary reading specialist. Dr. Young's primary research interests include reading fluency, supporting struggling readers, and integrating technology in elementary literacy instruction. He served as the editor of the *Journal of Teacher Action Research* and the co-editor of the *Texas Journal of Literacy Education*. He has also co-authored *Tiered Fluency Intervention: Supporting Diverse Learners in Grades 2–5*. His research has appeared in the *Journal of Educational Research*, *Reading Teacher*, and *Literacy Research and Instruction*. In 2014 the Association of Literacy Educators and Researchers selected him to receive the Jerry Johns Promising Researcher Award.

**Karen Soll** has an MEd in curriculum and instruction and several years of experience working on a variety of core and supplemental materials in the education market.

# Index

# Index of Authors

## Maupin House
# capstone

At Maupin House by Capstone Professional, we continue to look for professional development resources that support grades K–8 classroom teachers in areas, such as these:

| | |
|---|---|
| Literacy | Language Arts |
| Content-Area Literacy | Research-Based Practices |
| Assessment | Inquiry |
| Technology | Differentiation |
| Standards-Based Instruction | School Safety |
| Classroom Management | School Community |

If you have an idea for a professional development resource, visit our Become an Author website at: http://www.capstonepub.com/classroom/professional-development/become-an-author/

There are two ways to submit questions and proposals.

You may send them electronically to:
proposals@capstonepd.com

You may send them via postal mail. Please be sure to include a self-addressed stamped envelope for us to return materials.

Acquisitions Editor
Capstone Professional
2 N. LaSalle Street, 14th Floor
Chicago, IL 60602